Zukofsky's "A"

Barry Ahearn

Zukofsky's "*A*"
An Introduction

UNIVERSITY OF CALIFORNIA PRESS

BERKELEY | LOS ANGELES | LONDON

University of California Press
Berkeley and Los Angeles, California

University of California Press, Ltd.
London, England

Library of Congress Cataloging in Publication Data

Ahearn, Barry.
    Zukofsky's "A".

    Includes indexes.
        1. Zukofsky, Louis, 1904–1978. "A".
    1. Title.
PS3549.U47A6833   811'.52   81-13000
ISBN 0-520-04378-2   AACR2

Printed in the United States of America

1 2 3 4 5 6 7 8 9

to my mother and father

For a good Poet's made, as well as borne. And such wert thou.

Ben Jonson

Contents

Preface

The creation of Louis Zukofsky's long poem *"A"* took almost fifty years. It will probably be another fifty before we have a good idea of what it all amounts to. This book is not a guide to the poem; no one knows enough about *"A"* to write one. It is rather a history of the poem's growth.

Zukofsky himself is partly my subject, simply because he made himself so much a part of *"A"*: no other poet has given such a detailed account of his daily life. Yet at the same time he was one of the most reticent of men. Much is given—and much remains hidden. In the first chapter, I present some of the influences that formed him: birthplace, heritage, family, and education. Zukofsky's own words tell us a good deal about his upbringing, but not enough. Chapter 1 is designed to reveal more of the man behind, and in, the work.

Chapters 2 through 5 follow the growth of the poem through its twenty-four parts, or movements. Different preoccupations color the different stages of its development, and these stages can be roughly divided into four sections: movements 1–7, movements 8–12, movements 13–20, and movements 21–24. *"A"* 1–7 is concerned with the self cut loose from the family circle and an ancient, cohesive culture. The individual under inspection is the one Zukofsky knew best—himself. In *"A"* 8–12 the poet examines and creates connections between past and present, specifically the relation of himself and his poem to history and literary tradition. As a consequence, this section of *"A"* is dense with quotation, and I have tried to direct the reader through some of the thickets. *"A"* 13–20 catalogues mingled disasters and good fortune. Zukofsky's declining vitality, the withdrawal of his son Paul from the household, and his continuing obscurity provided the poet with materials for remarkable laments and even more remarkable consolations. Finally, in *"A"* 21–24 the poem expands to a comprehensive view of personal, human, and natural history. In these final movements Zukofsky makes a final accounting of those things he loves best and places them in the context of history.

Each of the four major concerns I have identified is present everywhere in the poem. One could, for example, investigate at great length the uses of quotation in *"A"* 13–20. But my study is concerned with Zukofsky's main emphasis in each of the four sections, a purpose that sometimes produces close readings of particular movements and passages, but not of every line. Readers of *"A"* wanting quick access to close readings can refer to the Index of Movements, which lists first lines of the passages explicated in the book and is keyed by movement and page number to the edition of *"A"* published in 1978 by the University of California Press.

The final chapter takes up a problem that Zukofsky worried about from the beginning: the question of unity. Zukofsky contended that *"A"* was a whole, but he spoke rather cryptically about its wholeness. Certain questions are inescapable: Is "A" a unit? If so, what sort of a unit, and how did Zukofsky build in (or coax in) unity? As my remarks at the beginning of that chapter suggest, these questions cannot be answered simply by looking at "A". Zukofsky's solutions force us to consider how other poets such as William Wordsworth, David Jones, and William Carlos Williams handled the problem. And that is the subject for another book altogether.

For their assistance in advancing this one, I am grateful to Mortimer Adler, Cid Corman, Peter Crisp, Guy Davenport, Leon Edel, Daniel Fallon, Jill Farmer, Donald R. Howard, Jerome McGann, Walter Benn Michaels, Paul Palmer, Moses Rischin, Hugh Seidman, Michael Silverblatt, Eliot Weinberger, Jonathan Williams, and Dr. William E. Williams. Donald Gallup assisted me at the Beinecke Library; David Farmer and Ellen S. Dunlap showed me every consideration at the Humanities Research Center at Austin. I am indebted to the editors of *ELH*, *Montemora*, and *Paideuma*, wherein earlier versions of some chapters appeared.

Grateful acknowledgment is also made to W. W. Norton & Company, for permission to reprint from *All: The Collected Short Poems*; the Humanities Research Center at Austin, Texas, for permission to quote from previously unpublished manuscripts in the Zukofsky Collection; James Laughlin and the Estate of William Carlos Williams, for permission to quote from a Williams manuscript in the Zukofsky Collection at the Humanities Research Center; and Paul Zukofsky, for permission to quote from his father's published and unpublished writings.

Three others did much more than help. Louis Zukofsky read and commented on the dissertation that eventually grew into this book. Celia Zukofsky generously provided information available nowhere else. Hugh Kenner, who introduced me to Louis Zukofsky, and whose good influence assisted this study at every stage, deserves more thanks than I know how to give.

Note on Texts

Though Louis Zukofsky did not live to see his poem bound in one volume, he did approve the galley proofs for the University of California Press edition of *"A"*, and that is the edition referred to throughout, with the single exception of a quotation from the early version of *"A"*-1 in chapter 2. The cited manuscripts at the Humanities Research Center (abbreviated HRC in the notes) at Austin, Texas, are all part of the Zukofsky Collection there. Quotations from Shakespeare are taken from *William Shakespeare: The Complete Works*, ed. Alfred Harbage (New York: Vintage, 1969).

ONE

Character

> Poets are proverbially born, not made; and, because
> they have been born rarely, the conditions of their
> birth are singularly interesting.
>
> Henry Adams, *The Life of George Cabot Lodge*

In 1904 Henry James set sail for America—first class—to
"take in" as much of the democratic scene as he could. It
was to prove a considerable taking. Like Rip Van Winkle,
he would have to assimilate the changes of twenty revolutionary years. But the opening pages of *The American Scene*
show James sufficiently aware of the immensity of his task.
One of his strategies for "taking" involved old friends,
such as William Dean Howells ("dear old W. D. H."),
who had chosen to stay at home. James sought him out not
only because of the claims imposed by long acquaintance,
but also because Howells could supply the expatriated
observer with information about democracy's impact on
literature since 1880. James knew very well that the vigi-
lant Howells had kept his eyes and ears open for talent
from sources not authorized by the Lowells, Adamses, and
Jameses.

One of these sources that his friend had watched and encouraged was located on New York's Lower East Side. Toward the close of his American journey—in the summer of
1905—James, accompanied by the Yiddish playwright Ja-

cob Gordin, sampled the exotic mysteries of the ghetto.[1] Strolling into the heart of that district, James rubbed and bumped elbows with its inhabitants as they swarmed in and out of shops, around pushcarts, and through tenement doorways. He was forcibly impressed: "As overflow, in the whole quarter, is the main fact of life—I was to learn later on that, with the exception of some shy corner of Asia, no district in the world known to the statistician has so many inhabitants to the yard—the scene hummed with the human presence beyond any I had ever faced in quest even of refreshment. . . ."[2] There are few Americans still living who saw, let alone existed in, such crowding. We are told, but cannot fully comprehend, that the Tenth Ward, which included Hester, Canal, Broome, Orchard, and Chrystie streets, had a population of over 300,000 souls per square mile in 1890.[3] And this preceded the greatest wave of immigration. Here was an intensity of sheer human presence sufficient to match the intensity of the Jamesian gaze. Face to face with the crush, he retreats at first into levity, suggesting, in the passage quoted above, that in the course of an ordinary evening the crowded streets of the ghetto surpassed the concentrated turbulence that invariably assembles around open bars.

As James maneuvered through this density, he passed near, perhaps traversed, Chrystie Street. Here lived the family Zukofsky: father, mother, daughters, elder son, younger son. The last held a special place in the family; he was the first born in America, and he was only a toddler—seventeen months old that June. The building that first sheltered Louis Zukofsky still stands, but Chrystie Street

1. Leon Edel, in a personal letter, identified Gordin (author of *A Yiddish King Lear*) as one of James's guides.
2. Henry James, *The American Scene*, ed. Leon Edel (Bloomington: Indiana University Press, 1968), pp. 131–32.
3. See the table in Jacob Riis, *How the Other Half Lives* (New York: Dover, 1971), p. 232.

has changed. A park now runs the length of the street, the space for it created by the demolition of rows of tenements. Vacant lots have proliferated in the area. To those who knew the street in its heyday, the scene now appears almost deserted. Another, less numerous generation of immigrants continues the battle to survive and eventually escape.

Though that old struggle goes on, it seems certain that the Lower East Side will never again be so densely packed. The incredible crowding brought repeated expressions of astonishment from outsiders. In 1911 Arnold Bennett chose blunt words to express his amazement. "The architecture seemed to sweat humanity at every window and door."[4] In that assessment we can hear echoes of "sweatshop"—which the tenements often were. The image of humanity as something like sweat should give us pause. The most crowded spot in the world might be the place where life was valued most cheaply. If Bennett so concluded, he was wrong.

James, for one, considered whether life in such conditions was meanly discounted. He does not answer the question directly, but offers a brilliant metaphor to illustrate Jewish humanity en masse. "So the denizens of the New York Ghetto, heaped as thick as the splinters on the table of a glass-blower, had each, like the fine glass particle, his or her individual share of the whole hard glitter of Israel."[5] One can read that comment two ways, but if considerable condescension lurks in his analysis, there is a compensating recognition of the latent power inhabiting each "splinter."

No wonder, then, that Hutchins Hapgood found it necessary to structure *The Spirit of the Ghetto* as a series of biographical sketches. Seemingly all of a type, on closer in-

4. Quoted in Moses Rischin, *The Promised City: New York's Jews, 1870–1914* (Cambridge, Mass.: Harvard University Press, 1962), p. 79.
5. *American Scene*, p. 132.

spection the ghetto dwellers revealed fierce individuality. This may help explain why Louis Zukofsky would one day acquire the reputation of being difficult to deal with— an unbending, self-centered man.

The street scenes that passed before James's wondering eyes yielded most of the data for his pages concerning the ghetto. He apparently made no attempt to discover what went on inside tenement walls. We may pardon the elderly novelist's reluctance to attempt the narrow, gloomy (hardly "bosky") stairs. Perhaps James, who knew exactly the extent of his vision, gauged correctly the degree to which the reverberations of Jewish family life would be lost on him. This New York bore little resemblance to the one he had known as a boy. A ghetto child's family lived in one or two rooms, and privacy was only a word. James really had no standards for correlating his childhood with that of a Zukofsky.

One day the poet would take up where the novelist of international episodes had left off, filling in areas unexplored by James. The matter of earning one's living, for example.

> The miracle of his first job
> On the lower East Side:
> Six years night watchman
> In a men's shop
> Where by day he pressed pants
> Every crease a blade
> The irons weighed
> At least twenty pounds
> But moved both of them
> Six days a week
> From six in the morning
> To nine, sometimes eleven at night,
> Or midnight.[6]

6. Louis Zukofsky, "A" (Berkeley and Los Angeles: University of

It was presumably a "miracle" that he (Zukofsky *père*) could carry on under such conditions. Of course, wage slavery had other effects also. The wife had to assume responsibility for the children. In Jewish families this had always been the case, but with his father absent almost all of Louis's waking hours, the bond between mother and child grew even stronger. The central figure in Zukofsky's early life became his mother. In surroundings hostile to families, she was the nurturing presence that lent stability and security. Zukofsky never quite got over her loss, and it is one indication of her importance that *"A"'s* last page remembers her.

When Zukofsky grew old enough to venture into the street, he would be surrounded by a phenomenon we might describe as linguistic goulash. James had noted the unfamiliar accents that rose on every side; these "torture-rooms of the living idiom" left him apprehensive and mystified concerning the "Accent of the Future."[7] The children of the Lower East Side accepted as normal a mingling of tongues that must have made the story of the Tower of Babel plausible. The common language was, of course, Yiddish, but fragments of Russian, German, Polish, Slavonic, and Rumanian also punctuated the American air. Language must have seemed a jumble of disparate, conflicting parts. The notion of "native" languages probably seemed fanciful to young Zukofsky. The notion of any single language having absolute priority—a concept most of us grow up with—had no hold on him.

Other problems associated with growing up in the ghetto—explosive problems—seem to have escaped James altogether: at least he chose not to mention them. Crucial political differences distinguished ghettos in Russia from

California Press, 1978), p. 152. All subsequent references to this edition will be followed by the page numbers in parentheses.

7. *American Scene*, p. 139.

the one in New York. Jews in America had escaped the pogroms. For the first time in centuries, they did not have to cling together behind bolts and bars while armed men rioted in the streets. This sudden relief from fear had unforeseen complications. The pogroms had forced cohesion; the end of persecution undermined that unity. Many of the children and grandchildren of the immigrants had no use for cultural bonds that had persisted for centuries. A family pious for generations might suddenly find that its youngest, dearest son had lost the faith—as Louis Zukofsky did.

America presented a new kind of government to Jewish immigrants, people accustomed to thinking of pharaoh, czar, and Theodore Roosevelt in the same terms. In this contrary land, Jews were not systematically excluded from Gentile society, but encouraged to participate—at least to some extent. Take the matter of public schooling, for example. Many public schools in Europe were closed to Jews. In the United States, however, Jewish children were required to attend. A special police force—truant officers—even made sure they put in a daily appearance. Once immigrant parents got over the shock of this reversal, they seized the opportunity to educate their children. The youngsters were ordered to become first-class scholars, and children who brought home bad report cards suffered parental displeasure. No matter that the classes were all in English, or that the curriculum consisted of topics unknown to the parents. There was, after all, the *chaider* to take care of religious education. Anxious to please his mother, Louis Zukofsky applied himself at school and became one of the brightest students on the Lower East Side.

But our subject is Zukofsky the poet, and his introduction to the arts took place before formal schooling. His *Autobiography* tells the story. "My first exposure to letters at the age of four was thru the Yiddish theater, most memorably the Thalia on the Bowery. By the age of nine I had seen a good deal of Shakespeare, Ibsen, Strindberg and Tolstoy performed—all in Yiddish."[8] In "A"-8 he allows us a brief glimpse of his passion for the theater:

> His older brother took him (the baby)
>   to the theatre (mezzanine always)
> Saturday matinee and night
> And Sunday matinee and night.
> Sunday you wished it were Friday.   (p. 83)

At the Thalia, he first learned that poetry is fundamentally a matter of someone speaking. Further, drama emphasizes unity of speech and action. Zukofsky's unending fascination with sounded words and the way they issue from our bodies can be traced back to the mezzanine of the Thalia.

"Theater depends on its words,"[9] he would later propose, then remarking offhandedly that another theater drew him out of the ghetto.

> Even before I read Stevens, growing up with the kind of theater that interested him I finally walked out of the East Side, it seemed then for miles and miles, to find this place called Greenwich Village and the Provincetown Playhouse. I expected palisades of course as pictured in the early Dutch history of New York. I was disappointed. Still it was a new world.[10]

Growing up on the Lower East Side meant growing up in a world sufficient unto itself. Zukofsky seems perfectly serious in remembering how he relied on books when learning about Greenwich Village, only blocks away. That

8. Louis Zukofsky, *Autobiography* (New York: Grossman, 1970), p. 33.

9. Louis Zukofsky, "For Wallace Stevens," in *Prepositions: The Collected Critical Essays of Louis Zukofsky* (Berkeley and Los Angeles: University of California Press, 1981), p. 29.

10. Ibid.

clinching line—"it was a new world"—makes the act of walking out of the ghetto equivalent to crossing the Atlantic.

Jewish children who went off to public schools were completing their families' passages to the New World. There they learned about the Pledge of Allegiance, Washington and Lincoln, Betsy Ross, the Alamo. Columbus was also on the curriculum with the Pilgrims (the implication being that the last significant boatload of immigrants had disembarked in 1620). More strenuous material than this, however, was presented to the children in the elementary schools of 1910. In his lecture on Wallace Stevens, Zukofsky remembered one task that faced him at P.S. 7. "I owned an illustrated Shakespeare, and my English teacher was offering a prize to everyone in his class who would read all the Plays and answer his questions about them—pretty stiff questions. I read all the Plays—that was at about the age of eleven."[11] Voices in the street, the intonations of actors—to these examples we can add another influence that helped form Louis Zukofsky's sense of language. Picture a child of eleven pondering the intricacies of Elizabethan English in a tenement household where only Yiddish was spoken.

The contending voices that filled the Lower East Side were also used to debate a variety of social issues. Political questions were some of the most popular topics for formal and informal discussion, and the ghetto's political spectrum was distinctly shaded toward the Left; many immigrants were refugees from the Russia of Nicholas II. In 1905 and 1906 there was an especially large influx of socialists and communists; the aftermath of failed revolution drove fresh supplies of Russian radicals across the ocean. The political creeds that young Zukofsky heard expressed

11. Ibid., p. 28.

were almost entirely revolutionary and left-wing. No wonder he flirted with the Communist party through the 1920s and 1930s, though never making an irrevocable commitment to it. One reason he kept his distance might be found in the profusion of other, competing *isms*, adherents of which were anxious to snare Louis Zukofsky—whose verbal abilities would have boosted their propaganda efforts. Zukofsky might have been captured by the Zionists, who were actively recruiting in those days. The Orthodox were less zealously evangelistic, but the upright conduct of Zukofsky's father may have been the most seductive invitation of all to the youth.

Somehow Zukofsky learned to thread his way through the surrounding maze of orthodoxies and enthusiasms. All his life he made a point of maintaining a safe distance from such systems. When he promoted a group of poets (himself among them) in the early 1930s, he insisted that they were only "Objectivists" and that they did not represent anything called "Objectivism." He kept pointing to individual poems, picking up the delicacies of nuance, and trying to avoid any generalities that might coalesce into "Objectivism."[12]

His persistent refusal to be a docile member of any group gave one evidence of strength of character. (And it helped him to acquire his reputation for stubbornness.) That trait helped him to stick with his writing even when it became clear that ten, twenty, perhaps thirty years might pass before a particular work made it into print. Such determination is uncommon. Did the intense concentration of the Lower East Side have some share in its making? An anecdote Zukofsky once told may have application here.[13]

He was assisted into the world in January 1904 by a Jew-

12. Louis Zukofsky, "Sincerity and Objectification," *Poetry* 37 (February 1931): 272–85.
13. Conversation with Louis Zukofsky, January 15, 1978.

ish midwife. She entered the date on the birth certificate and handed it over to his parents. This document was meaningless to them—they couldn't read it—and they carefully squirreled it away and forgot it. The question of the exact day of Louis's birth became problematic. In his early years Mr. and Mrs. Zukofsky chose a day "close" to the event. This was his "first birthday." Some years passed, and Louis learned to read and write. Happening upon his birth certificate, he discovered what he took to be the correct date—his "second birthday." More years went by, and one day he took a closer look at the certificate. He then discovered that he had misread the midwife's handwriting. At last the genuine date of his birth was determined—the third and final birthday. Or was it final? At any rate, Zukofsky thereafter considered that he was "a man with three birthdays." Astrologers are not the only people who consider birthdays talismanic. Zukofsky once remarked that his interest in numerology was not "cabalistic," but only superstition.[14] The distinction is nice, and it is characteristic of someone who made an art out of coordinating bundles of words. He neatly avoided a rigid conception of numerological influence, but preserved the assumption that something "out there" was linked to our essential selves. The whole fascination with numbers, anniversaries, and birthdays may have begun on the Lower East Side, where, if one were anxious to differentiate oneself from a multitude of other small boys—and one's birthday shifted alarmingly from year to year—having control over numbers could boost self-confidence. To the exceptionally bright student, certain numbers (93, 95, 98) and letters ($A-$, A, $A+$) can be all-important. They offer validation from authoritative sources of one's worth. And they please one's parents. Zukofsky was used to winning

14. Conversation with Louis Zukofsky, December 8, 1977.

such letters and numbers. His achievement and ambition propelled him to Columbia in January 1920. He had just turned sixteen.

The 1923 *Columbian*, thick and green, provided ample space for the immortalization of senior-class countenances. But not everyone was included: only a small percentage of the graduating students appear in individual photographs with the obligatory captions. The editors may have charged extra for the service; they may simply have decided that some were more deserving than others. Being Jewish was no bar to admission. Mortimer Adler came first, and the captioner took due note of his already fearsome breadth of learning: "they call him 'Plato.'" Top intellectual honors, however, went to Henry Morton Robinson. "'Rondo' is generally conceded to be our most learned undergraduate" was *The Columbian*'s grudging accolade. The lack of complete enthusiasm may be due to Robinson's status as class poet. There is something decidedly outré about poets.

The Columbian's editors would have objected if accused of making invidious distinctions. Hadn't they, after all, included a page of "Columbia men not listed elsewhere"? There are a good many names on that list. It runs the gamut from *A* to Zimmerman, J. A.; Zit, W. L.; Zukofsky, L. Nobody was left out, even though appearance on that list marked one as a nonentity.

Others at Columbia knew Louis Zukofsky as more than the last name on a roll call of the negligible. Adler counted him among his wide circle of acquaintances, and fifty-five years later would remember how exceptionally pale and frail Zukofsky looked.[15] He also remembered the young poet's quiet, shy manner. Zukofsky was not a good conversationalist in his early years. It was this retiring nature

15. Telephone interview with Mortimer Adler, December 6, 1977.

and uncommon pallor that led Mark Van Doren to characterize him as "a pale and subtle poet who was not in fact lazy, but the memory of whose painfully inarticulate soul forbids me to use him for any purpose however respectful. . . ."[16] At least Zukofsky could take comfort that his old teacher referred to him as a poet.

Zukofsky seems to have been interested in only one extracurricular activity. He joined a group of poets—the Boar's Head Society. Its members had at their disposal a slim periodical, *The Morningside*. They styled themselves on the masthead as "associate editors" and took turns being chief editor. Most of them were not destined for literary fame. Betram A. Lutton, Dusham Podgorshek, and Stanley Hart never made it to the anthologies. Still, they were poets, and this meant they had some fire in their hearts. Of Hart *The Columbian* tut-tutted, "'Stan' has certainly approved strongly of the radical aspect in American literature—one has to if one is to edit *Morningside*." What standards the commentator used to detect "radical" phenomena are not clear. He may have thought it daring to abandon rhyme. Perhaps the basis for his comment lay in a recent incident. One of the Boar's Headers had caused quite a stir; his name was Whittaker Chambers. A budding radical in those days, and a close friend of Louis Zukofsky's, Chambers also wrote for *The Morningside*. In November 1922, he took his turn in the editor's chair, and the next issue of the magazine featured one of his short verseplays, "A Play for Puppets." It dealt rather irreverently with the life of Christ. The college authorities did not condone atheism: they expelled him forthwith.[17] The scandal did not, however, interrupt the regular appearance of *The*

16. Mark Van Doren, "Jewish Students I Have Known," *The Menorah Journal* 13 (June 1927): 267.
17. See the account in Allen Weinstein, *Perjury: The Hiss-Chambers Case* (New York: Vintage, 1979), pp. 89–90.

Morningside. Chambers's piece had been an aberration. The poetry in previous and subsequent issues could not have offended anyone.

Even in Zukofsky's case the quality was distressingly low. He wrote brief, painstaking poems empty of wit.[18]

Youth

The opal dawn, that bathed the silent mountains
In its light, found a youth, proud, strong and tanned,
Against the blue. With legs fixed firm, he spanned
Two cliffs, dumb space between. The leaping fountains
Of Life and Hope within him sung; his face
Glowed, ruddy from the breeze; he knew no dearth,
But, holding forth his tawny hands, to earth
He poured out sunshine from a marble vase.

Undulations

Stopping mine ears to the noise of the world
I shall hear the distant murmur
                of a great sea . . . .

Under the blue expanses
I shall dream to the surge
                of the far-sweeping forest . . . .
Nirvana: The taking up unto the ceaseless
                pulsation of eternity . . . .

The figure of Phoebus Apollo in "Youth" wielding that "marble vase" suggests that Zukofsky imbibed at the well of Keats and his imitators. More to the point is the formula evidently generating these verses. A rule of contraries seems to be operating here; the landscapes tentatively and sketchily depicted are precisely the opposite of urban America. That brawny, bubbling figure in "Youth" has all the physical attributes so emphatically missing in Louis

18. "Youth," *The Morningside*, December 1920, p. 99; "Undulations," *The Morningside*, February 1921, p. 152.

Zukofsky. Still we should not press this too far. Zukofsky's manner cannot be distinguished from that of his
peers in the Boar's Head Society. The group had a common style, full of interchangeable themes and images.
Their poems expressed only the desire to be "poetic."
They were derivative of derivatives.

Late in Zukofsky's Columbia years, he redeemed himself with a work that broke from the soporific pattern. In
this poem he tried to define himself in terms not of a vague
aspiration, but of his family. The turn to autobiography
seems to have released powerful feelings that hitherto had
been buried under "poetic" ideals.[19]

> *Youth's Ballad of Singleness*
>
> Youth wrote a song of heart and head,
> White sages thought him old—no less!—
> They smiled that one as new to life
> As youth should sing of singleness.
>
> To seek out a life in himself and alone,
> Wistfully, slowly,
> Be as single a thing as a single stone
> In a field: solely
>
> To seek a peace of self's making, yet outerly hear,
> Wistfully, slowly,
> The clock bring its hour; know the days round the year
> For the high and the lowly:
>
> And at the twilight to feel that the white hairs waver,
> Wistfully, slowly,
> On the head of his mother, in the shadows that lave her,
> At twilight, all holy
>
> With her: then suddenly rise and go to his room,
> And his dog wondering

19. "Youth's Ballad," *The Morningside*, March–April 1923, pp.
47–48.

Why he stands and offers no hand for his stare in the
    gloom,
Why this vast sundering:

Somewhere to meet one, all kind and beautiful,
Perhaps make her his own,
And regret when at fault that she is too dutiful
Towards one much alone:

To love a few out of many far more than himself,
Still let them not know,
Have his father, winding the clock on its shelf,
Think, why his son is so:

To live within with those who sung and were fire,
Who were themselves wholly,
And look up as he reads, find others never tire—
Laboring folk and lowly:

To see the sun rise and to watch how it sets
From a hill against the sky,
See rain sink in black earth and rivulets
In curves pass by:

And when stars dawn as at their first birth
To see the blue loom higher,
While the stilled life of earth seeks closer the earth,
And each house lights its fire:

To know all these things have a place in life
For they are life wholly:
Then, to know it is good to engage in strife,
But wistful and lowly,

To know beyond all colors and aspects, unchanging,
One, nor wistful, nor lowly,
Is Change, unlike all things in their tireless ranging
To death, wistfully, slowly—

Is to live as though stars had elevation of stars,
And things not of earth their own aim,
As though a spirit moved in the shadow of bars
And still had the strength of flame,

> Youth ended his song of his heart and head,
> Sages thought him wise—no less!—
> Not old, nor young, nor growing wise—
> For he had sung of singleness.

The attempt to get a fix on himself by reference to father, mother, dog, sages, and an impression of the ultimate tendencies of the natural and social worlds, represents the earliest instance of Zukofsky working toward an "objectivist" vision of himself. That elusive character Zukofsky, he had discovered, could not be pinned down as a single object at a fixed point in time. Not a new idea, so far as the history of human thought is concerned, but new to him. And he was to take it to unprecedented lengths. "Youth's Ballad" was only the first step in a series of autobiographical essays that Zukofsky was to produce throughout his life, a series Sterne and Whitman would have appreciated.

Zukofsky received his M.A. in English from Columbia in 1924. This ended his formal education. The same year coincidentally marked the real beginning of his literary career. He wrote four poems that would eventually survive his critical eye and be included as part of his permanent contribution in *All*, the volume containing his collected shorter poems. One of these ("Poem 2" of *29 Poems*) was unlike anything he had done before.[20]

> Not much more than being,
> Thoughts of isolate, beautiful
> Being at evening, to expect
>   at a river-front:
>
> A shaft dims
> With a turning wheel;

20. In Louis Zukofsky, *All: The Collected Short Poems* (New York: W. W. Norton & Company, 1965), p. 24.

Men work on a jetty
By a broken wagon;

Leopard, glowing-spotted,
    The summer river —
Under: The Dragon:

It begins like one of his Columbia cream puffs, but quickly shifts into unexpected, discordant precisions. Where did this new style come from? Nothing comparable can be found in *The Morningside*. The impetus must have come from outside the Columbia circle of teachers and friends. He may have been inspired by a close study of William Carlos Williams's *Spring and All* (1923), a text he was later to praise as potentially comparable in influence to Wordsworth's *Lyrical Ballads*.[21] Both Williams and Zukofsky aim for unity of effect by incorporating complex linking sound patterns into poems whose syntax and vocabulary seem at odds. Poem XIX of *Spring and All* is a simple instance of Williams's careful handling of three sounds: *r*, *s*, and *z*. They wander aimlessly through the poem until the last three lines, when they suddenly sound for the first time in lockstep order (*r*, *s*, *z*)—no less than four times, twice in the concluding line.[22]

adorned with blossoms

Out of their sweet heads
dark kisses—rough faces

In "Poem 2" we are watching an exercise in *n* and *r*. Lines 7 and 8 are tied together by *n* ("men," "on," "broken," "wagon"), and are linked to lines 6 and 9 by the guttural components of "turning," "work," "broken," and "leop-

21. "Sincerity and Objectification," p. 279.
22. In William Carlos Williams, *Imaginations* (New York: New Directions, 1970), p. 136.

ard." Until this poem, Zukofsky had restricted his sensuous investments to images; now he moved into the sounds of the poem, making audible equivalents of his emotions.

In 1968 L. S. Dembo managed to persuade Zukofsky to consent to an interview. When asked about the significance of "Poem 2," Zukofsky cited it as an instance "of what happens if you deal mostly with sight and a bit of intellect."[23] It might have been profitable to pursue the question along those lines, but the hint was not taken. Instead, the subsequent exchange floundered into a bog of cross-purposes.

> Q. Where do the leopard and the dragon fit in?
>
> A. That's the constellation. "Leopard, glowing-spotted, / The summer river— / Under."
>
> Q. Why do you refer to the constellation?
>
> A. There I'm . . . I'm not for metaphor unless, as Aristotle says you bring together unlikes that have never existed before. But they're in words; they're in verbs: "the sun rises." My statements are often very, very clipped.
>
> Q. Well, the colon in the last line after "Under" would seem to imply that the dragon is under the river.
>
> A. "Summer river— / Under: . . ." There is a question of movement and enough rest; notice the space after "Under." The dragon is also reflected in the river— inverted.

Zukofsky was not comfortable in interviews, and eventually he avoided them altogether. Still, that remark about metaphor is enlightening. Zukofsky's work exhibits hardly any metaphors in the usual sense. In his own particular sense of the word, however, they are one of the defining

23. "Interview with Louis Zukofsky," *Contemporary Literature* 10 (Spring 1969): 210–22.

features by which we may identify an anonymous passage as Zukofsky's.

In 1924, then, he began compacting "unlikes" into dense matrices. This practice detached him from the Boar's Head style once and for all. Lyrical mood lingers in "Poem 2," but that mood is subordinate to Zukofsky's new interest in assembling odd words, strange spaces, and free-floating punctuation marks. The object of attention is no longer the mood that the poem supposedly enshrines, but the poem itself.

Zukofsky's next few years were taken up with his first experiments and explorations in the new idiom. Occasional excesses cropped up along the way. In the fourth number of Ezra Pound's *The Exile* appears a poem Zukofsky penned in praise of George Antheil's music.[24] In this case his ardor got out of hand. His attack on the unappreciative members of the audience was colored by a dreary crankiness. It concludes:

> No wail can be too loud to drown this milksop audience
> No piano too many-teethed for their banality,
> No percussion too strong to indent their brains.
> . . . .
> And from where I sit
> I can look down into the expensive pit
> And spit.

This is the manner of someone determined to be offensive. But who was supposed to take offense?

John Erskine, faculty advisor to the Boar's Head Society, would have been upset—if he read *The Exile*. He is remembered today chiefly as the author of such works as *Galahad*, *Adam and Eve*, and *The Private Life of Helen of Troy*. His contributions to education were, however, more

24. "Critique of Antheil," *The Exile*, no. 4 (Spring 1928), pp. 83–84.

important. Zukofsky's first year at Columbia coincided with a major addition to the curriculum. That was the year Erskine introduced the Great Books method of instruction, which, carried on by his student Mortimer Adler, came to have a profound effect on the teaching of literature. As Erskine described the program in his memoirs:

> I wanted the boys to read great books, the best sellers of ancient times, as spontaneously and humanly as they would read current best sellers, and having read the books, I wanted them to form their opinions at once in a free-for-all discussion. It would take two years of Wednesday evenings to discuss all the books on my list. Even by the end of the first year all the boys in the class would have in common a remarkable store of information, ideas about literature and life, and perhaps an equal wealth of aesthetic emotions.[25]

Here was eclecticism with a vengeance: books from all times and places where Western civilization had flourished, jammed together as never before. What effect this kind of packaging may have had on Zukofsky is hard to judge. He seems to have responded to the generous sweep of inclusiveness, but his later judgment of the man responsible was not favorable. In "Poem Beginning 'The,'" Erskine is placed in an unflattering light:[26]

173   On weary bott'm long wont to sit,
174   Thy graying hair, thy beaming eyes,
175   Thy heavy jowl would make me fit
176   For the Pater that was Greece.
177   The siesta that was Rome.

25. John Erskine, *The Memory of Certain Persons* (Philadelphia: J. B. Lippincott, 1947), p. 343. See also Mortimer Adler, *Philosopher at Large* (New York: Macmillan, 1977), pp. 55–66.
26. In *All: The Collected Short Poems*, pp. 17–18.

178   Lo! from my present—say not—itch
179   How statue-like I see thee stand
180   Phi Beta Key within thy hand!

The scrutiny of Erskine is, of course, patterned on Poe's "To Helen"—a gentle indication, perhaps, that the professor's knowledge of literature was a bit outmoded. Erskine goes on to tell his class that "Poe, / Gentlemen, don'chew-know, / But never wrote an epic." One year before "The" Erskine had published *Helen of Troy*, an event that may have influenced Zukofsky's choice of lines on which to grill his unfortunate teacher.

But what about the other members of the Columbia faculty? Late in his life, Zukofsky singled out two of his instructors for special mention:

> I was fortunate to have one of the finest professors of philosophy, who . . . acted his thoughts in his lectures. He did not write very much—respected for one concise slim book called *The Purpose of History*—a man named Homer Woodbridge. Dewey had something else for me. It's how he inflected his voice that mattered—stressing an active-*ing* or a passive-*ed* that made the point of his course—sometimes as he sat on the radiator, and when it was hot of course he moved away. His educational philosophy did not interest me. The preoccupied man did.[27]

It is as if Zukofsky the attentive student were actually Zukofsky the theatergoer—back at the Thalia. The terms of this passage make the classroom a stage. The professors are performers. Is the description a smokescreen thrown up to conceal an early interest in John Dewey's philosophy, an interest Zukofsky is anxious to deny? Perhaps, but we

27. "For Wallace Stevens," pp. 29–30. Zukofsky confused his teacher's name (Frederick J. E. Woodbridge) with that of American educator Homer E. Woodbridge.

cannot really charge him with duplicity; the orientation toward the physical neatly reconciles the class as theater and Dewey's pragmatism.

This arch reduction of pragmatism—noting that Dewey wisely avoided hot radiators—shows a keen wit. It also reveals a mind attentive to such mundane items as radiators and the patterned meanderings of a lecturer. But did young Zukofsky come to the classroom equipped with that sort of attentiveness? Or did something he learned there influence his perception? His account of the professors does, in fact, resemble something that was in the air during the 1920s; certain philosophers were beating the drum for "contact"—contact with immediate experience. In 1925, for example, we find Alfred North Whitehead complaining about the influence of the scientific method on civilization. He suggests that the seventeenth century had bequeathed an alienating point of view. "This conception of the universe is surely framed in terms of high abstractions, and . . . we have mistaken our abstractions for concrete realities."[28] Dewey voiced similar sentiments in his essay "The Need for a Recovery of Philosophy."[29] He presents the crisis of philosophy in terms of a series of dichotomies. In traditional, orthodox views, he writes, experience "is regarded as primarily a knowledge affair." It exists mainly in the mind and can be known through retrospection. What we need, Dewey argues, is a "forward looking" interaction with "a genuinely objective world," and we must regard experience as "an affair of the intercourse of a living being with its physical and social environment." Zukofsky's account of Dewey stressing active and passive suf-

28. Alfred North Whitehead, *Science and the Modern World: Lowell Lectures, 1925* (New York: Macmillan, 1926), pp. 80–81.
29. John Dewey, "The Need for a Recovery of Philosophy," in *Creative Intelligence: Essays in the Pragmatic Attitude* (New York: Henry Holt, 1917), pp. 7–8.

fixes seems to reflect the kind of "passive" and "active" polarities that Dewey outlined. More interesting is Zukofsky's remark that Dewey's philosophy left him cold, but that the "preoccupied man" held his attention. Dewey's philosophy, strangely enough, seems to have dictated how Zukofsky would remember him.

Zukofsky always professed to reject epistemology vehemently, and we should not overlook Dewey's influence in this area. That metaphysical brier patch drew harsh criticism.

> The problem of knowledge as conceived in the industry of epistemology is the problem of knowledge *in general*—of the possibility, extent, and validity of knowledge in general. What does this "in general" mean? In ordinary life there are problems a-plenty of knowledge in particular; every conclusion we try to reach, theoretical or practical, affords such a problem. . . . But there is no problem of knowledge in general.[30]

We can glean any number of examples from Dewey's writings that seem applicable to Zukofsky. But if we insist on rigorously applying the Deweyan formulas to *"A"* we will not get very far. More often than not, Zukofsky creates by showing as much interest in what Dewey rejects as in what Dewey champions. It seems that the legacy Zukofsky acquired from his teacher consisted of an intriguing set of opposites, which the poet could use to make something shapely.

The question of the proper relation between science and philosophy produced remarkable disagreements among eminent thinkers. Whitehead, as we have seen, singled out the scientific method as one of the villains responsible for aberrant philosophizing. Dewey, however, promoted the scientific method as the cure for philosophy's ailments.

30. "Recovery of Philosophy," p. 32.

> Pragmatism is content to take its stand with science; for science finds all such events to be subject-matter of description and inquiry—just like stars and fossils, mosquitoes and malaria, circulation and vision. It also takes its stand with daily life, which finds that such things really have to be reckoned with as they occur interwoven in the texture of events.[31]

Zukofsky must have been attracted by the appealing inclusiveness that Dewey recommends. Here was a program aiming to bring everything together—to make room for an infinite variety. One of our defining national myths affirms that America was founded on such a principle, and it would be difficult for a first-generation American to remain unmoved. But, fresh from the ghetto, he would also be acutely attentive to the ways that inclusiveness was more dream than fact.

Other aspects of Dewey's program would also have appealed to Zukofsky's visionary capacities. At one point, Dewey echoes Karl Marx's declaration that the modern task of philosophy is not to interpret the world but to change it. "Philosophy recovers itself when it ceases to be a device for dealing with the problems of philosophers, and becomes a method, cultivated by philosophers, for dealing with the problems of men."[32] We can almost hear young Zukofsky applauding those statements. How could a socialist not agree?

Dewey preached strenuously on behalf of progress and amalgamation. He exercised a powerful influence partly because he offered his students that special American optimism that sees opportunities for improvement everywhere. By 1920 the frontier had long since been improved out of existence, but as far as Dewey was concerned the

31. "Recovery of Philosophy," p. 55.
32. "Recovery of Philosophy," p. 65.

greatest challenge lay ahead. "Faith in the power of the intelligence to imagine a future which is the projection of the desirable in the present, and to invent the instrumentalities of its realization, is our salvation. And it is a faith which must be nurtured and made articulate: surely a sufficiently large task for our philosophy."[33] It sounds suspiciously like a proposal for an extremely sophisticated sort of Salvation Army, but the hope expressed here is most attractive. Immunity to such urgings comes only with more time and experience than most collegians can muster.

Frederick J. E. Woodbridge also professed optimism, but of a scrupulously qualified variety. It is, therefore, not as immediately appealing as Dewey's. Partly because of this reserved faith, and partly because of his disinclination to publish, Woodbridge today is little known outside philosophy departments. During his Columbia years, however, his local stature seems to have rivaled Dewey's. Those who came into contact with him testified to his extraordinary gifts as teacher and thinker. Mortimer Adler recalls that he lectured with "an eloquence that derived from the flow of his thought rather than from the flow of his words."[34] It was probably Woodbridge who introduced Zukofsky to the study of Spinoza and Aristotle, for Woodbridge particularly delighted in them. And Zukofsky revered them for the rest of his life.

Woodbridge's *The Purpose of History* (1916) is "concise" at eighty-nine pages, every one of which contains passages that could serve as apt commentaries on some of the poems containing history (Pound's definition of an epic) written in this century. Woodbridge begins by denying that there exists a purpose to history "if we mean by purpose some future event towards which the whole creation

33. "Recovery of Philosophy," p. 69.
34. *Philosopher at Large*, p. 29.

moves."[35] The study of history does, however, have a purpose. Man's intelligence permits him to take charge of events. Like the process of history itself, which "transforms the materials of the world without destroying them, and transforms them subject to laws of its own,"[36] mankind has the capacity to direct its own progress (though the will and wisdom may be lacking). The conclusion of Woodbridge's argument is worth quoting in full, for it could pass as a general explication of *"A"*.

> History is, then, not only the conserving, the remembering, and the understanding of what has happened: it is also the completion of what has happened. And since in man history is consciously lived, the completing of what has happened is also the attempt to carry it to what he calls perfection. He look at a wilderness, but, even as he looks, beholds a garden. For him, consequently, the purpose of history is not a secret he vainly tries to find, but a kind of life his reason enables him to live. As he lives it well, the fragments of existence are completed and illumined in the visions they reveal.[37]

Woodbridge anticipated the kind of effort in which Pound, Williams, Zukofsky, and others would become engaged. In 1926 Zukofsky would compose "Poem Beginning 'The'," which begins with a wasteland and concludes with a memory of lost gardens and a promise of future rebirth. *"A"* has as one of its aims a consideration of what the life of reason might be. The thought of Frederick Woodbridge colors both poems.

Woodbridge and Dewey inspired Zukofsky, but they were not the only men he admired, nor were they most

35. Frederick J. E. Woodbridge, *The Purpose of History* (New York: Columbia University Press, 1916), p. 4.
    36. Ibid., p. 82.   37. Ibid., p. 89.

important influences on his technique. We have to look elsewhere to account for the sudden, drastic change in his style.

Zukofsky himself was silent about the process that led from the Boar's Head mode to "The" and "A". But some of the writings of the contemporary New York avant-garde provide clues. They advocated precisely those traits that came to dominate his art. As early as 1915, some of Alfred Stieglitz's associates saw the opportunity to apply cubist and collage techniques to literature. Their little magazine 291 featured, in its first issue (March 1915), an essay on something called "Simultanism." The editors waxed enthusiastic about the advantages of this principle, even though no specimens of it existed.

> The idea of Simultanism is expressed in painting by the simultaneous representation of the different figures of a form seen from different points of view, as Picasso and Braque did some time ago; or by the simultaneous representation of the figure of several forms as the futurists are doing.
>
> In literature the idea is expressed by the polyphony of simultaneous voices which say different things. Of course, printing is not an adequate medium for succession in this medium is unavoidable and a phonograph is more suitable.
>
> That the idea of simultanism is essentially naturalistic is obvious; that the polyphony of interwoven sounds and meanings has a decided effect upon our sense is unquestionable, and that we can get at the spirit of things through this system is demonstrable.[38]

Space was limited in 291's first number. Those three short paragraphs contain all that the editors had to say on the subject. The next step, obviously enough, was to produce a sample of "Simultanism," and the following issue fea-

38. Unsigned note, 291 1 (March 1915): 1.

tured Agnes Ernst Meyer's brave attempt. She designed a single page for *291* consisting of abstract, multicolored designs upon which sentences, single words, phrases, and advertising slogans uneasily consorted. The function and necessity of the colored designs is not clear. Apparently it was thought necessary to provide something soothing to eyes adrift among print. Further developments of "Simultanism" were never realized. Suddenly born, it suddenly expired: its premises were too narrowly based. The kind of scattered auditory data that Simultanism sought to grapple with would not become pervasive until radio caught on in the 1920s. What was primarily an urban, public experience would then spread into every living room. The cacophony of competing voices would then become familiar as the air.

The editors of *291* had stumbled upon possibilities that could almost be taken as a blueprint for "The" and *"A"*. Of course, Zukofsky could not have seen the magazine in 1915. He was then only ten years old (and too busy reading Shakespeare). Williams probably owned a copy, but he and Zukofsky did not meet until 1928, two years after "The". The significance of Simultanism is simply that some American writers wasted no time in trying to exploit innovations imported from France. That these innovations and the American response to them should foreshadow Zukofsky's work was not coincidental.

The Frenchman he most admired in his early years was someone who championed the work of Picasso and Braque—Guillaume Apollinaire. We do not know when Zukofsky first became excited about the author of *Calligrammes*, but in 1932 he composed a long critical essay titled "The Writing of Guillaume Apollinaire." It appeared (incompletely) in a little magazine soon after. A French translation was made, but most of this edition was destroyed when the publisher's warehouse burned down.

The manner in which Zukofsky praises Apollinaire is

especially important. He does not point to this or that poem as a monument of genius erected at a certain stage in the artist's life. He does quote extensively, but only to assist his argument that Apollinaire aimed for, and achieved, the unification of his aesthetic and his life. Apollinaire, he concludes, not only advocated an art of "simultaneity" that would attempt to combine in some concrete medium many different facets of what one daily sees, hears, feels, and thinks, but actually embodied that aesthetic in his life and productions. Zukofsky presents him as a steadfast and supremely gifted synthesizer.

> Inevitably as well as consciously having to partake of the simultaneously conceived and received construction of the esthetic feeling of his culture (his time's), Apollinaire infused the contemporary principles of a dominant (if not the dominant) industry of the arts—painting—into the implicit judgement of his composition as action—poetry and prose being so-called.
>
> In Apollinaire the whole art would seem to be telescoping, into the choice of words, of times, existences and their thoughts composing into the dominant arts (writing, painting, music) of his era—the intelligence moved by passion and repaying by composition as action.[39]

"Composition as action" suggests that the dividing line between artist and art works is strangely tenuous. Distinctions between the artist and what he produces (or consumes) grow fuzzier and fuzzier. Though still identifiable as separate entities, they seem to have more in common than not. Whether Apollinaire's work exemplifies this seamlessness is debatable. Zukofsky nevertheless convinced himself that he had found a precursor.

Eliminating distinctions between artist and artifacts was

39. Louis Zukofsky, "The Writing of Guillaume Apollinaire," *The Westminster Magazine* 23:1 (Spring 1934): 15, 19.

only one of the shifts that Zukofsky adopted to get on with his work. The revolution in the arts at the beginning of our century generated other possibilities for change. One of these, which Zukofsky delightedly seized upon, is a tension that charges some of the most important works produced during the last sixty years. On the one hand, we find an emphasis on subjects and materials that are local, mundane, and commonplace—sometimes exasperatingly so. On the other hand, we find opposed to this tendency, yet coupled with it, an equally powerful demand for brilliant new feats of artistic innovation. *Ulysses* is perhaps the most perfect example of this tension. It arranges ordinary people and events in startlingly novel fashion. The critics who charged that "nothing happens" in *Ulysses* could see only trivial events enacted by unimportant people. Where was the critical probing of the malaise of the upper classes? What about the sufferings and sordid lives of the proletariat? It was hard to take seriously a long story whose most stirring incident featured a hurled biscuit tin. Of course, the clash between the inglorious events of June 16, 1904, and the prose that manhandled those events was the life of *Ulysses*. Since 1922 we have become more attentive to the author as cunning contriver, though he still lacks the following of the author-sociologists and author-entertainers.

Another tension that bears directly on Zukofsky's art and that connects with the split between materials and intellect is the rivalry pitting the "innocent eye" against the mind—which is presumably guilty. In our time the "innocent eye" has been put on the shelf. It reposes in the museum of intellectual history close by "tabula rasa." Fifty years ago, however, it was a hot issue. Apollinaire found it necessary to argue for the primacy of mind over eye in the visual arts.

> Cubism, which was the art of painting new configurations with elements borrowed, not from visual, but from con-

ceptual, reality. Every human being is conscious of this internal reality. One need not, in fact, be a cultivated man in order to understand that a chair, for example, in whatever position one places it, will always continue to have four legs, a seat, and a back.[40]

Apollinaire's distinction between visual and conceptual reality persists in Zukofsky's aesthetic. It exists comfortably in tandem with the materials/intellect tension. Zukofsky continually stresses the superiority of the "natural human eye" over the "erring brain," reversing Apollinaire but maintaining the dichotomy. Other voices of the period were saying much the same thing. In *Port of New York* (1924) Paul Rosenfeld observed that "on his Watman sheets, John Marin records what his eyes perceive, just as it is perceived; unconcerned with what records itself, or is supposed to record itself, on other retinas."[41] Clear seeing, emphasis on the mundane, feats of mental gymnastics, abstract organization—all are bound together in Zukofsky's art. Anyone who takes Zukofsky at his word when he protests that he is all for the "eye" should recall that he also said, "I can't help thinking."[42]

Nor should his liking for the local blind us to his appreciation of the abstract. Bram Djikstra has shown us that there existed in the early 1920s a pervasive inclination among artists to get back to local subjects, to familiar terrain.[43] The immediate scene: that was what one should paint, photograph, and write about. Williams's concern

40. Guillaume Apollinaire, *Apollinaire on Art: Essays and Reviews, 1902–1918*, ed. Leroy C. Breunig, trans. Susan Suleiman (New York: Viking, 1972), p. 260.

41. Paul Rosenfeld, *Port of New York* (1924; rpt. Urbana: University of Illinois Press, 1961), p. 159.

42. Louis Zukofsky, "About *The Gas Age*," in *Prepositions*, p. 169.

43. Bram Dijkstra, *The Hieroglyphics of a New Speech: Cubism, Stieglitz, and the Early Poetry of William Carlos Williams* (Princeton, N.J.: Princeton University Press, 1969), p. 123.

with "contact" was part of that trend, and it paralleled Whitehead's and Dewey's drive for "contact." A passage from Marsden Hartley's *Adventures in the Arts* (1921) indicates how the urge to be autochthonous influenced him. "There will be no magic found away from life. It is what you do with the street-corner in your brain that shall determine your gift." [44] All well and good, but the unavoidable counterpart of the local intrudes when Hartley elsewhere posits the mind as the place where artistry really takes place. "It is, as we know, brain matter that counts in a work of art, and we have dispensed once and for all with the silly notion that a work of art is made by hand. Art is first and last of all, a product of the intelligence." [45] Intelligence, not localization, becomes the acid test of contemporary art.

Self/art, materials/intellect, eye/mind: these dualities were important issues when Zukofsky was learning his craft. They remained important for him throughout his career. "A" would hardly have the shape it does but for the friction developed by the conjunction of concrete, local materials and the play of the author's mind over them. Despite Zukofsky's avowed inability to resist "thinking," he could not have been counterattacking very strongly. Williams made an astute observation, in his afterword to the first edition of "A" 1–12, about Zukofsky's approach to the world of words.

> After all a poem is a matter of words, the meaning of words. The *meaning*. I was seeking, perhaps, a picture (as an imagist poet) to relate my poem to; the intellectual meaning of the word, the pure meaning, was lost, we'll say, on me. Zukofsky when he thought of a rose didn't

44. Marsden Hartley, *Adventures in the Arts* (1921; rpt. New York: Hacker Art Books, 1972), p. 9.
45. Ibid., p. 105.

think of the physical limits of the flower but more of what a rose meant to the mind. . . .[46]

"The" and "A" actually resemble physical collages, in which ordinary things (often junk) serve as an arena where the real focus of interest is artistic intelligence. In retrospect it seems that the 1920s were a fortunate time for a young man to be exposed to new trends in the arts—at least if the young man came equipped with as various a background as Zukofsky had. This incessant contention of opposites helped him get a grip on the diversities of his own history.

We can trace an unbroken line of evolution from Zukofsky's *Morningside* poems, through "Poem Beginning 'The'," to the first few movements of "A". "Poem Beginning 'The'" is partly his forum for disowning the brand of poetry he had practiced at Columbia. At one point he takes a poke at Erskine's influence.[47]

168   Engprof, thy lectures were to me
169   Like those roast flitches of red boar
170   That, smelling, one is like to see
171   Through windows where the steam's galore
172   Like our own "Cellar Door."

Since "cellar door" would be the most beautiful phrase in English (barring its meaning), the indictment Zukofsky brings against himself, Erskine, and his peers, charges them with being overly concerned with mellifluous sounds. Their poems, he hints, sound fine—but mean nothing. Hence the hint of a pun on boar/bore in line 169.

"The"'s overall form is that of an academic satire, albeit

46. William Carlos Williams, "Zukofsky," in "A" 1–12 (Kyoto: Origin Press, 1959), pp. 292–93.

47. All: The Collected Short Poems, p. 17.

much more ambitious and sophisticated than most specimens of the genre. The complications begin early, before we get to the main text. In advance stands a pre-text in two parts.[48] First comes the title: "Poem Beginning 'The'." True enough—a glance ahead confirms our suspicion that the first word is indeed *the*. The title does not lie, but we feel cheated nonetheless. The second segment of the prefatory apparatus is a long list of the sources for quotations and paraphrases in the poem. Unfortunately, the more closely we inspect this so-called dedication, the more puzzling it becomes. Like the title, it contains no help for the reader seeking a message. The whole prefatory section makes gestures of accommodation, cumbering the seeker of "ideas about literature and life" with useless help.

What happens if we approach these prickly pre-texts at a different angle and inspect the nature of the obstacles? The title demonstrates how irritating the bare truth can be to lovers of "aesthetic emotions." It is utterly lacking in romance. The list of acknowledgments seduces our attention and leaves us struggling in a textual morass, for it is designed to resemble (1) the usual acknowledgments prefacing a scholarly work, (2) a dedication, and (3) notes unlocking an esoteric text, a key to "The". It is none of these completely. The acknowledgments are flippant, the dedication so dilutes itself as to be worthless; and knowing the sources of the quotations rarely helps us to understand why they were chosen or how they fit together. The ostensible dedication introduces the poem by its form; it squeezes three conventional forms into a new shape that is annoyingly familiar. At the age of twenty-two, Zukofsky had mastered the technique of collapsed collage.

48. Much later Zukofsky added a Persian epigraph to the poem. He got it from Basil Bunting, who had lifted it from Omar Khayyam.

All the fragmentation in Zukofsky's life before 1926 does not explain why he could write "The". There were, after all, plenty of young men with similar histories who never wrote a line. But the problem of squeezing his heritage, education, and ambitions into 330 lines makes the poem live. The first of the six movements, headed by an epigraph from Chaucer—"And out of olde books, in good feith"—consists largely of quotations from a score of contemporary authors: Joyce, Eliot, Cummings, Lawrence, and so forth. It seems to be a highly digested version of a Great Modern Books course. At the end of the movement it becomes clear why these recent works are "olde books." They complain about alienation, disintegration, and exile—conditions Jews have lived with for centuries. Old themes make for old books. Such unexpected, but justifiable, coalitions of "unlikes" provide the poem's energy.

"The" depends for its effects on the juxtaposition of academic styles, popular songs, literary allusions, translations from Yiddish folksongs and poems (principally the poems of Solomon Bloomgarden, pen name "Yehoash"), and divers other storehouses of diction. Strange, witty torsions are produced when these voices blend into one another. In the fifth movement, we find Zukofsky addressing his mother in English, a language she did not understand. He assumes the voice of Shylock in a performance resembling a Columbia dramatic production of *The Merchant of Venice*.[49]

254   I'll read their Donne as mine,
255   And leopard in their spots
256   I'll do what says their Coleridge,
257   Twist red hot pokers into knots.
258   The villainy they teach me I will execute.

49. *All: The Collected Short Poems*, p. 20.

259   And it shall go hard with them,
260   For I'll better the instruction.
261   Having learned, so to speak, in their colleges.

The passage, and the whole poem, is partly a demonstration in complicated knot-tying. Observe also that the phrase "so to speak" means both "after a fashion" and "to speak like this." Zukofsky often insisted on his right to say two or more things simultaneously.

"Poem Beginning 'The'" carries itself with perfect assurance, as if this were the logical mode of expression for a young New York Jew. It is a triumph, and not just technically so. The author's passions come through strongly. His anger and frustration over displacement, poverty, injustice, intellectual corrosion, and so forth tally exactly with the broken, spotlit, warped contortions of the verse. His emotions *are* the lines of "The": intense, self-centered, ardent, and swift in their alternation.

The poem's obvious predecessor is "The Waste Land." In an attempt to surpass Eliot, Zukofsky pushes formal details to an excessive, but liberating, limit. Eliot numbered every tenth line, Zukofsky numbers all of them; Eliot appended witty notes, Zukofsky confounds us at the start with his daunting dedication; Eliot divided his poem into five parts; Zukofsky has six movements. Zukofsky stretches and pummels the modern idiom until he can call it his own. This seizure and recalibration of "The Waste Land" is consistent with "The"'s feverish engorgement. Zukofsky seems to want his poem to devour everything within range.

But "The" could also be described as an introspective's house of mirrors—potentially a deceptive, dangerous locale. Someone less intelligent and less ambitious might have spent years pursuing the same vein before discovering that investigations of the self require constant invention. But Zukofsky had found a voice something like his own, and he wasted no time in expanding its range. As soon as he had finished with "The", he started planning a more comprehensive work.[50]

50. While he planned, however, he submitted "The" to Pound, as a calling card presented by one poet to another. Zukofsky did not know of the extent to which "The Waste Land" was an editorial achievement, but he did know that Pound was encouraging, promoting, and publishing new talent. The calling card was accepted, and the friendship between Zukofsky and Pound lasted until Pound's death. Through Pound's good offices, Zukofsky found other valuable friends, such as Basil Bunting, Carl Rakosi, and William Carlos Williams.

TWO

The Resurrectionist: *"A"* 1–7

And he is not likely to know what is to be done unless he lives in what is not merely the present, but the present moment of the past, unless he is conscious, not of what is dead, but of what is already living.

T. S. Eliot, "Tradition and the Individual Talent"

WHAT SEEMS to be the earliest sketch for *"A"* still survives. In faded pencil on one side of a small, creased piece of paper ranges a list of the section titles for a poem in twenty-four parts.[1] Some jottings were added in the mid-thirties, but at least the outline of intended section titles seems genuinely of 1927–28 vintage. This initial schema suggests that Zukofsky originally thought of *"A"* as more widely ranging than "The", but not greatly so. *"A"* grew directly out of "The", and the ur-plan shows close thematic ties between the two projects. *"A"*'s proposed section 2 was to be entitled "The Dead"; section 6 would take another look at feminine attractions under the mysterious aspect of one "Helena E."; section 16 would rehash "Ye-hoash"; section 18 would be "Couer-de-Leon"; section 21 aimed at "Johann Sebastian"; and section 24 would yoke "The" and *"A"*. In short, most of the names and preoccupations that populated "The" would appear in *"A"*.

1. This manuscript is now in the Zukofsky Collection at the Humanities Research Center, University of Texas at Austin (hereafter referred to as HRC).

Apparently the "*A*" that Zukofsky had in mind could have been completed in a few years. Perhaps it was intended as an intermediate step to something truly epic. (There are references to a proposed "*An*" in his letters to Pound.) What little evidence we have indicates that the actual composition of "*A*" created unexpected problems. Zukofsky dropped his plan and concentrated on finishing the first seven parts of "*A*". It would still have twenty-four movements when completed, but the completion date was pushed into the indefinite future.

Writing to Carl Rakosi in 1931, after finishing movements 1 through 7, he was uncharacteristically dubious about his work. "The Seventh Movement still seems to me the best I've done and Pound, fortunately, thinks '*A*' is better than 'The'. I think so and hope so. If not—well— . . . ." [2] The new work was already three times longer than "The". Zukofsky may have been wondering if it held together. Compounding the problems of length and unity were the new uses Zukofsky had found for verbal collage. "The"'s juggling of voices seems mainly a demonstration that such a technique could delineate character. "*A*" refines and extends that method. In the new poem, Zukofsky gives wider scope to other individuals and presents versions of himself—a series of self-caricatures.

"*A*" begins with Zukofsky in Carnegie Hall, observing a performance of Bach's *St. Matthew Passion*.

> A
>> Round of fiddles playing Bach.
>>> *Come, ye daughters, share my anguish* —
>> Bare arms, black dresses,
>>> *See Him! Whom?*
>> Bediamond the passion of our Lord,
>>> *See Him! How?*

2. Letter of February 6, 1931, HRC.

His legs blue, tendons bleeding,
   O Lamb of God most holy!
Black full dress of the audience.
Dead century, where are your motley
Country people in Leipzig,
Easter,
Matronly flounces, starched, heaving,
Cheeks of the patrons of Leipzig —
"Going to Church? Where's the baby?"
"Ah there's the Kapellmeister
   in a terrible hurry —
Johann Sebastian, twenty-two
   children!"

The Passion According to Matthew,
Composed seventeen twenty-nine,
Rendered at Carnegie Hall,
Nineteen twenty-eight,
Thursday evening, the fifth of April.
The autos parked, honking.   (p. 1)

It shortly becomes clear that "Zukofsky" is as much the focus of interest as the activity he reports. The scene unfolds at sufficient length and with sufficient detail to assure us that we, as readers, and Zukofsky, the main character, are solidly grounded in a fairly ordinary time and place. We even know the exact date. But we arrive at that basic ground after surmounting some obstacles, such as that vignette of townspeople in Leipzig watching Bach hustle to the church on Easter Sunday, 1729.

How can we account for this time-warp? The justification seems to be that the *St. Matthew Passion* provides a fixed point for comparison of audiences. Zukofsky peers sourly from the balcony at the upper classes, and, finding them disgusting, he constructs a pleasant, jocular, eighteenth-century miniature. The Leipzig scene is plainly a fantasy revolving in the head of Zukofsky the character. It isn't accurate either, since Bach had not fathered twenty-two children by 1729.

At the end of the concert Zukofsky slowly walks toward the exit, but loses his way. Confused, not knowing where to turn, he is overtaken by an usher, who then undergoes a peculiar metamorphosis.

> Galleries darkening.
> "Not that exit, Sir!"
> Ecdysis: the serpent coming out, molting,
> As tho blood stained the floor as the foot stepped,
> Bleeding chamfer for shoulder   (p. 2)

Another imagined scene, but here the setting is hell. "The serpent coming out" emerges from the twenty-fifth canto of the *Inferno*, where thieves are punished by being repeatedly changed into loathsome reptiles. "Bleeding chamfer" recalls the description of the amputated damned in the twenty-eighth canto. The hell Zukofsky envisions is supplied with props taken from literary tradition. We begin to perceive that *"A"*-1 is a scrupulous investigation by the author of the psychology of a less mature version of himself.

As might be expected, "Zukofsky" undergoes a temptation—a rather subtle one. He is invited to give up his sense of righteous indignation and accept things as they are, to drop idealism and get what he can for himself. The issues involved are hard to follow in the final version of *"A"*-1. The 1928 version has more substance.[3]

> "Blood of your desire to graft what you desire,
> Consider the Angels who sang in the boys' choir

---

3. *Pagany* (Summer 1932): 10. The first seven movements of *"A"* appeared in *Poetry*, *The New Review*, *Pagany*, and *An "Objectivists" Anthology* (Le Beausset, Var, France, and New York: To Publishers, 1932). In the summer of 1942, Zukofsky revised the first six movements. Most of the changes were deletions.

> God's cherubs,
> If seen near the ocean, stripped white skins, red
>   coat of the sunburn,—
> They have mothers."
> "No, Satan, not heart that bled
> Over boy's voices, nor blood
> Flowing for lost sons
> I have harbored perfection."

The temptation tacitly assumes that earthly existence is reducible to mere sweaty flesh, rutting and working, and "Zukofsky" doesn't have the wit to see that he is playing the devil's game by accepting that reduction. The noble young idealist rejects the base proposal; instead, he loftily chooses something he calls "desire longing for perfection" (p. 2). He strikes a pose modeled on Christ spurning the wiles of Satan in the wilderness.

> And as one who under stars
> Spits across the sand dunes, and the winds
> Blow thru him, the spittle drowning worlds —
>
> (p. 2)

This grand gesture inflates "Zukofsky" like a balloon. He then steps into a few lines that show him in a more practical light.

> I lit a cigarette, and stepped free
> Beyond the red light of the exit.
>
> The usher faded thru "Camel" smoke   (p. 2)

In addition to this descent from the sublime to the inane, there is another joke working to undercut pomposity. Those sand dunes have an inglorious origin, and the cigarette is the clue. In 1928 a pack of "Camels" depicted a camel, two pyramids, and three palm trees, all supported by a desert.

By now we understand that "Zukofsky" is victimized in *"A"*-1 by an assumption that some vague, ethereal sphere tagged "Art" contains the answers to his problems. We recognize that the contents of his mind are considerably less grand than "Art," containing as it does specimens of commercial art alongside the Bible and Dante. We suspect, and rightly so, that the "Zukofsky" fulminating in *"A"*-1 bears a strong resemblance to the member of the Boar's Head Society who dreamed of fauns and nymphs. Pained by the tragedies of modern life, he plans to flee to the world of beautiful illusions. *"A"*-1 works to subvert and make ludicrous such intentions.

After renouncing the world and the devil, Zukofsky slowly makes his way home, falling along the way into a revery nourished by his memories of the concert.

> The blood's tide like the music.
> A round of fiddles playing
> Without effort —
> As into the fields and forgetting to die.
> The streets smoothed over as fields,
> Not even the friction of wheels,
> Feet off ground:
> As beyond effort —
> Music leaving no traces,
> Not dying and leaving no traces.   (p. 4)

This private euphoria seems dangerously insubstantial. How did those fields creep into lower Manhattan? Wherever they came from (Flanders?), they are surely not discoverable among the skyscrapers. Shouldn't one have a little more respect for the rough edges of city life? Furthermore, this bubbleheaded approach to music ignores what effort may have gone into its composition and performance. At this juncture, young Zukofsky seems inclined to believe that Bach merely sat down with quill in hand

and let divine inspiration take its course. Walking on air, he eventually floats home, begins to deflate, and jots down a few notes.

> Not boiling to put pen to paper
> Perhaps a few things to remember —
> "There are different techniques,
> Men write to be read, or spoken,
> Or declaimed, or rhapsodized,
> And quite differently to be sung";
> "I heard him agonizing,
> I saw him *inside*";
> "Everything which
> We really are and never quite live."
> Far into (about three) in the morning   (p. 4)

That "Zukofsky" is not boiling to put pen to paper is another disheartening sign, but at least he begins to show some life: the notes stress the necessary complications of art. His selections show hope for him because they are all comments by contemporary poets who valued innovation.

The first quotation comes from Pound's *Antheil and the Treatise on Harmony*:

> Lawes' work is an example of how the words of a poem may be set, and enhanced by music. There are different techniques in poetry; men write to be read, or spoken, or declaimed, or rhapsodized; and quite differently to be sung.[4]

This is a useful caution that inspiration is only part of the poet's equipment. The craft is various, and each technique has to be learned slowly, patiently. "Zukofsky" will never bother with "different techniques" while mooning over the comforts that may be derived from listening to Bach.

4. Ezra Pound, *Antheil and the Treatise on Harmony* (Paris: Three Mountains Press, 1924), p. 61.

The second extract can be found in Williams's *A Voyage to Pagany* (1928). Chapter 26 ends with some enthusiastic words from Dev (the protagonist who stands in for Williams) after hearing a performance of Bach:

> Funny old figure he must have been going across the street having generated another child in the night. Over to the old organ loft. Something uncanny about it. —Dev was concerned. A light—coming, I saw him, I heard him and not like a man on the street. I heard him agonizing. I saw him *inside*, not cold but he *lived* and I was possessed by his passion.[5]

"Zukofsky" is too wrapped up in himself to hear any agonizing. The passage from *Pagany* presents an alternative, more fitting, approach to music.

E. E. Cummings's *Him* provides the last quotation. The play opened at the Provincetown Playhouse just a few days after the performance of the *St. Matthew Passion*, but had been published the year before. At that time (1927) Zukofsky wrote a highly favorable review of the play and sent it off to Pound for publication in *The Exile*. The quotation is lifted from this speech:

> When I could see, this other person's eyes and my eyes were looking at each other. Hers were big and new in the darkness. They seemed to be looking at me as if we had known each other somewhere else. They were very close—so close that my breath almost touched them. . . . I can't describe it—a shyness, more shy than you can ever imagine, a shyness cohabiting very easily and very skillfully everything which we really are and everything which we never quite live.[6]

5. William Carlos Williams, *A Voyage to Pagany* (1928; rpt. New York: New Directions, 1970), pp. 179–80.

6. E. E. Cummings, *Him* (New York: Boni and Liveright, 1927), p. 120.

An unusual choice to make if Zukofsky is really a solipsist. Perhaps he is not so much in the clouds as we had thought.

What this and the other selections do is double; they act as comforters to the young man, but they also tend to bring him back to the world. Note the ambiguity in the Cummings selection: the question of what we "really are," as it stands in *"A"*-1, hints that Zukofsky may be considering a necessary self-examination. The pull of the verse back to particulars continues in the deft parenthesis of "Far into (about three) in the morning." The preliminary phrasing suggests the hackneyed "far into the night," but changes in mid-sentence to a less romantic statement.

"A"-1 follows Zukofsky into the next day, Good Friday, and by then the uplifting effects of the music have completely worn off. Sinking back to the grubby, everyday world, the young man gloomily announces he is "ready to give up the ghost in a cellar" (p. 5). The correlation between Christ's burial and young Zukofsky's despair suggests that the ensuing resurrection will produce a quite different Zukofsky.

The figure of "Zukofsky" in *"A"*-1 is basically the personality sketched in "The", but with one crucial difference. In *"A"*-1 he lacks the wit, discipline, and ironical self-consciousness that went into the making of "The". To put it another way, author and subject were identical in "The", but are several years apart in *"A"*-1. "Zukofsky" in the poem's first movement has potential, but is deliberately stripped of synthesizing power. This "pre-poet" disappears into the cellar at the end of the first movement, to be replaced in *"A"*-2 by the figure of the "real" Zukofsky, the author of *"A"*-1.

We find him engaged in debate with someone named "Kay," but the tables have been turned. Kay adopts the position espoused by the Zukofsky of *"A"*-1, while the Zukofsky of *"A"*-2 vigorously dissents. The argument seems to have been underway for some time, and we join it *in medias res*. It presumably started in response to the indecorous "name calling" that Kay claims Zukofsky is guilty of perpetrating in *"A"*-1. Thus Zukofsky as author in *"A"*-2 defends *"A"*-1 against its first critic. Kay condemns Zukofsky's grumbling about social evils in the first movement. Instead, he should be producing the kind of poetry Kay terms "clear music" (p. 6). This evidently is an aesthetic of scrupulous isolation from everything troublesome, a program resembling the young Zukofsky's "desire longing for perfection" in *"A"*-1. Kay defines poetry—true poetry—as an insular activity worthy of the name so long as it avoids unpleasant matters. After all, how can one glory in Art's perfection if it includes the imperfections of the world?

But since *"A"* is the kind of poem it is, and Zukofsky is in charge, that position gets short shrift. Kay's argument covers only six lines, while Zukofsky replies in the next sixty-five, demonstrating graphically the narrowness of "clear music" and the expansiveness of his art. The sea enters *"A"* for the first time as Zukofsky's metaphor for the complications of the world at large, which poetry cannot afford to ignore. To avoid (he says) all that is around "in the sea / . . . with you" (p. 6) is to be a victim of the tides, as the "Zukofsky" of *"A"*-1 is a victim of his own isolated ways of thinking. Opposed to Kay's wish for autonomous music (which verges on solipsistic muttering), Zukofsky affirms that music is ubiquitously present in nature in many forms. That assertion works not only as a bare statement, but through a series of metaphors. As Zukofsky continues, his rhetoric weaves a web of relations.

> The music is in the flower,
> Leaf around leaf ranged around the center;
> Profuse but clear outer leaf breaking on space,

> There is space to step to the central heart:
> The music is in the flower,
> It is not the sea but hyaline cushions the flower —
> Liveforever, everlasting.
> The leaves never topple from each other,
> Each leaf a buttress flung for the other.
>
> Ankle, like fetlock, at the center leaf —
> Looked into the mild orbs of the flower,
> Eyes drowned in the mild orbs   (p. 7)

The order of the day in "A"-1 was invidious judgment. But in this passage music, flowers, architectural details, horses, and eyes, looking into flowers and out of them, all connect. Zukofsky as debater is overdoing it a bit here, but at least he shows a healthy interest in the objects around. The end of "A"-2, with its glance at young lovers in a field, even borders on voyeurism.

The principle of inclusion, with the artist playing the role of seer, lies at the heart of "A", as does a faith in the powers of harmony. What Zukofsky seems to be doing in "A"-2 is encouraging himself with a bit of fervor because he faces the burden of organizing all the voices, images, and attitudes that will inevitably crowd into such an expansive poem. The "Zukofsky" of "A"-2 may be another projection of the author with characteristics slanted to meet the demands of the moment. In "A"-1 we saw a "Zukofsky" helpless in the grip of events and emotions, yet potentially capable of organizing them. "A"-2's Zukofsky, an artist, faces large challenges and welcomes them. He even makes bold to don the voices of Christ and Walt Whitman at the close of "A"-2:

> I walked on Easter Sunday
> This is my face
> This is my form   (p. 8)

echoing Christ's "This is my body . . . This is my blood" at the Last Supper (Mark 14:22–24).

> Faces and forms, I would write
> you down
> In a style of leaves growing.   (p. 8)

By issuing versions of himself to act within the poem at its beginning, Zukofsky deftly avoids the burden of starting the poem as if it were the justification and repository for his thoughts and hopes. He is determined not to be the "star" of the poem (at least not yet), and the first two movements operate to provide enough ironic distance between his real self and the poem to permit him to enter it at a later point. By then the poem will, so to speak, have a life of its own, and Zukofsky will make his entrance onto a fully developed and functioning stage. "A" is not the first work in which the author aims to be both the creator and a character. Very few poems, however, have exhibited such a painstaking, subtle, and extended concern with double acting.

Part of the reason for this multiplication of Zukofskys can be traced to the aesthetic he advocates in "A"-2. If one is dedicated to garnering the external world, a single personality may be insufficient as a container. Kay's poetics lean in the other direction. But if one ignores the unpleasant, one may wander away from reality. Once headed down the road to "clear music," where do we stop? Kay's sex is deliberately left ambiguous, suggesting that she/he has written herself/himself into limbo.

Granted the admirable inclusiveness so firmly announced in "A"-2, what then? That ambition entails a problem. Life and expansiveness may be dominant powers in the world, but death also has claims on the attention, and cannot be ignored. In "A"-3 the poem takes up the challenge of dealing with it. This movement is an elegy for someone named "Ricky," and we are told no more than his first name and that he died young. It is as if he had barely existed, and the spareness of the verse seems a measure of how little there was to his life and what little remains in memory. Yet the ambiguity achieved through condensation allows Zukofsky to exploit disturbing effects that excite rather than dampen our curiosity about Ricky. Those effects rely on a curious property of language: words are charged with most meaning just when they approach the point at which the tenuous links between them threaten to evaporate. The problem for any poet working so economically is to know when to stop paring away. Zukofsky's whittling produces this—

> Automobiles speed
> Past the cemetery,
>
> No meter turns.
> Sleep,
>
> With an open gas range
> Beneath for a pillow
> . . . .
> "Who smelt gas?"
> "— Would I lie!"
>
> "No crossin' bridges,
> Rick' —
> No bridges, not after midnight!"
>
> "— God's gift to woman!"   (p. 9)

Is that meter a gas meter or a taxi meter? Should we rule out poetic meter? There are hints that Ricky may have died from suffocation by gas, but there are also suggestions he may have been killed in a car crash. Mysteries multiply as the exuberant Ricky becomes entangled by images of constriction. Consider the phrase "open gas range," which seems to connote a placid suicide, yet also contains the words "open" and "range," a detail connecting with the later images of Ricky as untamed cowboy and knight. For every bit of vitality there seems to be a matching breakdown. The phrasing of "A broken stanchion. / Of leaves" (p. 11) invites us to combine those conflicting images, even though punctuation and common sense set them apart. After the exuberance of "A"-2, "A"-3 strikes us as something like driving with the emergency brake engaged. This sudden change, taken together with the flipflop of "Zukofsky" between "A"-1 and "A"-2, reveals one of the poem's guidelines. It advances by alternation. (This phenomenon is treated more fully in chapter 6.)

As if sobered by "A"-3, the fourth movement shifts emphasis to the problem of the poem's continuation. The "adventures of 'Zukofsky'" are no longer sufficient to sustain "A". In fact, the poem begins to take on some of the narcissism that tinged "Zukofsky" in "A"-1. Like a hypochondriac fearful of drafts and damps, movements 4, 5, and 6 show increasing concern over their own viability.

"A"-4 takes up the matter of origins, the first instance of "A"'s continuing fascination with genesis. Three particular voices sound within the movement, each dwelling on origins. First come the Jewish elders, highly orthodox and passionate men. They look to God, who seems to be painfully distant—as distant as the stars. They lament in the accents of those who feel abandoned. "Even the Death has gone out of us — we are void" (p. 13). Yehoash (whom we last saw in "The") also considers the roots of his race, but finds it possible to regard them as terrestrial, not in terms that put them centuries or light-years away. He is also willing to explore the songs of other cultures—the "jargon" the elders condemn. The brief extracts from Yehoash suggest that his poetry, not limiting itself to a straitened tradition, finds strength in the natural world. Finally, J. S. Bach himself speaks. The passage (from Charles Sanford Terry's *Bach*) jestingly points out that the foundation of the family's musical talent was a grinding millstone—a quite solid and substantial base.[7] Passing from the elders to Yehoash to Bach, we witness a narrowing of the gap between the speaker and his point of origin. The elders see that locus as distant and fragmented, Yehaosh finds it dispersed, but vitalized, in the world about him; Bach treats it as monolithic and available at the nearest mill.

The problem of origins is, of course, intimately connected with the discovery of an authentic voice. "A"-4 suggests that authenticity is made rather than found. "We had a Speech," claim the elders—one they inherited. If the speech has subsided into a jargon studded with alien expressions, as they fear, then it no longer transmits the ancient traditions. The elders have a point. Their claim that the younger generation uses a corrupt language mirrors the poem's coming difficulties. If "A" continues to introduce new material (and the ground rules dictate such addition), the sheer multiplicity of items may overwhelm the poem. It could collapse into an olio of unrelated items.

"A"-6, longer than the first five movements put together, exemplifies the crisis. Here, for example, Zukofsky uses part of his space to tabulate what has gone before, as if lassoing stray details. Lines 71–101 of "A"-6 (pp. 23–34) are a retrospective of themes seen before in "A" 1–5. Inventory in this fashion is mere addition; the poem cannot continue for any great length along this path and still maintain unity. The language of the poem has been singing; will it drop into stammering and then to silence? Zukofsky's program, as announced in "A"-2, would then be

7. Charles Sanford Terry, *Bach: A Biography* (London: Oxford University Press, 1928). Quotations from Terry's book are scattered throughout "A".

no better than Kay's. The last words of the movement succinctly state the problem; "With all this material / To what
distinction —" (p. 38). That query elicits a proper answer,
one that can only be appreciated after rummaging in "A"-6.

The structure of this movement appears at first to be exceptionally slack. It allows enough room for Zukofsky to
travel to California and back. Though not actually a baggy
monster, it pretends to be one. It starts with a mention of
the sea: shorthand for chaotic, vast, multitudinous form
(or lack of form). "Environs, the sea of —" (p. 21), it begins. Sea of what? The incompletion of the first line con-
denses the new difficulties in the burgeoning poem; if no
way can be found to orchestrate the themes and "jargon"
of "A", it will simply come to a stop. Extinction is a theme
as well as a threat, and develops in the movement along
such lines as these.

> Saying, It's a hard world anyway,
> > Not many of us will get out of it alive.
>
> But who would say —
> If this world, the sources,
> Fathers, wherever they put their hats,
> Spiralled with tessellation as sands of the sea,
> The Speech no longer spoken and not even a Wall
> > > > to worship,
> Holy, laundered into a blank and washed over
> Tradition's pebbles, the mouth full,
> The fugue a music heap,
> > only by the name's grace music
> (Fate — fate — fate — void   unable to write
> > > > a melody —
> Ludwig and Goethe of one century,
> Forms only in snatches,
> Words rangeless, melody forced by writing,
> Walk, as arms beat in circles, past each other) —
>
> > Would you persist?   (p. 22)

It appears that the true corrupters of the speech are the "Fathers," who so fervently clutch it to themselves as a sacred relic that they have wrung the vitality out of it. The passage rhymes this kind of enervation with decadent versions of Romanticism, suggesting that all cultures suffer from the steady fossilization of living traditions. The triple rap of "fate" followed by a "void" reproduces a way of attending to music we saw before in *"A"*-1. Beethoven's Fifth Symphony, opening with three repeated G's followed by an extended E-flat, prompted some misguided appreciation. The gloss "So pocht das Schicksal an die Pforte" (Thus Fate knocks at the door) was even ascribed to the composer by romantic generalists. *"A"*-6, worried about loss of distinction, tussles with "forms only in snatches," the last stage before disappearance of form altogether. Of course it exploits that stage as well: "forms only in snatches" describes Zukofsky's approach, though not his intentions.

The problem of any tradition's continuation is that it must change to live. (*"A"*'s line of development constantly alters, yet it grows by such deviations.) The "speech" so jealously preserved by the elders is rendered sterile and threadbare by isolation. It dessicates in splendid solitude. The passage reminds us of a connection raised in *"A"*-1; solipsism, private salvation, private appreciation, and the cult of Art are related.

"A"-6 could be described as a catalogue of slides toward the void. Traditions, imperialism, capitalism, popular taste, contemporary morality—all seem to be going downhill fast. The movement spotlights retrogression, selecting representative details from the eighteenth, nineteenth, and twentieth centuries. The eighteenth seems to come off best, since it has for its ambassadors Bach and Mozart, masters of fugue and melody.

> Ours is no Mozart's
> Magic Flute —

Tho his melody made up for a century
And, we know, from him, a melody resolves
                              to no dullness —   (p. 24)

With the arrival of the nineteenth century comes Romanticism, which has the unlucky faculty of being easily cheap-
ened into crude versions. So we find Henry Ford, master
of the assembly line, opining that

> "We need beauty in everything, and culture
> Should be a thing of practice,
> Not something apart.
> Everything should be a thing of beauty,
> Well made and well thought out."   (p. 26)

Somewhere he picked up a debased version of a line of
thought that extends from Keats ("a thing of beauty") to
Pater and Wilde. His understanding of it is so reduced to
worn-out phrases that we cannot locate a definite source
for the generalities—one sign of ignorance. Trained in
a superficial comprehension of the less mechanical arts
("History is bunk"), Ford can only find the modern poets
meaningless.

> "I read poetry, and I enjoy it
> If it says anything,
> But so often it doesn't say anything."   (p. 26)

The transition from *Endymion* to the sage of River Rouge
suggests that those who are ignorant of poetry are con-
demned to repeat it, badly.
    There are a few upholders of distinction working in this
century to renovate civilization; Einstein gets a nod of ap-
proval. Another artisan receives brief acknowledgment.

> Histories, differences, walls,
> And the words which bind them no more than
> "So that," "and" —   (p. 27)

A tribute to Pound and his *Cantos*, where "so that" and "and" serve as mortar binding different voices, different ages.

"A"-6 examines other areas of contemporary collapse. In one passage, sexual indefinition links with imperialism. The scene begins in Haiti, where "Mars / Bloody / Tinkered with the other / Stars" (a synopsis of American interventions in the Caribbean?). "Tinkered" suggests Yankee know-how. Mars cheating on Venus is perhaps a code for the "Stars and Stripes" straying too far south.

> An accent, not any one nation's
> . . . .
> The hands wandering over each other,
> A hole and entered.
> And above terraces of the city, a hill,
> Night, Aldebaran,
> Young, no differences in ages, a hole.
> 'Disturbed?' 'What's in the underbrush?' A white rabbit
> Plumped on his belly, Reassured. Thru trees,
> White teeth perhaps
> Laughed. . .   (p. 31)

Speech is reduced to no definable accent; it is all homogenized. Sexes are no matter; re-creation is merely a question of finding someone else with a hole, and what hole is entered is immaterial. The cancellation of distinctions leads to serious consequences—the abyss of nothingness gapes wide. Thus the allusions to the particularly ephemeral parts of *Alice in Wonderland*: the hole into which the White Rabbit disappeared and down which Alice tumbled, the fading grin of the Cheshire Cat. This scene tells us something important about cultural entropy; one of its symptoms is a regression to childishness. The poem reports that the highest ambition of a "Septuagenarian actor" (p. 27) is to own a "personal locomotive / For retired estate which his boy day dreams realized." So our century labors to achieve placid juvenility.

Even "Zukofsky" suffers from regressive symptoms: he shows bad taste. "Cut short the night's work, / Took her to see 'Connie's Hot Chocolates'" (p. 37). We began "A" with the St. Matthew Passion, but wind up at a minstrel show. Zukofsky tries to cushion the fall by noting that Bach was not always serious.

> He wrote a Kaffee Cantata
> Spelling it "Coffee" as we do (sounded contacts)
> A kind of "Hot Chocolates" five years after the Passion
> (p. 37)

Just the same, Zukofsky seems to have strayed from his course, and at the conclusion of the movement has to remind himself what "A" is all about.

> Forgetting
>   I said:
>   *Can*
>   The design
>   Of the fugue
>   Be transferred
>   To poetry?
>   *At eventide*
>   Venus come up
> How shall I —
> Her soles new as the sunned black of her grave's turf,
> With all this material
>   To what distinction —   (p. 38)

The author has not really forgotten about fugal design. If there is any authorial amnesia in "A"-6, it is only pretense, for the slides toward extinction that the movement displays are counterpointed by examples of poetic organization. A small sample of such vitality hides in the section quoted above. It begins with a return of awareness, is followed by a phrase from the *St. Matthew Passion* ("At eventide") that accompanies Christ's burial (which in *"A"*-3 was associated with Ricky), and concludes with a view of Venus rising from the sea and a memory of Zukofsky's recently buried mother. So two promising regenerations balance and are balanced by two deaths. The sexes also are equal: two males, two females.

Playing against the themes of descent and dissolution, the movement includes material suggesting ascent and solidity; it even employs two small but sturdy words to help out: "hard" and "up." *"A"*-6, though apparently verging on collapse, contains plenty of material about shoring up, maintaining, and growing. Especially important to *"A"* at this juncture is the emphasis on "particulars."

> Inextricably the direction of historic and
> > contemporary particulars
>
> J.S.B.: a particular,
> His Matthew Passion, a particular   (p. 24)

> On that morning when everything
> > will be clear,
> Greeting myself, despite glasses,
> The world's earth a rose,
> > rose every particle
> The palm open,
> > earth's lily,
> One will see
> > gravel in gravel
> . . . .
> Not that one will get, see
> > more than particulars   (pp. 27–28)

In the "Objectivist" issue of *Poetry*, edited by Zukofsky in 1931, he tried to explain—with a tip of the hat to Marianne

Moore—that he had a rather broad definition of "particulars" in mind, a definition suitable for abstract organization:

> It is understood that historic and contemporary particulars may mean a thing or things as well as an event or chain of events: i.e., an Egyptian pulled-glass bottle in the shape of a fish or oak leaves, as well as the performance of Bach's Matthew Passion in Leipzig, or the Russian Revolution and the rise of metallurgical plants in Siberia.[8]

"A"-6 therefore includes cultural developments as particulars as well as humbler "parts." The words "hard" and "up" combine with one "part" and produce this risqué passage, part of "A"'s fertility theme.

> Ricky's romance
> Of twenty-three years, in
> Detail, continues
>
> He — a— pyjamas off —
> Invites ants upon his ankle
> Up-up, ta-ta,
>   minus, but quite there:
>
> "I beg your pardon
> I've a— "h" begins the rhyme here,
> Shall we now?   (p. 23)

The phallus hardening up, and Venus rising at the close, are part of a continuity circumventing entropy. But "A"-6 at times seems troubled by this very dichotomy. Solidity can be taken too far. As Zukofsky visits the West Coast, he finds fixation produces a

> Type of mind faking a thirst for itself —
> Land's jest —
> Concocters of 'hard' poetry —

8. Louis Zukofsky, "Program 'Objectivists' 1931," *Poetry* 37 (February 1931): 268.

Dramatic stony lips, centaurs, theatrical rock —
Living in a tower beyond rock,
In the best imitation of Sophocles. (p. 35)

(Zukofsky actually did visit this fellow in the tower, Robinson Jeffers.) He discovers a compromise in the conjunction of flux and solidity.

While in the sea
The seals pearled for a minute
In the sea as they sank (p. 35)

The sea superficially resembles the undifferentiated mass produced by entropy, but there the likeness ends. Standing on the shore, we front fertility. Pearls are solid beauty grown in the sea; Venus rises from the foam. The opposition in "A"-6 between up and down, simple and complex, is a limited construct. One can more profitably think of contraries moving into and out of each other.

The next step "A" takes is to tighten its structure, discarding the two-sided view of "A"-6 and severely condensing its themes. "A"-7 solves the overloading problem that had threatened. But Zukofsky had begun to solve the problem before "A"-6 was composed (1930), since he had started work on "A"-7 in 1928. We do not know what form Zukofsky may have envisioned for "A"-7 in 1928, but the movement's complexities ultimately required two years' labor.

Six movements, followed by a seventh that brilliantly recapitulates their themes—such was the plan. We do not know how much of the detail Zukofsky mapped out beforehand. Did he manufacture the crisis of "A"-6 so that "A"-7 could come galloping in, flags flying and bugles blowing, to save the poem? Or did "A"-7 take its shape gradually, in response to the development of movements 1–6? Whatever strategy he followed (or happened upon),

Zukofsky intended from the beginning that *"A"*-7 should carry considerable weight. As the culmination of *"A"* 1–7, it would have to bear that weight gracefully or the entire opening section of the poem would fail.

Zukofsky had turned his back on the aesthetic of the beautiful image, or "clear music," and embraced the art of clutter. Now that clutter had to be orchestrated. He chose to make a difficult job almost impossible by limiting himself to a string of seven sonnets—Shakespearian sonnets. A surprising reversal, after pages of the best modern "free" verse; what would the author of *Spring and All* have said?

"A"-7's dense texture partially obscures the scene. We began *"A"* with glimpses of Zukofsky at a performance, one in a crowd. *"A"*-7 is another performance, but here Zukofsky is conductor, audience, and reviewer all rolled into one. He sits alone near a street which is under repair. The locale is fitting, since, following the simulated breakdown of *"A"*-6, the poem too is under repair. Zukofsky's company consists of seven wooden horses barricading the work area. By dint of poetic effort, he turns the barren street into a private circus, putting the wooden horses (and words) through complicated paces.

> You're cut out, and she's cut out, and the jiggers
> Are cut out. No! we can't have such nor bucks
>   As won't, tho they're not here, pass thru a hoop
>   Strayed on a manhole — me? Am on a stoop.
>
> Am on a stoop to sit here tho no one
> Asked me, nor asked you because you're not here,
> A sign creaks — LAUNDRY TO-LET
>   (creaks — wind —) — SUN —
> (Nights?) the sun's, bro', what month's rent in arrear?
> Aighuh — and no manes and horses' trot? butt, butt
> Of earth, birds spreading harps, two manes a pair
> Of birds, each bird a word, a streaming gut,
> Trot, trot — ? No horse is here, no horse is there?

> Says you! Then I — fellow me, airs! we'll make
> Wood horse, and recognize it with our words —
> Not it — nine less two! — as many as take
> To make a dead man purple in the face,
> Full dress to rise and circle thru a pace
> Trained horses — in latticed orchards, (switch!) birds.
>
> (pp. 39–40)

Clarity falls by the wayside, and all of the reader's attention, intuition, and fancy are needed. As we hack a trail through this tangle, we must exercise uncommon resourcefulness.

Along the way, however, one can pause and enjoy "A"-7's punning verve. A clever denunciation of Prohibition lurks in the passage, reminding us that "A" got its start in the era of Izzie and Moe. "Jiggers" refers not only to streetcars and dancers, but also to measures of whiskey. The line urging "make a dead man purple in the face" not only continues "A"'s resurrection theme, but also suggests that it would be wise to put wine back into bottles. "Dead men" is slang for "empty bottles"; Swift used it in *Polite Conversation*.[9]

> LORD SMART: Come, John, bring us a fresh bottle.
>
> COL ATWIT: Ay, my lord, and pray let him carry off the dead men, as we say in the army.

Putting the "spirits" back into the bottles, into the wooden horses, and into the poem, are three of the many isomorphic operations conducted simultaneously by the author/ringmaster.

Verbal fireworks lend the movement a special kind of difficulty. When the poem announces that "each bird [is] a word" (p. 39) we may be taken aback. There is, however,

---

9. Jonathan Swift, *Swift's Polite Conversation: With Introduction, Notes, and Extensive Commentary*, ed. Eric Partridge (New York: Oxford University Press, 1963), p. 160.

something to be said for this proposition. The phrase "birds spreading harps" baffles us until we recall that the Australian lyrebird is so named because, when courting, it spreads its tail in the shape of a lyre. (Remember the assertion in *"A"*-2 that music is universally present.) Of course, the linkages don't stop there, for the lyrebird, as Guy Davenport observes, is of the genus *Menura* ("moonlike," because its tail is crescent-shaped), which generates a pun on the menorah, or candelabrum with seven branches, used in Jewish worship.[10] So, by virtue of the words attached to it, the lyrebird becomes part of the menagerie of *"A"*-7.

Menura and menorah are words that do not appear in the movement. But if we are to make sense of *"A"*-7, we have to make room for them. They seem to be part of a constellation of shadow-words influencing the tide of the movement. We might extend the list to include the French *meneur* (a manager of animals), the Greek *hae maenae* (the moon), and *mene-teon* ("one must remain"). Zukofsky is certainly a herdsman in *"A"*-7 (as was the composer of the Psalms). He has his own flock to take care of, even though friends such as Whittaker Chambers would have him busily proselytizing. The moon? It is night, and those horses dance by its light. The movement plays on man/manes ("manes" being a horse's neckhair and/or a Latin name for the spirits of the dead). Zukofsky apparently began work on *"A"*-7 by selecting a few key words—common words—such as the building blocks men-/man-. By choosing from among the many words to which they are related, he could construct the body of *"A"*-7. This would account for such peculiarities as the presence of a lyrebird on an American street. It is there because *Menura* entered the structure. Words determine the landscape of the movement.

This punning method of making a poem—all within the

10. From a personal letter, June 1, 1976.

rigid limits of the sonnet—points us in the direction of Shakespeare. Under the pressure of his greatest challenge to date, Zukofsky seems to have turned to the *Works* for guidance. Shakespeare's presence is felt not only in the profusion of puns, but in certain images. If we balk at seeing "two manes a pair / of birds" and condemn it as a strained, nonsensical conceit, we need to look again at *Venus and Adonis*.[11] Of course, Shakespeare says it in a more leisurely fashion:

> For through his mane and tail the high wind sings,
> Fanning the hairs, who wave like feath'red wings.

Zukofsky had first absorbed the *Works* in P.S. 7, in surroundings marked by poverty and leftist politics. By 1930 the distress that had always plagued the Lower East Side was beginning to engulf the nation. As the numbers of the poor increased, so did their cries for help. (*"A"*-1 contains anticipations of their pleas.) A few authorities considered the demands of the unemployed to be seditious.

Flavius and Marullus would have agreed. In the first scene of *Julius Caesar*, they demand that the mechanicals peaceably return to work—which is what the ruling class always demands of the laboring class. Browbeaten by their betters, the commoners try to defend themselves with puns.[12]

> FLA: What trade, thou knave? Thou naughty knave, what trade?
>
> COB.: Nay, I beseech you, sir, be not out with me. Yet if you be out, sir, I can mend you.

11. *William Shakespeare: The Complete Works*, ed. Alfred Harbage (New York: Viking, 1969), p. 1409. All subsequent quotations of Shakespeare are from this text.
12. *Julius Caesar* 1.1. 15–19.

MAR.:   What mean'st thou by that? Mend me, thou saucy
        fellow?

COB.:   Why, sir, cobble you.

The workmen finally slink away, defeated by the crushing
rhetoric of their betters. "They vanish," as Flavius aptly remarks, "tongue-tied." Shakespeare's elementary lesson in
language as well-defined political instrument reminds us
that the people on top forge weapons out of words. This
is more than just a rhetorical tradition. Shakespeare also
knew how the legal code works to the advantage of the
privileged classes. As the fisherman in *Pericles* testifies:
"Here's a fish hangs in the net like a poor man's right in the
law." [13]

A conflict of languages—legalese versus "plain speaking"—would appeal to Zukofsky. In *"A"*-7 we find

A sign creaks — LAUNDRY TO-LET
            (creaks — wind —) — SUN —
(Nights?) the sun's, bro', what month's rent in arrear?
                                                (p. 39)

"Rent in arrears" is the language of the law, and might be
found on an eviction notice. Whoever owned the laundry
could only reply: "How do you expect me to pay? I don't
even own a decent pair of pants. Look, these I'm wearing
have a rent in the rear." When we read "rent in arrear," we
see only the legalism; sounded, the line utters the complaint of a harassed debtor. It is the conflict of *Julius Caesar's* first scene—commanding rhetoric versus pun—tele-
scoped into a phrase.

"A"-7 is, among other things, Zukofsky's defense of the
downtrodden. He offers them what resources of language
he can command. This includes those elements not usually

13. *Pericles* 2.1. 112–13.

available to the masses (Shakespeare, judicial jargon). Admittedly, he has not given all, or even a substantial dose. But as a trial run, "A"-7 demonstrated that Zukofsky's talents shouldn't be wasted in tasks such as distributing leaflets on streetcorners. "One must remain," apparently doing nothing, rather than rushing off to the barricades. A genuine poet can make those barricades dance, demonstrating that words, as well as machines, are the means of production.

In "A"-7 Zukofsky tried to be a modern Orpheus. But why was he so anxious to succor the oppressed? Why so fervent an insistence on resurrecting dead words, dead hopes, and dead men?

The years 1927 and 1928, when Zukofsky began "A", were shadowed by four deaths: those of his mother, Yehoash, Ricky, and Thomas Hardy. The most important of these is the most private grief of the first seven movements, and can only be extracted from a few obscure details. The clues, as is characteristic of "A", decline to be definite. In "A"-5,

> Purple clover,
> She wore her shoes three years —
>   (The soles new as the sunned black
>   of her grave-turf)   (p. 18)

From this smidgen of information, we learn only that someone has died, evidently three years before the movement was composed (1930), and we may wonder if "she" ever owned many new pairs of shoes when alive. "A"-6 concludes with "Her soles new as the sunned black of her grave's turf" (p. 38), shortly after Zukofsky and some friends sing "Waken my fair one from thy slumber, / The gentle mother that thee bore" (p. 36). If Zukofsky's mother lies in the grave, never to be awakened by song, the reticence of reference could be a measure of grief too fresh for disclosure. Twenty years must pass before *"A"* indirectly acknowledges that Zukofsky's mother died in 1927. It does so because *"A"*-12 (1950–51) contains the death of Zukofsky's father.

> Buried beneath blue sky, bright sunlight.
> You'll remember:
> The eleventh of April
>   1950
> The twelfth —
> Snow flurries —
> Tasting all unseasonable weather early
> Alongside his "little fish"
> There 23 years before him.   (p. 154)

We, strangers to this family, suddenly realize that the poem remembered her as early as *"A"*-5. Joined in death in 1950, the Zukofskys are also joined that year in the poem—so far as the public reader is concerned.

Yehoash died in 1927 too. *"A"*-4 is partly his memorial; the "Shimaunu-Sān" poem is Zukofsky's translation from Yehoash's Yiddish—which the elders denounced as jargon. The fragments in quotations following "Shimaunu-Sān" are also translations from Yehoash.

As for "Ricky," it seems almost a sacrilege to reveal his identity, so tenderly has Zukofsky sung him to rest. The reader curious for personal details can turn to Whittaker Chambers's *Witness*. Ricky was his younger brother: Richard Godfrey Chambers, whose brief and unhappy life grew ever more troubled. He seemed always to have been in scrapes, usually of the self-destructive kind. "Whit" Chambers and his friends found that Ricky needed constant attention. Zukofsky himself assisted one night in taking care of the crapulous Ricky when Whit was detained at work. *Witness*'s account of Ricky's decline contains fragments of some anecdotes that were obviously passed on to Zukofsky in the 1920s, for they appear recognizably in "*A*"-3. From *Witness*:

> He is standing on our front porch, dressed in one of those shapeless wraps children used to be disfigured with. It is raining softly. I am in the house. He wants me to come out to him. I do not want to go. In a voice whose only reproach is a plaintiveness so gentle that it has sounded in the cells of my mind through all the years, he calls: "Bro (for brother), it's mainin (raining), Bro." He calls it over and over without ever raising his voice.[14]

In "*A*"-3:

> Out of memory
> A little boy,
> It's rai-ai-nin'   (pp. 9–10)

Page 733 of *Witness* reveals that Ricky's nickname was "Dickie," and so the last line of "*A*"-3 ("dicky-bird") acquires further sense. *Witness* accounts for other events behind "*A*"-3: Ricky's reckless behavior in his last years, his suicide ("My brother was lying with his head in the gas oven"), and the automotive environs of Sand Hill graveyard ("Cars hurtled down the Merrick Road, filled with hooting, singing people").[15] Though Chambers does not supply the exact date, Ricky took his life in 1926.[16]

The death which probably touched Zukofsky the least is the only one explicitly mentioned.

> "Poor Thomas Hardy he had to go so soon,
> He admired so our recessional architecture —
> What do you think of our new Sherry-Netherland!" (p. 3)

14. Whittaker Chambers, *Witness* (New York: Random House, 1952), p. 95. See also Allen Weinstein *Perjury: The Hiss-Chambers Case* (New York: Vintage, 1979), p. 102, for another account of Ricky's suicide.
15. *Witness*, p. 186.   16. *Perjury*, p. 102.

Hardy passed away on January 11, 1928, aged four-score and seven. Though he is precisely the kind of cultural giant that the "devotees of arts and letters" who attended the concert might be expected to read—or pretend to read— the concertgoers are evidently ill-informed. Those remarks suggest that they think of Hardy as someone cut off in his prime. Not only do the "devotees" speak of him as though he were an acquaintance who had had to leave a social function rather abruptly, they manage to leap from Hardy to the latest New York hotel (someone seems at least dimly aware of Hardy's architectural training). We are to infer that the impoverished young Jew recording the comments is much the worthier reader.

A master of English, a master of Yiddish, his mother, and his friend's brother—all dead within the space of two years. No wonder the *St. Matthew Passion*, commemorating the most important death in the history of the Western world, serves as a starting point for the poem, and no wonder the seventh movement has resurrection as its central theme.

"A"-7 was also supposed to reanimate the dead art of poetry. It was the only section of *"A"* Zukofsky included in the "Objectivist" number of *Poetry*. He evidently hoped that the issue would spark a new movement, a new vitality in American poetry. It was not to be. The response from most readers wavered between puzzlement and irritation. But Zukofsky still hoped for a new beginning. In August 1931, he gave an address at the Gotham Book Mart, the text of which became "Recencies" in *An "Objectivists" Anthology*. Here Zukofsky outlined his hopes for the kind of poetry that would spring up in the 1930s:

> The desire for what is objectively perfect, inextricably the direction of historic and contemporary particulars—a desire to place everything—everything aptly, perfectly, belonging within, one with, a context—A poem. The con-

text based on a world—Idle metaphor—a lime base—a fibre—not merely a charged vacuum tube—an aerie of personation—The desire for an inclusive object.[17]

"A" could be called the product of that desire for an inclusive object, especially since phrases from this passage appear in "A"-6. Zukofsky went on to express impatience with the poets of America.

> Because writing is a swifly cleansing process some minds act as if they washed every day and do not wait for the weekly review. The "Objectivists" number of *Poetry* appeared in February. Since then there have been March, April, May, June, July and we are now past the middle of August. Don't write, telegraph.[18]

He did not expect a flood of cables from like-minded poets (though that would have been bracing). Rather, telegraphy was a metaphor for the kind of writing suitable to the times—writing that would consider each word as carefully as if one were paying for it.

Between the "desire for inclusiveness" and the urgent demand for a new kind of writing lies a chasm. Not unbridgeable, but daunting. Inclusiveness, as we have seen, tends to inflate the poem with detail until it loses direction and maneuverability. Yet Zukofsky, if he could, wanted to put the world into a sentence. If he had gotten the kind of response he desired from his fellow poets, "A" might have become a year-by-year chronicle, with Zukofsky only one among many recording the times. Without that encouragement and context, he was thrown back on himself. The effort he had begun in "A" was to be his sole responsibility. When it became apparent that the example of movements 1–7 was lost on the world, Zukofsky had to reevaluate its

17. *"Objectivists" Anthology*, p. 15.
18. Ibid., p. 22.

aim. He could no longer assume that many of his contemporaries would pay attention. What, then, would *"A"*'s function be? As sole proprieter of the "inclusive object" aesthetic, Zukofsky would make the poem include his entire life. It would therefore have to be composed at intervals, when enough time had passed to alter the poet's circumstances. Each new section would be written, in a sense, by a different Zukofsky. His personality and basic views would endure, but they would be enhanced and altered by time's ripening. "The" had been a poem of a year; *"A"* would be, in the author's own phrase, "a poem of a life."

THREE

The Art of Appropriation: *"A"* 8–12

> Every word in the language has once been used happily.
>> Ralph Waldo Emerson, "Quotation and Originality"

THE TIME, 1950. The place, *"A"*-12. The speaker, Paul Zukofsky: "Wait till they find out / Where you took most of 'your' poetry" (p. 214): implying a low opinion of his father's originality.

Louis Zukofsky took hold of words wherever he found them. Seemingly innocuous remarks made by his son, wife, or friends might appear in the poem years later, without any warning or comment by the "author." Such ephemera were laid into place next to quotations from written texts. He had his own list of Great and near-Great Books, and he liberally scattered portions of them through *"A"*.

Why this growing mass of quotation as the poem entered a new phase? Zukofsky's love of paradox may supply a clue. The knottiest problems were the ones that gave him the most pleasure. One's relation to other texts provided him with no end of fascinating entanglements. There are times when we suspect our general fund of intellectual capital is entirely borrowed, inherited, or filched. We all face those uncomfortable moments when we doubt that any original ideas—about *Hamlet*, primroses, gumdrops— will ever brighten the humdrum landscapes of our minds.

It helps to remember that the geography of any mind is unique. Our collection of ideas, and their assemblage, is as particular as our genetic codes, and though we must take our genetic constitution as it came, we are free to alter and amend our intellectual charter. Reading allows us to become more—not less—individual. Zukofsky's personality was enhanced, not overwhelmed, by his erudition. Through his reading he multiplied his contacts with the past and also made himself myriad-minded.

So the Zukofsky of 1928–30 was not the Zukofsky of 1935–37, and both differed from the Zukofsky of 1949–52. This is one reason that he dated the separate movements of *"A"*. The poet revealing his reading is not showing off; rather, he is placing his intellect in context, showing its sources. If *"A"* was to be the poem of a life, it had to examine the past as well as the present and to be mindful of the successive versions of the author and of itself. The first seven movements are retrospective; they begin with a character left over from the Columbia period and conclude with a movement designed to justify *"A"* 1–6. As it grows, the poem constantly expands toward a larger perspective that explains the origin and significance of its earlier stages. As each section appears, it acquires the status of an object that must be placed in context. This concern with placing everything showed Zukofsky to be a serious student of the history of ideas, the history of sounds, and the history of history.

Between *"A"*-7 and *"A"*-8, he fortified himself with book-learning: economic, social, political. When the time came to produce *"A"*-8, he endowed the quotation method with new responsibilities. First, many of the selections were taken from eminent thinkers—Henry and Brooks Adams, Karl Marx, Thorstein Veblen. Their words carry more weight than street-corner conversation. Second, the quotations sketch personality and the development of historical consciousness, set largely in a chronological schema.

Zukofsky had not attempted anything like this before. Third, the quotations had to conform to the structure of "A"-8, which is a broad fugal design. Keeping all these strands coordinated, yet distinct, must have been a maddeningly delicate task. The compaction of "A"-7 begins to look simple in comparison.

The fugal pattern is the easiest to explain, if not to follow. Insofar as he consciously composed literary fugues, Zukofsky aligned himself with structures, not with doctrines. He clearly did have personal opinions about the matters discussed in the quotations, but he insisted that their primary qualification for inclusion was how well they fitted into the design. William Carlos Williams took the trouble to single out this "sensual" dimension.

> The writing of it is not put down for the literal meaning of the individual items or their particular truths (tho it is understood that they must be true to be used) but for their sensual qualities—sensual at a stroke by the mind—*not* driven on so in a consecutive prose discourse.[1]

It was probably necessary for Williams and Zukofsky to put extra weight on the "musical" aspect of "A"-8, if only to bring it sharply to the attention of prospective readers. In one letter, Zukofsky even went to the trouble of explaining how to read the lines

> So the green mold grew.
>
> Peter's garden, Padre,
> The garden above Peter's face,
> Green, yellow   (p. 64)

His gloss:

> *So the green mold grew* to the *green* yellow of Peter's garden . . . food orchestration—(displaying all yr. timbres) sound

---

1. William Carlos Williams, "Statement Relative to the Last Part of 'A'." Holograph MS on eight prescription blanks, HRC.

capacity by various instruments but . . . passing from one
instrument to another and bringing out a dissonance—and
I do that both by suggesting individual sounds and groups
of 'em and single images and (star) clusters of 'em.[2]

(Probably Saint Peter, in a painting; the lines are a transition from the "cheese" section of *"A"*-8 to the Metropoli-
tan Museum in New York; both sections examine gusta-
tory and artistic preferences of American "big cheeses.")
Zukofsky's insistence on the musical organization led him
to assert that "it must be music of the statements, but not
explanation ever, that's why I seem to leave out—but the
reader will have to learn to read statement, juxtaposed
constructs, as music."[3] In the same letter stressing this approach, Zukofsky lists eight themes constituting a kind of
overture to *"A"*-8 (they appear on pages 43–49 of the
movement). His comments leave no doubt that their intellectual content is indispensable.

I – Labor as creator, as creature.

II – Burying Jesus, so connection with Bach's *Passion*,
and what is to be said now is bridged and one can go
on with what is to be said now. Also negative creating the positive . . . synthesized.

III – Bach's life in relation to all this; and to rest of poem
(1–7).

IV – How others, not me, might look at it (beginning)
"natural that Bach . . . and out of respect," which
is Ezra, different mentalities, friends and writing,
combination of Atheling theme, Kay etc., in earlier
movement.

V – IV as I synthesize it. Matters that relate, people,
composition as action, ("How journeyed?")

VI – V as Marx synthesized . . . a basis for right and

2. Letter to Lorine Niedecker of January 28, 1937, HRC.
3. Letter to Niedecker of November 9, 1935, HRC.

wrong action, related to economic structure of society.

VII – Reason for V and VI in general comprehension of the nature of things: matter thinking, bodily substance.

VIII – Parallels to V, VI, VII in contemporary science: physics, mathematics ("Infinite is a meaningless word.")

Each theme pumped on the organ as you say modulates or is heard against the other, then each one assumes phases of the others, appearing in different guises, but continuing to mean the same—till they'll all go together.[4]

Put this way, the "music" and the "content" of the movement cannot be separated; they shade into each other. In "A"-8 Marx asserts that "it is impossible / to separate thought and matter that thinks" (p. 46). The same can be said of thoughts and the words constituting them. One hesitates to single out a major component of "A"-8 for fear of neglecting the others. We might slight the way they go together if we concentrate on too narrow a theme. But the issue is really out of our hands; the movement's components are everywhere knotted together. A glance at one theme is necessarily a glance at eight.

One portion of "A"-8, however, really stands out. Here Zukofsky shows an interest in historians of development, an interest new to "A". Zukofsky may have been influenced by Pound in this regard. He first read the *Cantos* after completing "A" 1–4, and the rest of the movements were probably too far advanced for drastic change. In 1933 Zukofsky travelled to Europe and visited Pound, who was about to publish his *ABC of Reading* (1934). In 1935, the year Zukofsky started "A"-8, he began work on his own collection of constructive examples, *A Test of Poetry*. It is not surprising that fugal development, in terms of his-

4. Ibid.

torical growth (both individual and cultural), molds the movement. The coherences of change provided Zukofsky with sufficient momentum to advance *"A"*.

"A"-8 was long in gestation, since it demanded extensive research and a monumental organizational effort. Not only do the themes of *"A"* 1–7 continue, but also comprehensive new ones are added. Zukofsky listed these themes for his own reference on the inside front cover of his manuscript for *"A"*-12.[5]

8 themes – Labor – Bach. Econ. Math, Nominalism (Duns Scotus)

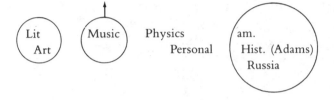

The listing presents some problems. How can we tell which are major themes and which are subsidiary? Why are three areas circled? Why does an arrow point from "Music" to "Bach"? Why do the 1950 notes differ from the list of overture themes made in the 1935 letter? Putting everything together and allowing for the author's possible changes of emphasis during the course of composition, we can come up with a compromise tally: labor, Bach, economics, science, nominalism, personal history, literature and art, and the Adamses. No one ever accused Zukofsky of lacking ambition.

The Adams family seems our best entry into *"A"*-8. The Adamses and their ancestral home are public property, and the sources Zukofsky used are readily available. One text significantly absent from *"A"*-8, *Mont-Saint-Michel and*

5. Holograph MS in the first of eight college examination bluebooks, HRC.

Chartres, was apparently intended for use quite early in *"A"*'s history. Item 10 of the projected twenty-four parts of the ur-*"A"* was titled "Tombeor." Henry Adams retold the story of the "Tombeor de Notre Dame" in chapter 13 of *Mont-Saint-Michel*, but no trace of the acrobat remains in *"A"*. It may be that the Adams who yearned for unity was too alien for Zukofsky's tastes. "The child born in 1900," Adams had predicted, "would be born into a new world which would not be a unity but a multiple."[6]

On the reverse of the ur-plan for *"A"*, which Zukofsky thriftily saved, are jumbled notes dating from 1934 and 1935. Among them we can trace out fragments of a sentence dotted with illegible words: "The Valley . . . by the . . . was called in Washington's. . . ."[7] In *"A"*-8 we discover some lines that are clearly a development of that note: "The valley bridged by this viaduct is / The Hollow Way of General Washington's time —" (p. 71). About ten lines further on, a quotation from John Quincy Adams appears. Why are viaducts, Washington, and the Adamses brought into conjunction? The connection lies in Zukofsky's presentation of the role of the Adamses in American history. Brooks Adams, in *The Degradation of the Democratic Dogma* (1919), offers this version of Washington's visionary plans:

> In his wanderings in early life in the western wilderness, Washington conceived the principle that a consolidated community which should have the energy to cohere must be the product of a social system resting on converging highways.[8]

6. Henry Adams, *The Education of Henry Adams* (1906; rpt. New York: Modern Library, 1931), p. 457.

7. Holograph MS, HRC.

8. Henry Adams, *The Degradation of the Democratic Dogma* (1919; rpt. New York: Capricorn Books, 1958), p. 14 (hereafter referred to as *DDD*). As a preface to the book, Brooks wrote a lengthy history of the intellectual tradition of the Adams family.

Washington's conception of a national capital corresponded in magnificence with his plan for the concentration of the nation. Built on converging avenues, it was to be adapted at once to military, commercial, administrative, and educational purposes, for at its heart was to be organized a university which was to serve as the brain of the corporeal system developed by the highways.[9]

Tantalized by the notion of unity, Brooks stresses that coherence is achieved by centralization. There was good precedent for thinking so; the Romans had known the value of excellent roads leading to and from the central authority. The Adamses confessed themselves products of the Age of Reason; hence the model city and state are based on a conception of the body that puts the brain at the center. Their premises were classically elegant—and totally unsuited to the times.

In his "Criticism" of Henry Adams (included in *Prepositions*), Zukofsky writes that "the general reader will perhaps give 'the cake' to the introduction" to *The History of the United States During the Administrations of Jefferson and Madison*. The introduction minutely describes the rigors of travel at the beginning of the nineteenth century. Adams indicates that

> nature was rather man's master than his servant, and the five million Americans struggling with the untamed continent seemed hardly more competent to their task than the beavers and buffalo which had for countless generations made bridges and roads of their own.[10]

Adams implies that the main issue confronting the young nation was whether man could subdue the wilderness or

9. *DDD*, p. 17.

10. Louis Zukofsky, "Henry Adams: A Criticism in Autobiography," in *Prepositions: The Collected Critical Essays of Louis Zukofsky* (Berkeley and Los Angeles: University of California Press, 1981), pp. 105–6.

the wilderness would absorb and bestialize man. Zukofsky follows that quote in his essay with another that serves to hone the point.

> A traveller on the levee at Natchez, in 1808, overheard a quarrel in a flatboat nearby . . . "I am an alligator," cried the other, "half man, half horse . . ." "I am a Mississippi snapping-turtle," joined the second, "I have bear's claws, alligator's teeth, and the devil's tail. . . ."[11]

Who would flourish in America, the Adamses or the Mike Finks? Henry answers the question in *The Education of Henry Adams* by comparing himself to a wilted begonia.

Henry and Brooks, looking back at Washington's generation, read into the effort at building a "consolidated community" a naive faith on the part of the founding fathers that good communications would ensure government by the best. According to this view, John Adams and his son trusted that the foremost men would be working at the center of a republic made strong by internal improvements. Brooks could only helplessly recount the betrayal of the hopes that they held for the nation. Referring to John Quincy Adams, Brooks writes that "he alone among public men of that period appreciated that a nation to flourish under conditions of modern economic competition must organize its administrative, as well as its social system upon scientific principles."[12] The "period" was that following the deaths of John Adams and Jefferson, when "scientific principles" meant Newtonian physics. As the last great exponent of Enlightenment doctrine, J. Q. Adams was left alone to discover that

> in 1828, democracy would not permit the ablest staff of officials to be chosen by him, to administer the public trust. Democracy, on the contrary, has insisted on degrading the public service to a common level of incapacity, thereby

11. Ibid., p. 106.   12. *DDD*, p. 61.

throwing the management of all difficult public problems, such as the use of railroads and canals, into private hands, in order that they might escape ruin, and thence has come the predicament in which we, in particular, and the world at large, now stand.[13]

So, according to a later scion of the Adams dynasty, the forefathers had staked all upon centralization, but in order to maintain the public weal were forced to turn control of communications over to those unscrupulous robber barons who throve on the democratic system. One hardly knows whether Brooks refers to the nation or to the Adamses when he uses "we" above.

Brooks dwells on the unfortunate last years of his grandfather as if he were Roderick Usher contemplating the effigy of an illustrious ancestor. His ruminations provide a good part of the Adams material in "A"-8. The last quotation, for example, serves as the source for

> Democracy would not permit John Quincy Adams
> The ablest staff of officials, to be chosen by him,
> To administer the public trust.   (p. 73)

If we pursue the thesis that the founding fathers based the national welfare on a network of roads and canals, and assume that this lies behind portions of "A"-8, some puzzling passages begin to make sense. Consider, for example, the following litany of discomfort.

> As cold as Nova Zembla.
> In the morning awakened by the hail — the
> Train frozen to the rails
> Could not be broken free for an hour.
> I felt as if I were incrusted in a bed of snow.
>
> Four of us slept, feet to feet
> Next to a stable bulging with horses,
> The boat staggered, a stumbling nag.   (p. 72)

13. *DDD*, p. 121.

This is Zukofsky's arrangement of the account of a journey
J. Q. Adams took in 1843. Brooks dwells at length on the
rigors of the trip that almost killed the old man.[14] He does
it with surprising verve, as though entertaining the notion
that it was all a punishment inflicted not by God, but by
Adams's own commitment to centralization, communication, and—worst of all—democracy.

For Brooks and Henry, and for "A"-8, J. Q. Adams
represents faith in science as an ameliorating influence.
Science, education, and rational self-government by the
masses are interconnected. So we are shown Adams taking
an interest in scientific pursuits with the public interest in
mind. The "forest of live-oak near Pensacola" (p. 73) was
one of his projects.[15] His plan for preserving the forest was
scrapped by the Jackson administration. The effect of the
new democracy coming to power in 1828 was to destroy
"everything of which I had planted the germ" (p. 73).[16]

Adams's scientific interests were not limited by gravity.
Pages 77–78 of "A"-8 are a capsule condensation of his desire to encourage astronomy. "Light-houses of the sky"
(p. 71) was his colorful locution for observatories. Brooks
adds one more detail to a portrait of his grandfather struggling vainly against public apathy: "The phrase light-
houses of the sky probably brought more ridicule on
Mr. Adams than anything he ever said."[17] Adams made
that terrible journey in 1843 to speak at the ground-break-
ing for America's first observatory—in Cincinnati. Brooks
concludes his sketch of the tribulations of J. Q. Adams by
claiming that the philanthropist died thinking his life had
been a failure, doubting himself, doubting science and education, and even struggling not to doubt his God.

The sad odyssey of John Quincy Adams serves as a pro-

14. *DDD*, pp. 68–69.   15. *DDD*, p. 53.
16. Cf. *DDD*, p. 53.   17. *DDD*, p. 61.

logue to the history of his grandsons. By 1869 public and private morality had declined considerably, and in the chronological section of "A"-8 for that year we find some quotations from Henry and Charles Francis Adams, Jr.'s *Chapters of Erie*—their joint diagnosis of financial chicanery in the Gilded Age. The railroads are in the clutches of crooks.[18]

> Ten o'clock the astonished police . . panic-stricken
> railway directors . .
> In their hands . . files of papers . . and their pockets
> Crammed . . assets and securities . . One,
> Captain, in a hackney-coach . . with him . . six
> millions in greenbacks.
> Under cover of night . . to the Jersey ferry.
> Some . . not daring publicity . . in open boats
> Concealed by darkness and a March fog . .
> A majority of the Executive Committee
> Collected at the Erie Station in Jersey City,
> (Ribbed Gothic and grilled iron)
> Proceeded to the transation of business.   (p. 76)

Zukofsky silently makes a few alterations in the text that render the case against these scoundrels even more damaging. "Captain" here is short for "captain of industry," Zukofsky's favorite designation for predatory capitalists. (His favorite probably because the phrase carries military overtones.) But in *Erie* the word used is simply "individual." Zukofsky had to change it, since, as he saw it, the thieves are hardly individuals. Stamped from the same rotten mold of selfishness, Vanderbilt and Gould are barely distinguishable.

In *Chapters of Erie*, the brothers Adams had laid bare the shame of the railroads. What then was the result? "A"-8's

---

18. Charles Francis Adams, Jr., and Henry Adams, *Chapters of Erie* (1886; rpt. Ithaca, N.Y.: Cornell University Press, 1956), p. 30.

chronology tells the tale. It skips to 1871 and shows the
"captains" brazenly in control.[19]

> By means of this simple and smooth machinery,
> Which differs in no essential respect from
>   roulette or rouge-et-noir . .
> I went down to the neighborhood of Wall Street . .
> And to my Newport steamer . . Mr. James
>   Fisk:
> In blue uniform, broad gilt cap-band,
> Three silver stars on coat-sleeve
> Lavender gloves, diamond breast-pin
> Large as a cherry, stood at the gangway,
> Surrounded by aides bestarred and bestriped
>   like myself . .
> And welcomed President Ulysses Simpson Grant.
>
>   (p. 78)

The account of the welcoming committee combines several portions of *Erie* for special effect. At first we assume
that the "simple and smooth machinery" must be some
sort of trolley or other public transportation. But how
does this fit in with references to gambling? Aside from
the continued use of the communication motif, and the
mention of roulette ("chance" is one of Zukofsky's interests in *"A"*-8), what are we to make of this gaudy show? A
glance at *Erie* reveals that the "machinery" is the process of
"buying on margin."[20] In other words, the anonymous
captain arrived at his bad eminence by speculation: gambling. One important distinction: with these operators it is
not gambling. The founding fathers' plan for an internal
binding network has become a rigged game.

> Three distinct railways, with all their enormous resources,
> became the property of Cornelius Vanderbilt, who, by
> means of their credit and capital, again and again swept

19. Cf. *Erie*, pp. 102, 116.   20. Ibid., p. 102.

millions of dollars into his pocket by a process curiously similar to gambling with loaded dice.[21]

The most promising experiment of the Enlightenment, the United States, has turned into a crooked casino.

After the passage recounting the flight of the captains across the Hudson to Jersey, the movement passes another judgment on them.

> Doll said: "A captain!
> God's light . . the word as odious as the word
> 'occupy' . .
>
> Excellent . . before it was ill sorted."   (p. 76)

As is so often the case in "A", we are reading a quotation of a quotation. In Erie, C. F. Adams, Jr., calls on Doll Tearsheet to comment on the titles Vanderbilt and his cronies adopted.[22] Doll complains about the word "admiral" and how it has been debased by those unworthy of the title. Adams quotes her only to put the barons of Wall Street in their place, but Zukofsky continues his own denigration of "captains." Following Doll's commentary comes a medley of quotations from Erie, in which Charles Francis Adams speculates on the future evils that corporate octopi have in store for the nation.[23]

> The old maxim of the common law,
> That corporations have no souls.
> Corporate life and corporate power,
> As applied to industrial development,
> . . yet in its infancy.
> It tends always to development, —
> Always to consolidation . .
> Even threatens the central government.

21. Ibid., p. 103.
22. Ibid., p. 95. See also King Henry IV, Part 2, 2.4. 133–35.
23. Cf. Erie, pp. 96–98.

It is a new power, for which our language
Contains no name.   (pp. 76–77)

If the corporations have no souls there can be nothing individual about them. Huge and amorphous, they cannot be located and held to account for their crimes because they are decentralized. Still more ominous, "it is a new power, for which our language / Contains no name."

Comparisons of the United States with the Roman Empire in its decline trouble the rest of C. F. Adams's text.[24]

It, perhaps, only remains for the coming man
To carry the combination of elements
One step in advance, and put Caesarism
At once in control of the corporation and of the
                                    proletariat.
                                    (pp. 77–78)

Zukofsky succinctly comments on the parallel of Rome and America in a parenthetical aside; "Him to — hymn to — Latinity" (p. 77). We see converging the "decline of the West" syndrome, Henry Adams's attraction to the Church of Rome (a centralized organization if there ever was one), the Adamses late interest in entropy, and the increasing alienation of the family from its surroundings.

After documenting the gross corruption of the postwar period, the chronology of "A"-8 leaps suddenly from 1871 to 1893. Zukofsky, monitoring the age through the Adamses, chose to keep step with Henry. The twenty-year hiatus coincides with the twenty years of which nothing is said in The Education of Henry Adams. (Henry skips from chapter 20, "Failure"—1871, to chapter 21, "Twenty Years After"—1892.) A score of years drops out because, according to Henry, his education ceased during that period. In 1871, too, Henry and his brothers seem to

24. Cf. Erie, p. 99.

have lost hope that their exposure of corporate corruption would have immediate impact. They retreated to other pursuits. Charles went to work on the railroad; Henry determined to study the situation more thoroughly and publish a few works that might guide the rising generation. He later concluded that during those two decades he had worked in vain. The portion of *The Education* that follows 1892 has no faith that the forces of history will be stayed by any man's books.[25]

The Degradation of the Democratic Dogma represents the last gasp of the family's pessimism. Though published in 1919, it supplies some of the material dated 1893 in *"A"*-8.[26]

> Henry, like the good brother he was . .
> Stayed with me in Quincy . .   (p. 79)

> Hot August . . and talked endlessly of panic.
> If I live forever, I shall never forget
>   that summer.   (p. 80)

The panic of 1893 severely jolted the Adamses. Henry and Brooks were together that summer keeping a close eye on the family finances. As Henry dryly observes, the collapse meant that "the community was bankrupt and he was probably a beggar"—or so it seemed at first.[27]

The Adamses were, as Henry and Brooks saw it, a product of the dead past. Their ideas and energies, they thought, were suited to a fixed conception that had grown obsolete. The theory of entropy they flirted with, in which the universe is a closed system running down like a complicated watch, is perhaps an agreeable notion if one's personal capacities, great as they may be, are geared to problems and opportunities that existed a century earlier. Though Henry and Brooks said nothing about the relation between en-

25. *Education*, p. 315.   26. *DDD*, pp. 90, 94.
27. *Education*, p. 337.

tropy and family character, "A"-8 invites us to make the connection.

The last stage of entropy would be an undifferentiated mass at a temperature of absolute zero, and at several points in "A"-8 the family members suffer from freezing chills. For example, the passage

> "To sponge in a brook
> before sunrise with the thermometer at thirty
> and a bracing breeze blowing
> tries the epidermis" (p. 58)

is Henry laconically describing the rigors attending cleanliness in the Wild West.[28] We have already reviewed the journey west of J. Q. Adams during which he almost froze to death. The quotations from the family conclude with Henry's Baltic and Russian journeys, where images of icy cold abound: "uniformity of ice and snow" (p. 81); "The glacial ice-cap" (p. 82); "Ice-cap of Russian inertia . ." (p. 82).[29] In only one instance does the family suffer from too much heat, during that "Hot August" of 1893. "A"-8 shows the Adamses sweltering when their capital is threatened. The legacy of Peter Chardon Brooks had put the Adamses on easy street in the third generation. Perhaps they would have been better off coping with straitened means, as did John Adams and his son.

It is not the business of "A" to speculate on what might have been. Instead, the movement suddenly veers to suggest that the decline of the Adamses comes to its conclusion just as another cycle of growth begins in Russia. "A"-8 seems to view Lenin and Stalin as new Adamses in the right time and the right place: quotations from Henry Adams and Josef Stalin are juxtaposed on page 78. On page 80 Brooks calls it quits.

28. Worthington Chauncey Ford, ed., *Letters of Henry Adams, 1858–1891* (Boston: Houghton Mifflin, 1930), p. 215.
29. Cf. *Education*, pp. 409–11.

"It is now full four generations since John Adams
Wrote the constitution of Massachusetts.
The world is tired of us
We have only survived because our ancestors
Lived in times of revolution."

The source of this passage indicates more clearly why the
American and Russian revolutions are rhymed:

> Here have I, for years, been preparing a book to show how
> strong hereditary personal characteristics are, while the
> world changes fast, and that a type must rise or fall accord-
> ing as it is adjusted to its environment. It is seldom that
> a single family can stay adjusted through three genera-
> tions. That is a demonstrable fact. It is now full four
> generations . . . .[30]

"*A*"-8 intertwines the decline of the Adams family with new
beginnings. Zukofsky elsewhere observes that Henry's theory of the acceleration of history (which Henry thought of
as the rush of disintegration) may have anticipated the Russian Revolution. That a Russian uprising might be heir to
the Spirit of '76 is further developed in "*A*"-8 by the last of
the Adams quotations. As Henry's voice fades out, dimin-
uendo, in the frigid darkness of northern Europe,[31] we
read:

> Nothing to say.
> For him, all opinion founded on fact must be error,
> Because the facts can never be complete,
> And their relations must be always infinite.
> Very likely, Russia, would instantly become —   (p. 82)

At the moment in "*A*"-8 when Henry Adams falls silent,
there is an interruption—

30. *DDD*, p. 93.
31. Cf. *Education*, p. 410.

Then feed, and be fat,
Come we to full points here; and are etceteras nothing?

(pp. 82–83)

These lines dismiss an overstuffed generation and look to a new people. The source is the same play, act, and scene, in which we heard Doll Tearsheet expostulate earlier. Here Pistol has the floor; the points to which he refers are "stops." In short, the end of the Adamses is not the end of all. What continues? Some immigrants—uprising Russians—from Eastern Europe (mere "etceteras" to patrician Adams?), among whom are the Zukofskys.[32] Henry's musings cease just as the poem picks up the earliest memories of Louis Zukofsky. (The tapering off of Adams followed by Louis's infant recollections may have helped Pound organize his long poem; the Chinese cantos conclude in the eighteenth century, and are followed by the Adams cantos.)

Zukofsky assumes a spot one step removed from the Adamses, and by hitching on to that dynasty takes considerable responsibilities upon himself. As heir to the Adamses, he inherits their problems along with their vision. The consequences of this assumption lead him toward another of "A"-8's themes: science. The Adamses were, like so many sedulous citizens of the eighteenth century, amateur scientists. In the world of John Quincy Adams, professional scientists were rare creatures. Even busy statesmen could hope to make important discoveries for the benefit of mankind. Within a few generations,

32. In his preface to *The Law of Civilization and Decay: An Essay on History* (London: Swan Sonnenschein, 1895), Brooks saw only one remedy for a senile civilization: "The evidence seems to point to the conclusion, that, when a highly centralized society disintegrates, under the pressure of economic competition, it is because the energy of the race has been exhausted. Consequently, the survivors of such a race lack the power necessary for renewed concentration, and must probably remain inert, until supplied with fresh energetic material by the infusion of barbarian blood" (p. viii).

however, the languages of science became mysterious to laymen. Henry Adams, baffled by such newly uncovered phenomena as radioactivity and X-rays, assumed his usual stance as spectator:

> If the physicists and physico-chemists can at last find their way to an arrangement that would satisfy the sociologists and historians, the problem would be solved. Such a complete solution seems not impossible; but at present,—for the moment,—as the stream runs,—it also seems, to an impartial bystander, to call for the aid of another Newton.[33]

It was a symptom of some kind of breakdown when so brilliant an observer as Adams threw up his hands.

"*A*"-8 studies the crisis with the aid of a few remarks by Poincaré and Einstein, but offers the most space to Thorstein Veblen, though his name does not appear in the movement. There are, of course, many disembodied voices in "*A*", but Veblen's concealment in "*A*"-8 is all the more puzzling in light of Zukofsky's high regard for him as expressed in 1931. At that time he hailed "Thornstein [*sic*] Veblen's masterly essay" as pointing out "the meaning, or what should be the meaning of science in modern civilization."[34] Zukofsky believed that Veblen had major insights to offer on that subject, and this warrants a look at Veblen's essay "The Place of Science in Modern Civilization."[35] Here Veblen argues that modern civilization perceives the world from a scientific point of view. (He was emphasizing this years before Dewey and Whitehead jumped on the bandwagon.) Every culture, he claims, has suffered from the common delusion that its methods of apprehension are pure. A companion essay, "The Evolution of the Scien-

33. *DDD*, p. 259.
34. An *"Objectivists" Anthology* (Le Beausset, Var, France, and New York: To Publishers, 1932), pp. 18–19.
35. Thorstein Veblen, *The Place of Science in Modern Civilization and Other Essays* (New York: B. W. Huebsch, 1919).

tific Point of View," develops a detailed history of how
the scientific bias came to dominate modern thought.[36]
Quotations from this essay are featured at length in "A"-8.
Though Zukofsky deletes some of the text, the original is
almost as obscure.

> Process: notion about which the researches cluster.
> The knowledge sought and the manner of seeking it
> Are a product of the cultural growth.
> All the generalities on motion belong here.
> Ions, together with what is known of the obscure
>   and late-found — .
> In so far as the science is of modern complexion,
> In so far as it is not of the nature of taxonomy simply,
> The inquiry converges upon a matter of process,
> And it comes to rest,
> Provisionally, when it has disposed of the process.
> Whereas it is claimed that scientific inquiry
> Neither does nor can legitimately, nor, indeed, currently
> Make use of a postulate more metaphysical
> Than the concept of an idle concomitance of variation,
>   such
> As is adequately expressed in terms of mathematical
>   function.
>
> Consistently adhered to, the principle of "function"
> Or concomitant variation
> Precludes recourse to experiment, hypothesis or
>   inquiry — indeed

36. Also in *The Place of Science*. Zukofsky sometimes took objects as
he found them, and, in one instance, the Veblen section incorporated a
lucky accident: "Ions, together with what is known of the obscure and
late-found—" ("A"-8, p. 56) is drawn from a footnote in Veblen's essay.
The break faithfully reproduces a textual accident. The footnote on
page 35 of the Huebsch edition ends with "obscure and late-found," but
continues on page 36 with "radiations and emanations." The reader's
bafflement (as he reads "A"-8), wondering as he does what those obscure and late-found phenomena might be, matches the puzzlement of
Veblen and physicists at the turn of the century.

It precludes "recourse" to anything whatever. Its
                notation (however)
Does not comprise anything so anthropomorphic.
              (pp. 56–57)

Veblen chose physics to illustrate our dependence on notions of "process." He treats the problem by discussing an
anthropomorphic tendency in human thought.

> Concomitance at a distance is quite as simple and convinc-
> ing a notion as concomitance within contact or by the in-
> tervention of a continuum if not more so. What stands in
> the way of its acceptance is the irrepressible anthropomor-
> phism of the physicists. And yet the great achievements of
> physics are due to the initiative of men animated with this
> anthropomorphic repugnance to the notion of concomitant
> variation at a distance.[37]

Veblen perceived physics to be in crisis because man's anthropomorphism had led to such remarkable success in the
past. By 1900, however, the chief obstacle that prevented
physics from making progress at the atomic level was that
same anthropomorphism. The science, according to Veblen, had entered a new dimension, where matters of action
and reaction passed into a twilight world closed to man.
But what yardstick would suffice? And how could "irre-
pressible anthropomorphism" be repressed?

As far as Veblen was concerned, the history of the growth
of science had revealed its sustaining props to be unscien-
tific ways of thinking. The crisis in physics, whereby the
very strengths that ensured its early triumphs now stymied
development, seems to rhyme with the fate of the last
members of the Adams dynasty. Zukofsky's detection of
this "Achilles heel" pattern in American thought suggests
that his training in "Objectivist" analysis was excellent

37. *The Place of Science*, p. 35.

preparation for the unraveling of intellectual tangles. Ideas in "A"-8 come to have as much shape and line as a piece of sculpture. An Egyptian pulled glass bottle in the shape of a fish begins to resemble a collection of ideas and images.[38]

Veblen's gloomy view of the future chances for progress in theoretical physics happened to be overly pessimistic, but a few of his propositions play a role in "A"-8: abstract instruments are grounded in culture; modern science claims not to be metaphysical or anthropomorphic, yet it is; a science that claims to be unbiased is only deceiving itself. The problem raised by the last conclusion put Veblen in a curious position; his essay on the development of the scientific viewpoint begins with the caution that "a discussion of the scientific point of view which avowedly proceeds from this point of view itself has necessarily the appearance of an argument in a circle; and such in great part is the character of what here follows."[39] This frank admission is charming, but the more closely we study Veblen, the less ingratiating it appears. Veblen's anonymity in "A"-8 may indicate that Zukofsky's enthusiasm had cooled between 1931 and 1935. Zukofsky probably realized that it is impossible to extract much that is positive from Veblen's analyses; they leave one stripped of settled norms without offering better approaches.

Veblen's probing of modern thought led him (in "The Instability of Knowledge and Belief") to widen his range and charge that

> point of view . . . is a matter of habit. It is common to modern civilized peoples only in so far as these peoples have come through substantially the same historical expe-

38. Zukofsky owed this image of the fish-shaped bottle to Marianne Moore's "An Egyptian Pulled Glass Bottle in the Shape of a Fish." For Zukofsky's use of the image in "An Objective," see *Poetry* 37 (February 1931): 268.
39. *The Place of Science*, p. 20.

rience and have thereby acquired substantially the same habits of thought and have fallen into somewhat the same prevalent frame of mind.[40]

As far as it goes, this cannot be called relativism. Veblen merely observes that men base their views on inadequate grounds—that they are unconscious of the extent to which they are enslaved by habits of thought. Zukofsky evidently found the proposition appealing. Such views are echoed elsewhere in "*A*". It harmonizes with Spinoza's interest in free will, with Marx's assertion that material conditions are instrumental in producing the world-view of each age, and with Brooks Adams's assertion that "men work unconsciously . . / perform an act, before they can explain why; / often centuries before" (p. 81). The succeeding age comprehends the thought of the previous generation; each era represents an advance in mankind's awareness. Veblen is only the loudest of many voices declaring that individuals and cultures suffer from handicaps invisible to them. "*A*"-8 seems to agree that there is indeed "cultural growth" (pp. 53, 89), but if we ask where Veblen stands in relation to that growth, we face difficulties. Though he acknowledges his scientific viewpoint, and admits he is as much a product of the age as anyone else, he seems to insist on his own neutrality.

One cannot build a system given Veblen's approach. But Zukofsky did owe a debt to Veblen's analysis of the connection between the history of thought and the history of technology. Veblen offered a brief sketch in "The Evolution of the Scientific Point of View" of the rise of industrial technology and its effect on metaphysics. He notes that during medieval times "the 'realities' of the scholastic lore were spiritual, quasi-personal, intangible, and fell into a

40. Thorstein Veblen, *The Vested Interests and the State of the Industrial Arts* (New York, B. W. Huebsch, 1919), p. 1.

scale of differential dignity and prepotency."[41] As industry increasingly dominated human affairs,

> the institutions of European civilization fell into a more intimate relation with the exigencies of industry and technology.
> In this way . . . modern science comes into the field under the cloak of technology and gradually encroaches on the domain of authentic theory previously held by other, higher, nobler, more profound, more spiritual, more intangible conceptions and systems of knowledge.[42]

Though Veblen offers no comforting values on which the mind can relax, he does provide the kind of pattern pleasing to a poet more interested in structure than ingredients.

A study of the interactions of thought and history must be placed in some sort of chronological schema. This necessity seems part of the justification for "A"-8's chronological development. Veblen had commented on the aversion of the scholastics to "matter-of-fact" concerns (God was the object of proper attention). Zukofsky follows the hint by suggesting that a chink appeared in the old order at a specific moment.

> Whether it was "impossible for matter to think?"
>   Duns Scotus posed.
> Unbodily substance is an absurdity
>   like unbodily body. It is impossible
> to separate thought and matter that thinks.   (p. 46)

It was a startling innovation to locate intellect in humble matter. Zukofsky revealed the quotation's force in a letter to Lorine Niedecker: "And at the beginning of his 'Historical Materialism,' Engels also suggests that the dialectic was *already* on its way when Duns Scotus asked the ques-

41. *The Place of Science*, p. 49.
42. Ibid., p. 50.

tion whether it was 'Impossible for matter to think'?"[43] During the early 1930s, Zukofsky evidently deepened his acquaintance with authors who see history as progression. The Adams brothers and Veblen fit into this category, but they cannot compare to Marx; he reaches all the way back to Scotus for his materials. Those comments grouped around Scotus's question are Marx's, as quoted by Engels.[44]

Zukofsky ushers in Marx, by name, on a promising note.

> Friends too tired to see differences,
> This, Marx dissociated:
> "*Equal* right . . presupposes inequality,
> Different people are *not* equal one to another."
> But to make the exploitation by one man of many
>   impossible!
> When the opposition between brain and manual work
>   will have disappeared
>   (p. 45)

We have to make the connection with "*A*"-6, where the line "everyone tired of trying to see differences" (p. 22) ominously introduced a movement on the verge of collapse because of undifferentiated morals in private and public life. Marx therefore vaults onto the stage as the feisty champion of differentiation and particularization. Dialectic becomes the art of arranging ideas in new patterns.

Writing to Pound in 1935, Zukofsky argued that "there's more material fact and more imaginative poetic handling of fact in that first chapter of Marx than has been *guessed* at in your economic heaven."[45] Zukofsky admires Marx for his poetic sensitivity (as he admired Henry Adams), and,

---

43. Letter of June 7, 1939, HRC.
44. Cf. Frederick Engels, *On Historical Materialism* (1892; rpt. New York: New York Labor News Co., 1938), p. 9.
45. Letter of June 7, 1935, HRC.

as with Adams, Zukofsky assembles a portrait of Marx as an individual, varying extracts from *Capital* with fragments of revealing correspondence. Marx's energy and incisive handling of facts gradually develops as a sharp contrast to the temperament of the Adamses. This juxtaposition, presented without commentary, seems to be the "personal" theme in action, proceeding by counterpoint. That a theme could proceed through the contrasting of statements, and not simply within the statements themselves, is no small achievement. It justifies Zukofsky's remark that "the reader will have to learn to read statement, juxtaposed constructs, as music."

Immediately following the passage that ends with Veblen commenting on anthropomorphism comes Marx, exclaiming: "I am now working like a horse" (p. 57). The transition is an obvious instance of the "musical" reading Zukofsky hoped the reader would discern, but it also contains another truth (which is one of the advantages of working with words rather than notes). Since Marx has all the energy and drive of a horse, he is a hard man to keep up with. So he manifests impatience with lesser minds:

> I have no patience to read anything else.
> Other reading always drives me back to my writing.
> Then there is still the fourth book, the historical-literary,
> to write —
> The easiest for me as the problems have been solved
> in the first three
> And this is repetition. (p. 57)

Marx's personality is sketched early in *"A"*-8, and, once established, defers to quotations from *Capital*. Zukofsky weaves them into the movement with the usual slight, but significant, alterations. The passage beginning "But the labor process" and concluding with "all comes to an end" (pp. 61–62) is assembled from pages 169–77 of the Everyman *Capital*. Zukofsky distills the couplet

The less it frees him body and mind —
The more is his care glued to the grind   (p. 61)

from this sentence in Marx:

> The less attractive he finds the work in itself, the less con-
> genial the method of work, the less he enjoys it as some-
> thing which gives scope to his bodily and mental powers—
> the more closely must he devote his attention to the task.[46]

Zukofsky's tinkering with the passage makes it more sen-
sually vivid. The worker becomes entangled in his work;
the next line—"Spins and the product is his web"—reveals
the unfortunate proletarian glued to the sticky web he fab-
ricates. Some such lurid, melodramatic scene—the capitalist spider forcing the victim to spin the filaments of the
trap in which he will be suspended while his vitality is
drained—lies behind the passage. Victorian melodrama
(with which Marx would have been familiar) seems closer
to the spirit of *Capital* than we might have thought.

But there is more to the passage than simple melodrama. Throughout *Capital*, Marx relies heavily on statistics garnered from the textile industry. Since the production of textiles was one of the first operations to be widely
affected by steam power, more complete statistics existed
for this industry during the Industrial Revolution than for
most others. Facts and figures drawn from the textile industry are constantly turning up; one of Marx's favorite
examples of a necessary commodity produced by factories
is coats. Zukofsky takes the hint and includes such lines as:
"Near Spinoza refusing a new coat" (p. 85).

As we near the close of the movement, it becomes apparent that the necessity of contrasting the Adamses with
Marx has left little room for an examination of Marx's
positive contributions to the understanding of economics.

46. Karl Marx, *Capital*, trans. Eden and Cedar Paul (1930; rpt. New
York: Dutton, Everyman's Library, 1974), p. 170.

To do him full justice, Zukofsky had to find a format for displaying Marx's thought in isolation—or as much isolation as Zukofsky's obsession with interconnection would allow. There was no room in *"A"*-8 for such a format.

As early as 1931, Zukofsky had a plan—albeit a dim one—for scrutinizing capitalism through the lens of poetry. Writing to Rakosi that year, he listed some of the difficulties he and Reznikoff were having in raising money for publication, and then remarked, "The only thing left for me to do is to make a canzone out of economics, which I'll do someday, wait and see." [47]

The next section of *"A"* (composed between 1938 and 1940) was the first half of *"A"*-9. Here we find Marxian phraseology laid upon a grid that happens to be Guido Cavalcanti's "Donna Mi Prega." For the first (and last) time Zukofsky went to the trouble of supplementing his poem with an exegetical apparatus. *First Half of "A"-9*, the poem with its accompanying explanatory material, includes a summary of the sources and method that went into that section. Zukofsky published *First Half of "A"-9* himself in an edition of only fifty-five mimeographed copies—the minimum number required to protect copyright. Its forty-one pages are full of useful information, but they presume a readership that did not exist in 1940 or for decades afterward. The Zukofskys sold a few copies, and the rest were eventually given away. They were still to be had for the asking in the 1960s. This thundering indifference to *First Half of "A"-9* was surely part of the reason for Zukofsky's subsequent disinclination to explain his work. But the crucial decision to let the rest of *"A"* stand on its own is quite consistent with his determination to make the reader respond directly to the poem, a determination present since the beginning. And, in fact, the crutch of *First Half of*

47. Letter of November 9, 1935, HRC.

"*A*"-9 (like the prefatory material introducing "Poem Beginning 'The'") is not much help.

For example, it does not point to the similarity between "*A*"-7 and "*A*"-9. We have to figure out for ourselves that the guiding premise of both movements is animation of the inanimate. "*A*"-9's first half features manufactured goods endowed with the ability to speak, an inspiration for which Zukofsky is indebted to Marx. In *Capital* we find this flight of fancy:

> If commodities could speak, they would say: "Our use-value may interest human beings; but it is not an attribute of ours, as things. What is our attribute, as things, is our value. Our own interrelations as commodities proves it [*sic*]. We are related to one another only as exchange-values."[48]

In the first half of "*A*"-9 this becomes

> So that were the things words they could say: Light is
> Like night is like us when we meet our mentors
> Use hardly enters into their exchanges,
> Bought to be sold things, our value arranges
>   (p. 106)

Nor does *First Half of "A"-9* cover all of Zukofsky's debt to Marx. The first few lines of the movement speak of "equated values," and that phrase can be traced back to *Capital*,[49] though Zukofsky did not list the pages in question as sources in *First Half*.

The capitalist system as described in the first half of "*A*"-9 seems to be legalized insanity. A case can be made for the malign influence of world affairs on the movement, especially since "*A*"-10, composed the same year Zukofsky completed the first half of "*A*"-9, concerns itself with the collapse of international order and the beginnings of World

48. *Capital*, p. 58.   49. *Capital*, pp. 5–6.

War II. "A"-10 shows the strain on its author; it is much less ambitious than its companion movements. Zukofsky would rather be shouting from the rooftops than laying the words on a page. "Let a better time say / The poet stopped singing to talk" (p. 120), he laments.

From 1940 to 1948, Zukofsky left "A" untouched, with the exception of his final revision of movements 1–6. Some of the despair that silenced him during those years, and the healing influence that brought him back to the poem, are suggested in a 1946 essay, "Poetry / For My Son When He Can Read." It begins: "When you were 19 months old your ability to say 'go billy go billy go billy go ba,' much faster than I could ever say it, made me take some almost illegible notes on poetry out of my wallet. The time had come for me to fill the vacuum I abhorred in my life as much as you had filled it in yours."[50] The portions of "A" written between 1948 and 1951 reveal a man content to find peace in his own family. (He had married Celia Thaew in 1939. Their son Paul was born in 1943, and within a few years was studying the violin.) No longer does the verse strain and collapse under the weight of the world's madness. Each of the three sections—second half of "A"-9, "A"-11, and "A"-12—shows increasing and unprecedented dexterity in his handling of materials. In "A"-12 Zukofsky achieves what might be called the high point of the entire poem: he manages to reconcile his cosmology with his family.

When he returned to "A", he took up where he had left off by considering how one could maintain one's sanity when others were losing theirs. "A"-9's first half had Marx for its patron. For the second half, an equally giant intellect was pressed into service. But this thinker prescribed remedies that do not require the restructuring of society.

50. "Poetry / For My Son When He Can Read," in Prepositions, p. 3.

The *elixir vitae* Zukofsky discovered was the *Ethics* of Baruch Spinoza. His choice forces us once again to confront the polarity of "abstract" and "particular" that Zukofsky loved to fuss with. In one respect, it can be argued that the *Ethics* is a perfect combination of these two strains, since it presents itself simultaneously as the most basic of systems and the most abstract. Zukofsky pointed out this paradox in "About *The Gas Age*."

> The wonderful thing about Spinoza's philosophy to me is that out of 8 definitions and 7 axioms he built the whole system. But that's late, that's very late in philosophy, and to me it's the end of philosophy. After that they're just finding other terms for it, which is alright, every generation ought to redefine, you know, use a different term, but it ought to be a better one.[51]

The economical system Zukofsky so admires is the *Ethics*; the elementary definitions and axioms from which Spinoza builds are at the beginning of the work. So Zukofsky presents the contradiction without fanfare. Spinoza's system has the fewest moving parts, yet it is philosophy brought to its highest development.

In 1947 Zukofsky began work on his longest critical essay, *Bottom: On Shakespeare*. Here Zukofsky "wrote 500 pages about Shakespeare just to say one thing, the natural human eye is OK, but it's that erring brain that's no good, and he says it all the time."[52] As usual, Zukofsky means what he says, but implies much more. The remark about "erring brains" applies directly to the second half of "A"-9, begun at the time *Bottom* was getting underway. The essay's intent to "do away with philosophy" suggests that "A"-9's second half is also Zukofsky's tilt with philosophy.

---

51. "About *The Gas Age*," in *Prepositions*, p. 170.
52. Ibid.

The second half of "A"-9 exists as a preindustrial scene, reversing the setting of the first half (which was apparently a factory or warehouse). Instead of wandering about in a nightmarish man-made world, we enter this half of "A"-9 to find ourselves in a garden or greenhouse—there is at least one different kind of flower in each stanza. We are confronted with a collection (an anthology) of wonders that some power other than man produces. We cannot make flowers. We can only imitate them in paper, plastic, and glass. The second word in the first stanza is "eye," something else man cannot manufacture. (And here we should recall the conjunction of eyes and flowers in "A"-2.)

The mixing of the mechanical and the human in the first half of "A"-9, where people became machines and commodities started to speak, was a monstrous inversion. That inversion is complemented in the second half by a different sort of topsy-turvydom. Here the assumption guiding the movement is that love is not abstract, but tangible. Thus we are invited to equate love with organic growth, and with the labor involved in making the poem. That love and the physical are not really so far apart in the normal world is hinted at by the phrase "related is equated" (p. 108). The poem claims to be specifying two areas that are—or should be—closely linked.

The poem assumes that men live in a world so benighted and confused that, in order to restore proper balance, received notions must be turned inside out and upside down. Stanza 1 wastes no time in so doing.

> An eye to action sees love bear the semblance
> Of things, related is equated, — values
> The measure all use who conceive love, labor
> Men see, abstraction they feel, the resemblance
> (Part, self-created, integrated) all hues
> Show to natural use, like Benedict's neighbor
> Crying his hall's flown into the bird: Light is
> The night isolated by stars (poled mentors)

Blossom eyelet enters pealing with such changes
As sweet alyssum, that not-madness, (ranges
In itself, there tho acting without right) is —
Whose sight is rays, "I shall go; the frequenters
That search our centers, love; Elysium exchanges
No desires; its thought loves what hope estranges."

(pp. 108–9)

As with other parts of *"A"*, we could appreciate the verbal music and leave it at that. If we want to examine the intellectual music, however, we have to read backwards and sideways as well as forward.

"Labor / Men see" says the verse; men see labor rather than feeling it in their bones and muscles. Contrarily, "abstraction they feel," rather than grasping it intellectually. The poem is obviously creating a bizarre dimension of inversions, in which we must learn to trust our eyes, not our brains. One cannot expect a sick brain to reason itself into health.

Further inversions clog the stanza. "Benedict's neighbor / Crying his hall's flown into the bird. . . ." Such backwardness seems nonsensical, but we know what the excited neighbor means even though his message comes out the wrong way round. The source is the *Ethics*, and "Benedict" is Spinoza:

> Now many errors consist of this alone, that we do not apply names rightly to things. . . . If this were not so we should not believe that they made mistakes any more than I thought a man in error whom I heard the other day shouting that his hall had flown into his neighbour's chicken, for his mind seemed sufficiently clear to me on the subject.[53]

53. Baruch Spinoza, *Ethics and On the Correction of the Understanding*, trans. Andrew Boyle (1910; rpt. New York: Dutton, Everyman's Library, 1970), p. 74. Zukofsky's early edition of this text contained an introduction by George Santayana, but no mention of the translator. Zukofsky assumed that Santayana had made the translation.

Men are led astray by the improper use of words. When messages are garbled, we can at least estimate how far we have strayed from "natural use." The verse hints at a whole spectrum of error in "hues."

In the middle of the stanza, a colon shifts the progress of the argument to particular examples. The poem grants us a vision that puts harmony back into nature. "Light" (in the passage from "A"-9 quoted above) can be read as "not heavy," because the stars are the upper ends of tent poles (the poles being the rays of light connecting stars with the earth) that keep blackness—the void—at a safe distance. "Light is / the night isolated by stars" also suggests that the stars overpower blackness. We usually think of stars as lonely beacons in a vast night. But since this is a poem of inversions, we have to consider the possibility that interstellar blackness is on the verge of being overwhelmed by blazing suns.

Zukofsky's description of the radiant canopy of the heavens locates its ground on earth (the base of those poles), where little stars ("blossom eyelet") mirror the larger canvas. These plants differ from those in "A"-2; much livelier, they enter the world like sounding bells, "Pealing with such changes." Nor are they merely decorative; these flowers are just the ones needed to heal human intellects. Sweet alyssum was once considered a cure for insanity, hence its name: "a-lyssum"—"not madness." The parenthesis following the mention of sweet alyssum might be translated "this curative power exists, though by human standards it should not, since man disdains to see a connection between his mind and so humble a thing."

"Sight is rays" asserts one line, and the "I" speaking in that line seems to be a ray of light speaking to other rays. This "I" promises rewards for the astronomers, botanists, and lovers who "search our centers," the centers being the stars and flowers from which light shines. Going is connected with paradise, because "I shall go" and "Elysium"

are related; "Elysium (Greek root) meaning 'I shall go.'"[54]
Elysium is not a place, or a stasis, but the exchange of love,
seen here under the guise of rays going from star to flower
to eye.

Love "exchanges / No desires," i.e., will not provide the
lover with anything more than what he already has. He
must settle for the complete adequacy of what is at hand.
Hope for something more "estranges." Desire for something more than love, desire for other terms than those on
which it is granted us, is a foolish wish. Those who refuse
to accept those terms are chasing airy Good—Kay's "beautiful music."

> Such need may see reason, the perfect real —
> A body ready as love's steady token
> Fed thought unbroken as pleasure induces —
> True to thought wearies never its ideal
> That loves love, head, every eddy. Broken
> Plea, best unspoken, a lip's change produces
> Suffers to confuse this thought and its loci,
> The foci of things timelessly reflected —
> Substance subjected to no human prevision,
> Free as exists it loves: worms dig; imprecision
> Of indignation cannot make the rose high
> Or close sigh, therein blessedness effected
> Thru power has directed love to envision
> Where body is it bears a like decision.   (p. 109)

The "need" is the human need for love and loving, and
such a need may in "A"-9 quite literally "see reason," since
love is being treated as a tangible object. Spinoza equates
love and reason at several points in the Ethics: "He who
lives under the guidance of reason endeavors as much as
possible to repay his fellow's hatred, rage, contempt, etc.,
with love and nobleness."[55] The perfect is real; it is no faint

54. Undated letter to Niedecker, ca. 1939, HRC.
55. Ethics, p. 174.

hope. "Reason" and the "perfect" are incorporated in "A body ready as love's steady token." The second and third lines of the passage propose the earthly trinity of Love, Reason, and the Body. Human desire has found its completion when love perceives itself in another: love is an act of recognition. Love can see, can "envision / Where body is it bears a like decision."

The danger always exists that "imprecision of indignation" will meddle with the processes of love. Spinoza exposed this human failing: "Human lack of power in moderating and checking the emotions I call servitude. For a man who is submissive to his emotions is not in power over himself." [56] Like flowers, love grows by its own rules and cannot be forced. The "real" and the "ideal" (the rhymes of the first and fourth lines of the passage quoted are one. In the first half of "A"-9 those rhyme words were used quite differently. There they demonstrated the divorce of the real and the ideal when economic error exists. In this half, however, love combines with reason to synthesize the real and the ideal. This stanza's flower is the rose, probably because it unites physical and ideal love.

Stanza 3 taxes the reader. Denser and more difficult than the first two, it tests the skills we have acquired thus far.

> Virtue flames value, merriment love — any
> Compassed perfection a projection solely
> Power, the lowly do not tune the senses;
> More apt, more salutary body moves many
> Minds whose directions make defection wholly
> Vague. This sole lee is love: from it offences
> To self or others die, and the extorted
> Word, thwarted dream with eyes open; impeded
> Not by things seeded from which strength increases;
> Remindful of its death as loves decreases;

56. Ibid., p. 141.

Happy with the dandelion unsorted,
Well-sorted by imagination speeded
To it, exceeded night lasts, the sun pieces
Its necessary nature, error ceases.   (pp. 109–10)

The sense of the first line is clear enough; the source of
value and love is not abstract, but comes from "virtue."
Reason, freedom of action, and love are concomitants.
Spinoza had this to say about merriment and how to tune
the senses.

> There cannot be too much merriment, but it is always good;
> but, on the other hand, melancholy is always bad. Merri-
> ment . . . is pleasure which, in so far as it has reference to
> the body . . . that the body's power of action is increased or
> aided in such a way as all the parts preserve the same pro-
> portions of motion and rest one with the other; and there-
> fore . . . merriment is always good.[57]

Merriment, therefore, is a fine-tuning of the body that assists the power of love. "Power" (the third line in the passage from "A"-9 quoted above) is not machine power;
whatever it may be, it projects "compassed perfection."
    The stanza distinguishes between the "lowly" and the
more "salutary body." The more perfectly tuned body has
a finesse and a power flowing through it that influence
other bodies. The power also seems to show defects in
their true light. In describing the salutary effects of love,
Zukofsky uses a pun to summarize those effects. "Sole lee"
can be taken as the substantiality of love (lees = dregs of
the wine), or as stressing that only love is a sure shelter—
the lee side of a blustery world. Also, "sole lee" sounds
like "solely," and rhymes with "lowly" in line 31. One of
love's powers is that it kills hatred—"from it offences / To
self and others die. . . ." (Spinoza: "Hatred is increased by

57. Ibid., p. 171.

reciprocal hatred, and on the other hand, can be destroyed by love."[58]) It also kills the "extorted / Word," for love is anything but a matter of compulsion or coercion. Love destroys the "thwarted dream with eyes open." To dream with one's eyes open could be an example of more brain-error. Spinoza: "Those therefore, who believe that they speak, are silent, or do anything from the free decision of the mind, dream with their eyes open."[59] Love cannot be separated from the physical act of love. "Strength increases" from the act; it is certainly not an expense.

The elements through which love works are mortal, common; and the flowers of this stanza are the kind we call weeds. But the word "weeds" is a human invention—there are no weeds so far as nature is concerned. Even the dandelion serves in wine and salads. So we and the poem should be "happy with the dandelion unsorted."

The theme of time passing, introduced at the close of the third stanza (in "Remindful of its deaths as loves decreases"), is amplified in the fourth.

> Love acts beyond the phase day wills it into —
> Hate is obscure, errs, is pain, furor, torn — a
> Lust to adorn aversion, hope — love eying
> Its object joined to its cause, sees path into
> Things the future or now, that poorer bourne, a
> Past, a step, a worn, a voiced look, gone — eying
> These, each in itself is saying, "behoove us,
> Disprove us least as things of love appearing
> In a wish gearing to light's infinite locus,
> Balm or jewelweed is according to focus.
> No one really knows us who does not love us,
> Time does not move us, we are and love, searing
> Remembrance — veering from guises which cloak us,
> So defined as eternal, men invoke us."   (p. 110)

58. Ibid., p. 114.   59. Ibid., pp. 89–90.

The word "time" appeared twice in the first half of "A"-9, and is used twice in the second half. It is introduced here as a limited power. "Time does not move us. . . ." Love, though it works in time through mortal objects, is itself timeless, and those who love are partly free from the ravages of time. Spinoza: "In so far as the mind conceives a thing according to the dictates of reason, it will be equally affected whether the idea be of a thing present, past, or future."[60] Hate is trapped in time; it tends to look backward, nursing old grudges and old enmities. Love looks forward; like someone escaping from the obscuring error of hate, it "sees path into / Things the future or now."

He who hates has only a perverted pleasure, "a lust to adorn aversion." The stanza echoes the method of the first half, with things doing the talking (a further concretization of the usually abstract conception of love). These things urge humans to see through the "guises which cloak us." Love seems to grant temporal eyes the power to see with love's eyes—that is, under the aspect of eternity. Light here represents love's creating power, a power with "infinite locus." But light must be focussed if it is to work, and human beings—who have lenses in their eyes—must do the focussing.

"Balm or jewelweed is according to focus." Balm: a plant yielding aromatic and medicinal fluid when crushed. Jewelweed: known also as "touch-me-not." These plants are at opposite ends of a "touching" spectrum, but both are (or can be) viewed as equally valuable if one goes about using them the right way. How to do so? The eleventh line of the passage claims that "No one really knows us who does not love us." The equation of loving and knowing might be another Spinozan influence. The *Ethics* defines love this way: "Love is a pleasure accompanied by the idea

60. Ibid., p. 184.

of an external cause."[61] One cannot know that which is not a source of pleasure: the will to know only exists when the external object is a source of pleasure.

The fifth stanza, just as intricate as the fourth, contains some of the elements that will blossom in *"A"*-11.

> A wise man pledging piety unguarded
> Lives good not error. By love's heir are asserted
> Song, light obverted to mind, joy enjoined to
> Least death, act edging patience, envy discarded;
> Difficult rare excellence, love's heir, averted
> Loss seize the hurt head Apollo's eyes point to:
> *Ai, Ai* Hyacinthus, the petals in vision —
> The scission living acquiescence, coded
> Tempers decoded for friendship, evaded
> Image recurring to vigilance, raided
> By falsehood burning it clear to the vision,
> Derision transmuted by laughter, goaded
> Voice holding the node at heart, song, unfaded
> Understanding whereby action is aided.
>
> (p. 110)

The stanza adumbrates its author's death. "By love's heir are asserted / Song," could well be a prediction that Celia and Paul will continue the music. There is a hidden apostrophe to the poem by its author in "goaded / Voice." Decoded: "Go, dead voice." The advice on what to do after Louis is gone merges into the myth of Hyacinth, a change that should not alarm us. Zukofsky loves to combine two or more variants of a pattern; numerous variants tend to validate a pattern.

Hyacinth was loved by Apollo (source of light, friend of poets, musician) and Zephyr. Hyacinth preferred Apollo, and one day, when the two were tossing quoits, the jealous Zephyr blew Apollo's quoit (turned aside—averted) so

61. Ibid., p. 130.

that it struck the youth on the head and killed him. So "averted / Loss seize the hurt head" is a telegraphic version of the bad news. Zukofsky manages to vary "love's dart" in "Donna Mi Prega," pun on "sees" in "seize," and include his beloved letters "*A*" (Apollo) and "*Z*" (Zephyr).

Hyacinth became a flower which the sun shines on and feeds with light ("Apollo's eyes point to"). A further complication: the letter "O" originally symbolized the eye. Hence Apollo's eyes are in his name as well. Here the poem grows literal: "*Ai, Ai* Hyacinthus, the petals in vision." Apollo's cry of grief over the dead youth can be seen and read on the petals of the flower, according to the Greeks. As in Apollo's name, we see the "*Ai*'s." In Zukofsky's system, the "eye" is equivalent to the "I"—an individual largely being his modes of perception—so "*Ai, Ai*" = eye, eye = I, I.

The canzone ends with a coda taking us back to the concerns of the first stanza and hitting the major themes of the second half. It also sweeps us from the eternal aspect of love into the particular time of 1948–50, when Asian and European cities were still wracked. However complex the verse, it is in and of its time.

> Love speaks: "in wracked cities there is less action,
> Sweet alyssum sometimes is not of time; now
> Weep, love's heir, rhyme now how song's exaction
> Is your distraction — related is equated,
> How else is love's distance approximated."
>
> (pp. 110–11)

In this time, sweet alyssum doesn't seem to work, and "love's heir" could be the poet himself. The poem has, therefore, been a distraction from the hellish state of the world. The "exaction," the tortuous inversions and sinuosities of the poem, its labyrinthine redirection of mistaken intellect, the work involved in writing and reading it; all these are measures of how distant love is from the world.

Many passages in the *Ethics* suggest why Zukofsky makes Spinoza the presiding genius of the second half of "A"-9:

> Men think themselves free inasmuch as they are conscious of their volitions and desires, and as they are ignorant of the causes by which they are led to wish and desire, they do not even dream of their existence.[62]

> Hence it follows that the human mind is a part of the infinite intellect of God, and thus when we say that the human mind perceives this or that, we say nothing else than that God . . . in so far as he is explained through the nature of the human mind, has this or that idea.[63]

Spinoza hopes to wake men up to their state of subjection, and to lead them to an understanding of the ultimate harmonies. In a letter to Niedecker, Zukofsky hints at a distinction between the first and second halves of "A"-9, while suggesting how Marx and Spinoza go together: "Read this against second stanza of the first half of "A"-9 (and of course following out of first of second half I sent last summer) and you'll see what I'm trying to get at: the Marx is in Spinny, but without (in Spinny) the hell in it."[64] One thing that "hell" might be is the hell of factories, but it also might be Marx's rage. Spinoza has no such rage, possibly because he lived before the Industrial Revolution, possibly because his philosophy aims at paradise. "A" calls him "the Blest," because "Baruch" means "blessed" (as does "Benedict"), and because the *Ethics* contains such statements as: "I shall endeavour to show what power reason has over the emotions, and moreover, what is mental liberty or blessedness (*mentis libertas seu beatitudo*)."[65]

62. Ibid., p. 30.   63. Ibid., p. 46.
64. Undated letter, HRC.   65. *Ethics*, p. 199.

Zukofsky's familiarity with "the Blest" evidently began long before *"A"*, probably back in Woodbridge's classroom. To Rakosi he wrote, "As a kid I wanted to be an engineer—I'd have been a swell one, but I met a fool philosopher or an epistemologist, and it really was easier doing nothing at Columbia."[66] The equation of philosophy with "doing nothing" is characteristic of the later Zukofsky. (Incidentally, the "fool philosopher" he refers to was neither Woodbridge nor Dewey.) In the same letter, Zukofsky indicated that Spinoza's system could be domesticated: "My father . . . the only pious example of Spinozisitic philosophy I've ever met."[67] It seems that this philosophy pleased Zukofsky because it could be embodied.

If *"A"*-9's second half is a prescription for recovering sanity, *"A"*-11 and *"A"*-12 are portraits of a sane family living in harmony. These are clearly companion pieces, viewing the Zukofsky family from inside (*"A"*-11) and from outside (*"A"*-12). "Inside" seems the appropriate term for *"A"*-11, since so much of the movement is based on inside information. At first it appears that the movement has a single frame of reference: the family made up of Louis, Celia, and Paul. But the problem of extracting meaning from the movement soon becomes almost impossibly difficult, for part of the meaning is deliberately concealed from the public reader. Words, phrases, and images that obviously have a private meaning for the Zukofskys keep obtruding.

Much that seems impenetrable clarifies if we just stay alert. In "If your father offended / You with mute wisdom," "mute" might be a synonym for "silent." But what kind of wisdom would that be? How could it offend? Surely something more fitting is called for. Hired mourn-

66. Letter of January 6, 1931, HRC.   67. Ibid.

ers? No. Common usages don't seem to work. We approach the meaning when we remember that Louis (or rather the poem) is talking to a violinist. To Paul "mute" would signify the clip attached to the instrument that deadens its resonance. "Mute wisdom" would be Louis's occasionally heavy-handed direction of Paul's upbringing. Common sense and a dictionary open up much of "A"-11.

A bit more than a dictionary is required, though, when we come to "For the flowing / River's poison where what rod blossoms." What rod, indeed? Tannhauser comes immediately to mind, and the connection is validated when Venus appears a few lines further on. Fertility has been a theme in "A" since the beginning. Thinking along those lines might direct us back to the Bible, specifically Num. 17:8 (where Aaron's rod blossoms as a sign of his election) and Exod. 7:20 (where the rod turns the waters of the Nile to blood). The complication here is the equivocal nature of the rod. On the one hand, it produces fruit; on the other, it poisons. Another referent for "rod" will help stabilize the image. Rods are retinal bodies that the eye uses to see in dim light, as when one is looking at stars. So the "flowing river" would be the stream of tears falling from the grieving eyes of Celia and Paul. Louis rejects this response as inappropriate. A paraphrase of his admonition might go like this: "Don't weep and wail after my passing. Tears poison the eye." Celia and Paul should instead dry their eyes and set "A"-11 to music. Then Louis will live again as Paul plays the accompaniment to its recitation.

Of course, the method of exhausting a single word's meanings has its limits. Zukofsky's real talents shine when he joins several words to spark significance. Rivers and lights have glimmered before in the poem (see "A"-2); no wonder Zukofsky introduces hydroelectric power into the movement.

> No, song, not any one power
> May recall or forget, our

Love to see your love flows into
Us. If Venus lights, your words spin   (pp. 124–25)

"Rod," just a few lines before, becomes a connecting rod. The constellation of "rod," "power," "flows," "lights," and "spin" permits us to apprehend the family Zukofsky as a generating unit.

The first two stanzas of "A"-11 cradle another delicate archipelago of sense. Its members: "river," "wrangling," "grazes," "bow," "stinging animal," "river's poison," and "dust." A western cattle drive? Something like that, with overtones of "Red River Valley" and "Bury Me Not on the Lone Prairie." To die is proverbially to "go west." As an American making a poem about his own death, Zukofsky has turned to a national ballad form—the cowboy's lament. There is just enough of its integument to color the poem: a coating of dust on an artifact that is composed of layered meaning.

A more intimate touch adds to the picture. "Whose losses show them rich and you no poorer" is an iambic rendering of a sentence from Henry James's "The Altar of the Dead"—"People were not poor, after all, whom so many losses could overtake; they were positively rich when they had so much to give up."[68] This consoling thought passes through Stransom's mind as he observes the anonymous lady who (though he doesn't know it yet) grieves for Acton Hague. James's tale, partly a study of the attitudes the living take toward the departed, and what might be called a comedy of mourners, is just the right choice. Acton Hague links Stransom and the unnamed lady, James's story links Louis and Celia (she greatly admired James), and "A"-11 will one day unite Celia and Paul as composer and performer. In all three cases, the acts of the absent one create a bond between the living.

68. *The Short Stories of Henry James*, ed. Clifton Fadiman (New York: Random House, 1945), p. 331.

The dead binding the living: as a general formula, it well describes the method of the middle movements of "A". Healing influences are available from the past, Zukofsky would argue. Even if the reader doesn't see precisely whose beneficent presence is working, the effect persists. This was one reason why Zukofsky thought it immaterial that his readers know every jot and tittle of his craftsmanship.

Toward the end of "A"-11 he refers to "four notes" but leaves them as notes. Those notes were once living men: two poets—Cavalcanti, Joseph Rodman Drake; two philosophers—Spinoza, Paracelsus. Cavalcanti seems to have priority; his *ballata* "Perch' io non spero" provides the bones for "A"-11. It determines the length and number of stanzas, and dictates that the word concluding each stanza will be "honor." (Cavalcanti was less strictly bound; he started with *onore*, but varied the rhyme with *dolore*, *del core*, *d' Amore*, and *valore*.) The basic premise of both poems is the same: the exiled poet commands his song to go to his beloved. Cavalcanti asks the *ballata* to conduct his soul to his lady and say a few kind words on its behalf. In both the *ballata* and "A"-11, the song receives its instructions in stanza 4.

Zukofsky, of course, diverges from Cavalcanti, but with cause. For example, in the second stanza of his *ballata*, Cavalcanti warns his song to be wary of interception; unless it reaches his beloved he will suffer doubly. Though Zukofsky does not have to worry about his poem going astray, he cautions his song to be sure and "graze" Celia's tears. The space "A"-11 must bridge is emotional.

Verbal echoes of the *ballata* dot "A"-11 in a kind of sonic palimpsest. *Tornar* in the first line of the *ballata* becomes "turn." *Ti miri*, ending line 9 of the *ballata*, peers through "you mirror," ending line 9 of "A"-11. A passage in lines 14–15 of Cavalcanti's poem seems to have given Zukofsky the idea for associating death with a stinging/stringing rhyme; "la morte / Mi stringe." "Great hem" (line 28) is a muffled counterpart of *che triema*. So our recitation of *"A"*-11 revives a bit of Cavalcanti. And Zukofsky will live again when his heirs breathe the words of the movement.

Though turning has been associated with rivers in previous movements (most notably in *"A"*-4), it was always a case of the river turning something else (a mill wheel), or objects revolving near a river (e.g., carousel horses). Now it is the river itself that turns. But "turn" is not the word one would usually plug into "River that must ⸺ full." "Full" tends to direct "run" into that space, or perhaps "flow." And, in the next line, "turn" would be the usual complement of "Song, my song, ⸺ grief to music." Zukofsky wrote with a considerable reservoir of English poetry in his head. His choice of "turn" runs counter to such precedents as "Sweete Themmes run softly, till I end my Song." The first word of *Finnegans Wake* floats prominently in modern awareness. And Alph, the sacred river, also ran. So Cavalcanti's *ballata* might be thought of as an interfering signal from Italy, jamming one traditional (English) coupling of words and generating a novel combination.

A particular river, the Bronx, flows through the borough of that name. Upon its shores are situated Bronx Park and the Bronx Zoo. Nor far from there, Celia and Louis Zukofsky made their home in the early years of their marriage. "We lived then opposite the park and not far from the zoo. The river that flowed from up the country, and passed the side of our house, fell in a cascade we saw from our windows." Thus Zukofsky, in "It Was" (1941).[69] The river had its poet long before the Zukofskys arrived on the scene. Joseph Rodman Drake (1795–1820) penned

69. Louis Zukofsky, *Ferdinand: Including "It Was"* (London: Jonathan Cape, 1968), p. 7.

"Bronx" in the days when the area was a rural retreat.[70] Drake's first stanza:

> I sat me down upon a green bank-side,
> Skirting the edge of a gentle river,
> Whose waters seemed unwillingly to glide,
> Like parting friends who linger while they sever;
> Enforced to go, yet seeming still unready,
> Backward they wind their way in many a wistful eddy.

Cavalcanti's *ballata* lent "*A*"-11 its structure. Drake's poem supplies the river and reinforces the tone. "Bronx" is a pastoral elegy; the poet has strayed far from the unsullied innocence of the natural world, and lost himself in a fallen social maze. He promises himself a respite.

> Yet I will look upon thy face again,
> My own romantic Bronx, and it will be
> A face more pleasant than the face of men.
> Thy waves are old companions, I shall see
> A well-remembered face in each old tree,
> And hear a voice long loved in thy sweet minstrelsy.

Part of the appeal of "Bronx" lies in the subsequent changes in the landscape. Drake turns from the face of men to regain his peace of mind beside the Bronx; today the river is surrounded with precisely those encumbrances that Drake fled. Drake's poem does not show through the diction as does Cavalcanti's, but some vocabulary can be traced back to "Bronx." "Sick," "light," "leaves," and "face" seem to have been carried over. The tree featured in Drake's last stanza might have produced the tree branching in the last stanza of "*A*"-11. Last, and probably least, Drake's middle name provides yet another referent for "the flowing / River's poison where what rod blossoms."

70. See Frank Lester Pleadwell, *The Life and Works of Joseph Rodman Drake* (Boston: Merrymount Press, 1935), pp. 224–26.

Since *"A"*-11 is also a sententious message to the living, it borrows some advice from Spinoza. "Honor, song, sang the blest is delight knowing / We overcome ills by love" has for its antecedents two passages: "Hatred which is entirely conquered by love passes into love, and love on that account is greater than if it had not been preceded by hatred" (*Ethics*, part 3, prop. 44); "hatred should be overcome by love" (part 4, prop. 73*n*).[71] No reason for us to carp at the switch from "hatred" to "ills"; one function of *"A"*-11 is to make the *Ethics* suit the needs of the Zukofskys, and "hate" would hardly describe their feelings.

"We are led in life principally by the desire of honour, and under the burden of blame we can scarcely endure it," says the Blest (part 4, prop. 52*n*), and the remark chimes twice in *"A"*-11: "Freed by their praises who make honor dearer"; "Live our desires lead us to honor."[72] But how can a close-knit family keep honor constantly in mind? Once the "ills" are taken care of, might there not remain such nagging thoughts as resentment and remorse? Spinoza offers good advice to the gloomy—advice that Zukofsky wants to amplify. "A free man thinks of nothing less than of death, and his wisdom is a meditation not of death, but of life" (part 4, prop. 67).[73] Using this as a backdrop, Zukofsky cautions his song: "Your heart in nothing less than in death." Good advice, if we could remember it.

Since *"A"*-11 presents itself as a kind of mnemonic device, Spinoza's comments on memory turn up. "No, song, not any one power / May recall or forget" borrows from "Again, it is not within the free power of the mind to remember or forget anything" (part 3, prop. 2*n*).[74]

The fourth major figure grafted on to *"A"*-11 surprises because unanticipated. Spinoza and Cavalcanti have visited

---

71. *Ethics*, pp. 114, 190.   72. Ibid., p. 177.
73. Ibid., p. 187.   74. Ibid., p. 89.

"A" previously, and even Drake appeared briefly in *Anew*, but Paracelsus arrives without warning. Historical accident (if such a thing exists) brought him into Zukofsky's range. While *"A"*-11 was still in progress, the Bollingen Series issued an English translation of Jolande Jacobi's *Paracelsus*.[75] What did Zukofsky see in this hermetic, nomadic, and prickly author? Paracelsus is a transitional figure, with one foot stuck in the past and the other tentatively planted in the future. His writings are a strange mixture of antique wisdom—his medieval heritage—and bold explorations in medical and chemical science. He fills an important spot in the history of Western thought that Zukofsky had been preparing to write since *"A"*-8, and which would eventually appear as *Bottom: On Shakespeare*. But what does Paracelsus have to say for the poet and his family?

Paracelsus's alchemical writings influence these lines of the movement:

> Take care, song, that what stars' imprint you mirror
> Grazes their tears; draw speech from their nature or
> Love in you — faced to your outer stars — purer
> Gold than tongues make without feeling
> Art new, hurt old: revealing
> The slackened bow as the stinging
> Animal dies, thread gold stringing
> The fingerboard pressed in my honor.   (p. 124)

When Paracelsus refers to gold, he does not mean the precious yellow metal beloved of speculators, but rather the spiritual and intellectual enlightenment attained in the striving for wisdom. In adapting the Paracelsian meaning Zukofsky retains some of gold's tangibility. Thread gold could be used for stringing musical instruments—e.g., violins.

75. *Paracelsus: Selected Writings*, ed. Jolande Jacobi, trans. Norbert Guterman (Princeton, N.J.: Pantheon Books, Bollingen Series XXVIII, 1951).

The alchemical cast of the passage leads us to the primary meaning of "tongues." The only tongues that assist in the production of genuine gold are tongues of flame—a refining fire. Zukofsky, like Paracelsus, is maintaining a delicate balance between gold as object and gold as symbol. Paracelsus: "This is an action which—like that performed by fire on gold—frees man from the impurities that he himself does not know"; "Alchemy is nothing but the art which makes the impure into the pure through fire."[76] Art itself is such a fire, turning ill words into loving words, defeating the power of poison. No need, it seems, to worry about the poisoned river: "He who despises poison does not know what is hidden in it; for the arcanum that is contained in the poison is so blessed that the poison can neither detract from it nor harm it."[77] All the bitter moments of domestic life are powerless to subtract from its virtues. Arts (Louis's, Celia's, Paul's) conjoined in "A"-11 will turn the family toward the "second paradise" mentioned in line 32. And what precisely is that? "The striving for wisdom is the second paradise of the world," according to Paracelsus.[78]

Paracelsian diction helps define one problem that troubles "A"-11: how to coordinate the family Zukofsky with those distant, dead eminences arranged on library shelves, of whom James, Spinoza, and Cavalcanti are only representatives. "The starry vault imprints itself on the inner heaven of man" advises Paracelsus; his way of saying that eternal truths are near at hand—as near as the person next to us—if we but look for them.[79] A fictional Paracelsus, Robert Browning's, mingles with the original at this juncture; a passage from *Paracelsus* seems to apply to "Take care, song, that what stars' imprint you mirror / Grazes their tears":

76. Ibid., pp. 168, 217.   77. Ibid., p. 169.
78. Ibid., p. 65.   79. Ibid., p. 114.

> Now, aureole, stay those wandering eyes awhile!
> You are ours tonight, at least; and while you spoke
> Of Michael and her tears, I thought that none
> Could willing leave what he so seemed to love:
> But that last look destroys my dream—that look
> As if, wher'er you gazed, there stood a star!
> How far was Wurzburg with its church and spire
> And garden-walls and all things they contain,
> From that look's far alighting.[80]

The "stars" of *"A"*-11 are those scintillating minds that tend to draw Louis away from his family. It is on record that Celia considered Louis's "meanest" action was "just never to hear what I was saying. He was oblivious when he was working or thinking about something."[81] In *"A"*-11 Zukofsky dives into that oblivion and brings back a gift for Celia and Paul. The stars he steers by in this movement guide him to his family.

The dates of composition for *"A"*-11 and *"A"*-12 that Zukofsky listed at the beginning of *"A"* are somewhat misleading. He places *"A"*-11 in 1950, but his manuscripts and the presence of material from Jacobi's *Paracelsus* indicate that he worked on it well into the next year. The manuscript for *"A"*-12 is dated June–October 1951; Zukofsky indicates that it took shape in 1950–51. Perhaps the actual writing of these movements was anticlimactic; the labor may have been in the preparation. If so, then Zukofsky's chronology records the time spent arranging his materials.

The planning of *"A"*-12 would, therefore, seem to coincide with the completion of *"A"*-11, only one of several indications that they are companion pieces. Both use the

80. *The Complete Works of Robert Browning*, ed. Roma A. King, Jr., Morse Peckham, Park Honan, and Gordon Pitts (Athens, Ohio: Ohio University Press, 1969), I, 71–72.

81. Carroll F. Terrell, "Conversations with Celia," *Paideuma* 7 (Winter 1978): 600.

family Zukofsky as a foundation, "*A*"-11 concentrating on the inner dynamics of the family, "*A*"-12 considering the interaction of the family with the world. (There is plenty of family chat in "*A*"-12, but exterior events persistently shadow that discourse.) Roughly speaking, "*A*"-11 presents the family as a closed entity, "*A*"-12 treats it as a cell within the universe.

In "*A*"-12 a quartet is once again summoned to the poet's aid. Zukofsky's brain trust for this movement: Aristotle, Paracelsus, Spinoza, and . . . Celia. He promotes her to that exalted rank by designating her "the lover of wisdom" (p. 237). As mediator between the flights of two artists (one creative, one performing) and the irregularities of daily life, she had to possess manifold wisdom, if only for self-defense.

The four appear in shorthand notation at the movement's beginning (p. 127) and end (p. 261) as *B, A, C* and *H*. "*B*" for Blest (Spinoza), "*A*" for Aristotle (referred to as "Ardent," apparently in recognition of his love of learning), "*C*" for Celia, "*H*" for Hohenheim (Paracelsus's real name was Philippus Aureolus Theophrastus Bombastus von Hohenheim).[82] Their voices sound through the movement, sometimes identified and sometimes not. At many points, their words and Zukofsky's become indistinguishable, especially since he continues his old habit of "correcting" their phrases. This is as it should be, for "*A*"-12 makes explicit Zukofsky's conviction that he participates in a common tradition that includes Aristotle, Lucretius, Ovid, Shakespeare, Spinoza, et al. Given such a tradition, it really doesn't matter whose voice is speaking. The tradition itself speaks, in many tongues. We have come a long way from "Poem Beginning 'The'," where the young Zukofsky

---

82. I am indebted to Mr. Peter Crisp for his help in determining the referents of *B, A, C,* and *H*.

seemed burdened by voices from the past. His style then was an attempt to shoulder that burden. By the time we reach "*A*"-12, however, his frame of reference is no longer temporal. Voices flow in and out of one another, existing in and affirming an atemporal body of truth.

One of "*A*"'s goals is the recovery and arrangement of the materials that permit an exact comprehension of history and culture. This project comes to fruition in "*A*"-12. The arrangement seems to be directed mainly by the *B*, *A*, *C*, *H* notation, but another quartet assists. The mind, active and searching, travels over an ineluctable ground—the world. It cannot be ignored, or the mind falls toward the limbo that threatened Kay in "*A*"-2. And what does the world consist of? So far as "*A*"-12 is concerned, it consists simply of the ancient tally of four elements: earth, air, fire, and water. They appear in some form on every page of the movement, a continual counterpoint to the ruminations of Zukofsky and the big four. Not that a conflict exists between mind and the elements; when the relations between mind and the world are properly seen, they are discovered to be harmonious. The trouble, Zukofsky hints, lies in man's chronic lapse into disharmony with himself. Because we are internally divided the outer world seems chaotic. This is not an original notion, but we should not rush to fault Zukofsky for want of originality. "*A*" is partly a critique of the concept of originality.

The old conflict in "*A*" between wisdom and error, which pervades the poem from the beginning, returns as a major theme in "*A*"-12, and Zukofsky gives it a name.

> From Battle of
> Discord and Harmony
> Come home beloved.   (p. 136)

The immediate source for that designation is Vivaldi (see page 212), but further back stands Empedocles, of whom

Diogenes Laertius remarked that "his doctrines were as follows, that there are four elements, fire, water, earth and air, besides friendship ($\Phi\iota\lambda\iota\alpha\nu$) by which these are united, and strife ($\text{N}\varepsilon\hat{\iota}\kappa\text{o}\varsigma$) by which they are separated."[83] So a Greek philosopher contributes to the structuring of "A"-12. But no single contributor can carry off all the credit. Such a monopoly of originality would contradict Zukofsky's convictions. So, joining Empedocles is Paracelsus: "The animal body . . . is in itself always dead. Only through the action of the sidereal body does the motion of life come into the other body. The sidereal body is fire and air. . . . Thus man consists of water, earth, fire, and air."[84]

The focus and ground for that body of truth is the family Zukofsky. The family provides a sure footing for the poem, a pivot the poem has been seeking since "A"-1. Cast adrift from secure moorings in the mid-1920s, Zukofsky has found in his new family a context for his finest work. The restless acquisition of voices that marked the first half of "A" is satisfied when, at the close of "A"-12, it becomes clear that Celia's words have as much, or more, value than Zukofsky's, Shakespeare's, or Spinoza's.

—Tell me

—Tell *you*

Tell me of that man who got around
After sacred Troy fell,
He knew men and cities
His heart riled in the sea
As he strove for himself and his friends:
He did not save them.
Tell us about it, my Light,
Start where you please.

83. *Diogenes Laertius: Lives of Eminent Philosophers*, trans. R. D. Hicks (Cambridge, Mass., and London: Harvard and Heinemann, 1970), II, 389.
84. *Paracelsus*, p. 92.

It's so simple,
Telemachos rose from his bed
And dressed   (p. 261)

"Tell *you*," Celia responds, surprised and unaware that she has the wisdom Louis seeks. Though the poem is only halfway to its conclusion, the journey to the place desired—the respite from fragmentation and isolation—has been accomplished. Celia is revealed as Zukofsky's true Penelope, the only voice that can tell him the meaning of his journey. Alone, Zukofsky could not "save them." In the company of Celia and Paul he is saved. His art, extraneous to his first family, is fully integrated with the life of his second family. The return to Ithaca finds Zukofsky enfolded in an adequate familiarity.

FOUR

The Recluse: *"A"* 13–20

> Thus we lived several years in a state of much happiness, not but that we sometimes had those little rubs which Providence sends to enhance the value of its favours.
>
> Oliver Goldsmith, *The Vicar of Wakefield*

AT THE beginning of *"A"*-15, we encounter a bewildering kaleidoscope of words whose purpose only clarifies when we learn that they are "English" versions of Hebrew passages from the book of Job ("Iyyob"): not a translation, but a rendering of the sounds as they might be heard in a synagogue. God is talking here, and if He is hard to understand . . . well, we have neglected the art of attending to messages in the wind. Nature in modern times speaks no intelligible language. Or does it? Putting aside the issues raised by the "Iyyob" passage (they are legion), we can at least note that the story of Job has some application to movements 13–20. And we are not likely to forget it, since Zukofsky constantly asks us to read his own troubles in a Jobian light, as he broadcasts in the language of complaint.

Job found some relief in lengthy, eloquent meditations on his plight. His losses, however taxing, provided an opportunity to develop and display verbal wealth. Not having Job's considerable supply of livestock, children, and ready cash, Zukofsky spends most of his time lamenting his physical ailments. Only part of this is hypochondria. When he resumed work on "A" in 1960, he was fifty-six years old, and the inevitable depredations of late middle age were beginning to register on someone who smoked constantly and took no regular exercise. So the second half of "A" records in detail its author's obsession with failing faculties of wind and limb.

Where does one begin to trace the arc of falling vitality? At the top of the curve, where strength still permits feats of invincible excursion. Section ii of "A"-13 tells us that on a summer's day in the late 1950s, Louis and Paul toured the streets of lower Manhattan, crossed the Brooklyn Bridge, and, after a brief rest at the Brooklyn Esplanade, returned to Celia and their home in Brooklyn Heights. All this was accomplished on foot. The movement as a whole is a story of that day in the life of the three Zukofskys. This fact, however, escapes immediate apprehension, since the first of the movement's five sections is not especially well an-chored in a particular time and place. It needn't be, for it could easily be subtitled "Any Father to Any Son." Louis's monologue in section i aims to impart pithy wisdom, with Paul as recipient. From what we learn of Paul in other sec-tions of "A"-13, it seems doubtful that he is listening. Thus the usual course of paternal instruction to a son depart-ing the domestic circle: father attends to his own pleasing sententiousness while son has other things on his mind. Sounding like George Herbert at the Church Porch or Po-lonius, Louis ladles out his free advice, gets carried away, and begins talking to himself.

The gentle humor in this tableau of parental admonition gone astray conceals a more serious intent. By installing so traditional a scene and rhetoric at the commencement of the poem's second half, Zukofsky hints at one of his inten-tions for "A" 13–20: the creation of a renovated language based on the field of cliché. Later movements of "A" will

push English beyond recognizable limits, but even in *"A"*
13–20, we find Zukofsky tugging and manipulating common parts of speech.

> If you talk to yourself
> Your love talks to you
> Your music meets her words   (p. 274)

"You" and "your" are pointedly indefinite here. They latch
on to any one of the three Zukofskys, suggesting that so
tightly knit a family finds its private thoughts forever
meeting and connecting. Perhaps talking to oneself is not
a futile type of communication. If family thoughts are
shared in common, what need for Louis to bother Paul
with nuggets of anecdote and sage advice? Since Paul has
been one of the three participants in this remarkable discourse for seventeen years, he has already imbibed them
through osmosis. His father's rambling speech is thus the
gist of a generation's worth of "mute wisdom." As a digest
it could hardly be pegged down to a specific occasion, another reason for the indeterminate status of time and place
in section i.

Section ii lands us at the Brooklyn Esplanade, which
provides one of the best views of New York Harbor. Here
in the gathering twilight sit Louis and Paul, taking in the
harbor, the island of the Manhattoes, and, to their right,
the Bridge. In short, they are reviewing the ground just
covered. This attitude, like the posture Louis assumed in
section i, hangs heavy with tradition. Addison, Gray,
Goldsmith, and Wordsworth have been there before Zukofsky, sounding the retrospective note that often begins
with the poet perched on a suitable eminence.[1] Paul, too
young for manifold memories, takes little interest in the

---

1. Also hovering in the background are Walt Whitman—crossing
Brooklyn Ferry—and Hart Crane, resident of Washington Roebling's
house.

scene, but time has brought his father to the point where his thoughts can drift back fifty years.

Paul's fascination with fire was recorded in "A"-12, and the excursion apparently began at the Duane Street Fire Museum. Father and son also have inspected the "rat lofts on Greene Street" (p. 281), unchanged since they were "rat lofts" in "A"-5. Our heroes seem to have gone as far as Gansevoort Street at the north side of Greenwich Village. That would be a long walk, in more senses than one. The span of Greene-Gansevoort measures two of Zukofsky's pasts: Greene—the Jewish; Gansevoort—the literary. Herman Melville, as Zukofsky reminds us (p. 282), regularly passed through Gansevoort Street as a customs officer. He found that no one knew for whom the street was named, even though the inquirer was a grandson of General Peter Gansevoort. Americans are famous for having short memories.

So much coverage takes its toll.

> —We *have* walked today
> My lean old shanks hurt.
> Twenty years since I've walked
> From 12 Street home all the way
> Across Brooklyn Bridge   (p. 280)

Contemplating his own aching pins, and comparing them with the remarkable spring in Paul's step, Zukofsky is moved to consider the vagaries of bipedal motion:

> He ambles
> She ambles with glasses
> The other with a feather.
> The old dowager again
> Crossing her ankles as she walks
> Reliving the ballet   (p. 277)

Zukofsky shows himself a connoisseur of diminished progress, perhaps suggesting that both the poet and his poem are running out of steam. The tip-off of that decline appears at the head of section ii: "Why hop ye so, ye little, little hills? / And wherefore do ye hop?" (p. 274) (a palpitation drawn from a considerably more exuberant text, Psalm 68: "Why leap ye, ye high hills?").

Eventually Louis summons up enough strength to make the short stroll home to Willow Street, only a few blocks behind the esplanade. The Zukofskys are now living on the tenth floor of an apartment building. Hence the comment by Paul, "Let's go upstairs" (p. 287) that precedes their ascent in an elevator. This proposal touches off a metaphysical discussion between father and son, proving that they really have "left the ground." The upward movement continues in an aside noting a truly remarkable thrust heavenward.

> —Before Lunik Three
> (the third)
> Which is now nearer
> The moon certainly
> Than either to Moscow or New York   (p. 289)

Dreamers and poets have made pretended voyages to the moon for centuries. In 1959, however, Russian spacecraft (extrapolations of the upward striving chronicled in "A"-8) actually extended man's dominion to that sphere. A triumph of science over art?

Zukofsky considered the "race" to the moon sheer folly. He condensed its causes and consequences in "A" 13–20 at tedious length. His response in "A"-13 takes the form of a modernization of a thirteenth-century English poem, "The Man in the Moon." Zukofsky's "man" has, like Zukofsky himself, a precarious sense of balance; his legs aren't what they should be. Alienated from the world, he fears to take the steps that will carry him to social redemption. Deaf to the poet's entreaties, he has lost contact with the language that will bring him back to his senses. Who is this "Man in the Moon"? We are probably not far from the mark if we assume that he is all those who ignore Zukofsky (which means just about everybody). But he is also a poet without a family, what Zukofsky might have become. In this, and in other instances, Zukofsky taps one American tradition: the author's creation of alternate versions of himself. The moonscape of this part of "A"-13 is another "Jolly Corner."

Despite divergences of this sort, "A"-13 presents a recognizable scene on a particular day. Nothing so reassuring has been offered the reader since "A"-1. This is no coincidence. Both movements function as entry ways to their respective halves of the poem. The unities of space, time, and action are more or less under strict control—the red carpet is unrolled for the reader. Other movements are less accommodating. Zukofsky seems to have thought of the second half of "A" as a starting over, not merely because twelve movements remained to be written, but because the first half's search for a mediating ground had been satisfied with the discovery of the family as a suitable field of discourse. What seems to trouble "A" as it moves forward is the prospect of steadily diminishing arenas of action: in the author's life, in the number of movements left, and in possibilities of finding a readership. What does not diminish is the author's command of language, and in the latter movements this comes to be the overriding concern.

Conversely, the poem's interest in public events falls off sharply. After "A"-18, in fact, public history is banished altogether. The news of the day, centrally significant in "A" 1–12, merely serves as illustration in "A" 13–20, as if what the media report has no significance except as further evidence of what the sage old poet already knows. When Zukofsky does cast an eye on what the news commentators have to say, bitterness tends to creep into his tone. It might be argued that rancor is the proper response, but Zukofsky seems to go beyond all reasonable bounds. His attacks on warped thinking are themselves rather warped, as they were in *"A"*-9. One such diagnosis, at the beginning of *"A"*-14, takes up the question of changed perspective in the Space Age. Mankind's view of the universe must be re-fashioned, now that human artifacts are whizzing through the void, but what progress has been made along these lines? Zukofsky bends his analytic faculties to the task. The first words of *"A"*-14, "An / orange / our / sun" (p. 314) advert to the popular texts that address the problem of unthinkable magnitudes. The average high school geology book and the Sunday supplement usually ask the reader to envision the sun as a beach ball set down on a football field or baseball diamond. One by one the planets are placed at proper range, all the way to pea-sized Pluto in the parking lot.

With the solar system disposed of, we are then invited to picture the earth as an orange—the rind serving as crust. Zukofsky's parody of this schema seems based on the assumption that the taxpayers (and congressmen) footing the bill were voting with little more than this sort of cosmology in mind. Zukofsky's version of the fruitarian universe posits the sun as an orange, and this shuffling of the schema's elements shows how simplistic such models are.

Zukofsky's cryptic broadsides in *"A"* 13–20 usually turn out to be solidly grounded. Just as the Sunday supplement can be discerned behind the first lines of *"A"*-14, the second half of the poem has plenty of contact with the everyday world. Up to, and including, *"A"*-18, there are public references aplenty, although *"A"* has no interest in dwelling on them long enough for the reader to recognize them and understand why they are used. Though it would be a mistake to approach the poem the way we approach trick pictures ("how many common household items can you find here?"), it is reassuring to discover recognizable phenomena. If we want to take the trouble, we can even distinguish discrete areas of reference. The most prominent, and easiest to track, limits itself to public figures. We can easily identify the "old man" and "bonny prince" (p. 350) as Robert Frost and John F. Kennedy. "Episcopal gold-wasser Polyuria" (p. 354) is plainly one of Zukofsky's splenetic swipes at a 1964 presidential candidate. But other clusters of reference take us away from the newspaper and steer us to the card catalog, a slight but significant narrowing of focus. Flipping through the index to *"A"* (and, incidentally, getting a covert glimpse of the poet's library), we discover that the text Zukofsky probes at the close of *"A"*-14 is E. A. Wallis Budge's translation of the Egyptian *Book of the Dead*. This represents middle-level arcana, but even the more common literary allusions cause trouble. Zukofsky seems much of the time to have been unaware that the practice of memorizing poems had fallen off in elementary schools. He therefore assumed a wider comprehension of the "classics" on the part of his readers than actually existed, or exists. Anyone can see the simple pun in "not / a / long / fellow" (p. 334), but the odds are that very few will recognize that Zukofsky's "sands of time" is an emendation of Henry Wadsworth Longfellow's "A Psalm of Life." It appears that many of *"A"*'s baffling passages were not deliberately intended as puzzlers. The same could be said for non-literary references, such as the use of local geography. Some material that seems totally gratuitous may turn out to be logically placed—if we consult a map of New York City. Directly below the esplanade, for example, are docks still in active use. So *"A"*-14 examines a Japanese freighter, one of many Zukofsky could not avoid seeing. Life-long residents of New York take its geography for granted. They tend to forget that there are tourists in the world.

So far as legibility goes, movements 15–17 present few

problems. Less challenging than the flanking pairs (13–14 and 18–19), they are also shorter, less intricately crafted, and plainer, as if calling for less than the full measure of a poet's skill. Three deaths seem to have called them into being: those of John Kennedy, Robert Frost, and William Carlos Williams—that is, a national leader, his unofficial poet laureate, and the poet who should have been laurcate. A question is raised by this conjunction: what does the poet owe his nation, and vice versa? Another question also needs an answer: what did Zukofsky owe Williams?

"*A*"-15 concentrates on JFK's assassination and funeral rites, and here Zukofsky relies heavily on radio, television, and the newspapers. The death of the president—a public event—allows the poet a rare opportunity to respond publicly. His "public" approach depends, for example, on millions of people remembering where they were and what they were doing when the news broke. Here the hermetic poet can show that he shares a common point of departure:

> that the teacher
> overhearing
> a student
> thought a stupid jest—
> the class
> shocked into a "holiday"   (p. 363)

Zukofsky did, after all, live in the same world that we do.

Yet the public world slowly and inexorably turns ephemeral. Its solidity depends on its being packed with bits of information, styles, and trivia common to everyone. But time turns these details into arcana. How many readers understand, at this late date, the reason for Franklin Delano Roosevelt's play on "Manifesto" in "*A*"-8?

> Or maybe as F.D.R., diverted at a
>   dinner the year after,

> Would jest,
> The invested Ambassador to Maine?   (p. 98)

Anyone reading those lines in 1937 would recall that only
Maine and Vermont went for Landon in 1936, and understand F.D.R.'s view of Maine as enemy territory to which
ambassadors might be dispatched. To most of us it is
obvious that "John-John" (p. 368) is John F. Kennedy, Jr.,
but readers born after 1955 may be puzzled. The sighs of
relief that we breathe when encountering stretches of "A"
causing no difficulty may well mark precisely those areas
where ensuing generations will discover impenetrability.

For four days "the nation grieved / each as for someone
in his or her family" (p. 368). Yes, that is how the nation
grieved, but how did the Zukofskys take it? We are not
told. Not that they were unmoved, but the emphasis on
"nation" hints that the familial solidarity known intimately
to the Zukofskys was briefly eclipsed by a semblance of
that unity on a national scale. If Zukofsky were to recount
the distress of himself, Celia, and Paul, it would be super-
flous, perhaps even patronizing. We should also remember
that Zukofsky habitually expresses deep emotion by a reticence and displacement that can easily pass unnoticed. So
he suggests his own response by considering how Williams
might have reacted, had Williams been alive. As Zukofsky
puts it,

> he would
> miss
> living thru the
> assassination   (p. 361)

"Miss" sounds an ambiguous note, and three different interpretations stem from it: (1) Williams would "not be
around" to see it, (2) Williams would "be spared the pain,"
(3) Williams would "be sorry for losing the experience."

The passage lies on the page with a deceptively casual air, in a "natural" order. But any tinkering knocks that three-way balance out of phase. "He missed" or "he would have missed" tend to emphasize readings (2) and (3). Of course, a poet's hunger for the events that alter and illuminate our times should not be confused with murderous intent. There exists, however, a desire for experience that moves the poet toward agonizing loci, his revulsion all the while mixed with fascination. That discordant approach finds adequate expression in Zukofsky's multivalent phrasing. His talent for making words deliver up all their meanings was always useful.

The floral tribute Zukofsky pays Williams in "A"-17 is more than just another funeral wreath. It takes its cue from Williams's own use of flowers; *Spring and All*, for example, concludes with a poem suggesting that we can profitably consider people as flowers. With a nod in that direction, "A"-15 closes with:

> *negritude* no nearer or further
> than the African violet
> not deferred to
> or if white, Job
> white pods of *honesty*
> satinflower   (p. 375)

Translation: race relations might improve if we would remember that American gardens hold, side by side, African violets (originally imported from the Dark Continent, as Africans were) and the satinflower, native to California. Extremes can grow amicably together. Given the right conditions, there may even be a mutually profitable exchange. Such an exchange is sampled in "A"-17, where Zukofsky finds Williams's influence in his own work.

If Williams dominates movements 15–17, Paul Zukofsky dominates 18–20. The dead artist, his distinguished

career completed, yields to a virtuoso just starting out. As
the poem trains its attention on Williams and Paul, we notice that public history seems to fade away. "A"-15 and
"A"-18 fret about world disasters, but movements 16–17
and 19–20 pay more and more attention to the artists. It
seems that human folly goes on and on in the same old circle, but the poet and the musician have something new to
show us.

The troubled course of human events makes its last major appearance in "A"-18, where the latest war (Vietnam)
supplies Zukofsky with various examples of stupidity. As
a parting shot at the big cheeses, he twists their names in a
fashion unseen since the heyday of the Augustans.

> I see with the inflation boys march West
> Less Land Ia Drang news one more less safer
>
> (p. 398)

We easily spot General Westmoreland leading the way,
scorching and defoliating the earth. Less conspicuous because "more [or] less safer" tagging along at the rear is CBS
correspondent Morley Safer. Like many another poet, Zukofsky ultimately finds human folly and criminality tire-
some. There are no grand, profound dimensions—only a
musty creaking. Therefore little effort is required to reduce
error to its basically narrow dimensions. The entire American war effort is captured in the anecdote of the "mi-
raculous fish" (p. 392). Its source is an article Zukofsky
clipped from *The New York Times*, edited by him to sharpen
its latent satire. A resort to massive firepower, mistaken
efforts, shooting in the blind, internal rivalries of reli-
gious/political factions—these are the dynamics of the
war, caught on a single page.

Public history disappears, Zukofsky retires from his
teaching job, and Paul begins to compete for a place in the
music world. This is the background for movements 19

and 20. The "real event" behind *"A"*-19 is a violin competition held in Genoa, where Paul comes in fourth after giving the best performance (at least according to the poem—we must allow for parental bias). But the texture of *"A"*-19 is not that of a solo recital. It seems more like a quartet, whose members are Paul, Louis, Paganini, and Mallarmé. Louis plays on texts by Mallarmé just as Paul plays on Paganini's own instrument. The quartet therefore has two members from the nineteenth century and two from the twentieth. (It is *probably* coincidental that the number of this movement is 19 and that the next is 20.) The ground staked out by *"A"*-19 turns out to be a space created by the intersection of quadruple talent.

"A"-20, like *"A"*-16, hardly seems serious. What value can be mined from a listing and shuffling of the titles of Paul's compositions? It appears to be mere frivolity, like the title, "the title of this piece is / the title of this piece doesn't matter" (p. 436). If we walk out in a huff, however, we simply show we haven't learned much in forty years. The composer's father used the same tactic with "Poem Beginning 'The'." *"A"*-20 reveals a continuity between the art of father and son. And at the end of *"A"*-20 comes a poem written by Paul at age nine (in 1952) to demonstrate that there was more than one poet in the family. The son's creative work becomes the cogent reply to his father's monologue in section i of *"A"*-13. *"A"*-20 as a whole also seems to be the reward that makes suffering negligible. This movement, so slight in appearance, works wonders for Zukofsky.

Though Celia and Paul could not always be an attentive audience for Louis, especially after Paul had left to seek his fortune, the poet had almost no other sympathetic listeners. During the years when movements *"A"* 13–20 were composed, his wife and son may have constituted his principal readership. His widely known hermeticism was probably deepened by a conviction that nobody cared for his work.

> "I am a man needed but not wanted."
> As to how much one is needed it has been hard
> To feel it these many years more than the light
> of that joke. (p. 276)

Zukofsky's audience, never large, was probably at its greatest in the early 1930s, and would not surpass that height until the late 1960s. He was acutely aware, as he began "A"'s second half, that his entire body of work was out of print—with the single exception of Cid Corman's two hundred–copy edition of "A" 1–12. Was there, perhaps, a faint hope on his part that further work on "A" might find a few readers? Two hundred readers. For Zukofsky that would constitute a multitude. A lifetime's effort had brought him to the point where publishers felt free to insult or neglect him—or so Zukofsky believed. Avoiding bitterness, he poked fun at his perpetual anonymity. In "A"-14:

> I
> stumbled into the
> TV—'you want?
>
> to be on
> television'—C.   (p. 334)

(C for "Celia," not "CBS.") Hollywood, the royal road to American fame, seems to beckon the poet:

> Imagine,
> said Celia, selling
>
> the movie rights
> to *Bottom: on
> Shakespeare*   (pp. 336–37)

> don't complain
> Hollywood bought 12
> copies of your
>
> *A Test*   (p. 349)

It hardly needs to be said that no amount of exposure on
the tube or the silver screen would further an understanding of his art. Rooted as his work is in measures that do not
lend themselves to short, simplified treatment, Zukofsky
would not have recognized Hollywood images of *Bottom*.
He could never make contact with a public enamored of
the transient, a public staring raptly at pictures of the eternal beamed from outer space.

> Ranger VII
> photos landing
> on the
>
> moon
> how deep
> its dust?   (pp. 315–16)

How deep? A puzzle of interest to scientists and astronauts, anxious that the first men on the moon not be swal-
lowed by fathomless seas. Yet also a comment by Zukofsky, noting the moon's total sterility, as if he considered it
one huge clump of dust. Nothing human, he suggests,
contributed to the layers of dust on the moon, and earth-
lings preoccupied with a foreign body neglect the dust in
their own back yard.

> Egypt
> Sumer's works
> whose foot
> has disappeared?   (p. 316)

Armstrong's first step sank only a little way into the moon
fluff, but what about the millions of feet that have disap-

peared into the dust of ages? Public awareness has flocked to the wrong end of the "dust scale." Eyes and energies bent on the planets seem to have no time for the successive human worlds of the past. Zukofsky would argue that Egypt, Sumer, Troy, and all the other vanished kingdoms of the world have a more legitimate claim on our attention than the bleak plains and mountains of the moon that will rise tonight.

What interests "A" is our own crowded planet, where each particle of earth was once, or may yet be, alive. Clay has the latent capacity to sing. Sumer's works may be moldering rubbish, and its poets gone with the duststorms of yesteryear, but the feet in a poem persist so long as there is someone to sing.

> *The* works.
> Hallel ascents
> degrees vintage   (p. 316)

The works because words—the first imperishable tools invented by mankind—survive. *The* persists, and "Poem Beginning 'The'" will last. Hallel (the hymn composed of Psalms 113–18) ascends through the ages, with greater endurance than that shown by rockets. We rise on wings of song, not by means of Saturns and space shuttles. And who do we have to thank for this? Our ancestors, the vintners of all past human experience, have handed them down ("degree" comes from *de gradus*, literally a "step down").

Zukofsky's want of an audience in "A" 13–20 shades into his growing conviction that he is obsolete. Not only that, he has become outmoded without ever having been put to use. The prime disseminator of cultural opinion in his home town, the *Times*, has ignored him; the public had never even seen (as of 1960) a review of his work.

> Grandsons and granddaughters who take courses eat —
> and learn

> From the newspaper how Downtown Business is saving
>   little
> Old New York, where today of its past I reappeared
>   (p. 283)

As he emerges unnoticed from the past, he is as out of date (and slyly playing that old-fashioned role) as Rip Van Winkle, Enoch Arden, Isabel Vane, John Harmon, or any of those nineteenth-century ghosts whose intense contemplation of all they have missed seems their sole reason for being. Zukofsky feels more and more like a living fossil, just as Henry and Brooks Adams did. Echoes of "A"-8 pepper "A"-13, as both movements juxtapose the decline of one generation and the emergence of another. In "A"-8 Zukofsky was part of the surging wave of the future; but that moment is long past. It is Paul who has the world before him.

At least Louis has the courage to laugh at this new alignment, though the jokes often recede into obscurity—as usual. One such moment occurs in section ii of "A"-13. We find Zukofsky disturbed by a noisy urchin:

> —That kid, banderlog singing.
> "I think, madam, you can hardly
> Be aware that your child's song
> Is a cause of annoyance to the rest of us"   (p. 278)

The formality of the quoted remonstrance should alert us. Zukofsky seems to be identifying himself with a period when such phrasing did not sound completely stilted. "Banderlog" suggests Mowgli, Kipling's obstreperous youth, and so directs us back to the turn of the century. All well and good, but without the complete text this is as far as we can go. We have to turn to Logan Pearsall Smith's *Unforgotten Years* to learn why the "child's song" suggests a pattern of isolation and decline:

He (William James) had gone . . . by tram that afternoon
to Boston; and as he sat and meditated in the Cambridge
horsecar two strains of thought had occupied his mind.
One of these was the notion, which Mrs. James had recently derived from the perusal of Kipling's writings, that
our social order . . . had for . . . ultimate sanction nothing
but force, however much we might disguise it—the naked
fist, in fact, the blow of the sword, the crack of the pistol,
or the smoke and roar of guns. Superimposed upon this
meditation began to recur, with greater and greater per-
sistence, the memory of certain remarks of his brother
Henry, who, on a recent visit to America, had indignantly
protested against the outrageous pertness of the American
child and the meek pusillanimity with which the older generation suffered the behavior of their children without
protests.

It was not long, William James said, before he became
aware of what had aroused this second line of thought; it
was the droning sound which filled the horsecar—the
voice, in fact, of an American child, who was squeaking
over and over again an endless, shrill, monotonous sing-
song. Growing more and more irritated by this squeaking,
William James resolved that he at least would not suffer it
without protest; so, addressing the mother of the vocal infant, he said politely, "I think, madam, you can hardly be
aware that your child's song is a cause of annoyance to the
rest of us in this car."

She ignores this comment, and, to his surprise, James finds
himself reprimanded by another passenger for this "ungen-
tlemanly" address. With Kipling's tough-minded analysis
of the social order still simmering in his brain, James threat-
ens to slap his interlocutor should he repeat the challenge.

The remark, to his consternation, was repeated and the
professor was compelled to make good his word. The slap
was conscientiously administered; the occupants of the
horsecar arose in indignation, pressing their cards upon the

victim of the assault, and protesting their willingness to be witnesses at any legal proceedings which might ensue. Then they all sat down; and as the car clattered along through the dust towards Boston, with the child still shrilly singing, the grave burden of the public disapproval which William James had encountered became almost more, he said, than he could bear.[2]

A hateful sense of personal antiquity haunts Zukofsky. As "A"-19 suggests, he seems to have abandoned the hope of ever finding an audience. That difficult quest is now Paul's.

Other problems plague Zukofsky, such as the maintenance of a steadily decaying body. As he and Paul rest at the esplanade, further passages from *Unforgotten Years* crowd in to broach the theme of old age and its attendant discomforts:

> We venerate our young
> Instead of feeling as the Chinese of the last century
> Proud of accumulating years . .
> Our bones ripen it is true
> For their ultimate repose . . but
> How small a price to pay . .
> For those adequate conceptions in whose possession
> According to Spinoza's wisdom true felicity consists.
>
> (p. 278)

The price paid and the recompense gained are calculations each of us has to weigh for ourselves. Zukofsky's eschatological concern is not new to "A"; his obsession with death was evident in the first movement. But the "distinguished thing" draws closer now, and his appreciation of its presence sharpens. Feeling his bones "ripening," he begins "A"-18 with a brief speculation on the nature of his and

2. Logan Pearsall Smith, *Unforgotten Years* (Boston: Little, Brown, 1939), pp. 117–20.

Celia's mutual relations after his death. This late meditation on the life of his survivors gains poignancy simply because it completes "A"'s series of posthumous ponderings.
Within the movement, there appears another variation on
the theme.

> When I am dead in the empty ear
> you might ask what was he like away
> from home. . . . (p. 393)

The English language has heard something like this before;
another old man's speculations about how the curious
would react to news of his passing:

> Behold the fatal day arrive.
> "How is the Dean?"—"He's just alive."
> Now the departing prayer is read;
> "He hardly breathes."—"The Dean is dead."
> Before the Passing-bell begun,
> The news thro' half the town has run.
> "O! may we all for death prepare.
> What has he left? and who's his heir?"[3]

This great original, "On the Death of Dr. Swift," lies re-
motely behind "A"-18, but other selections from the Dean
jostle each other at the conclusion of the movement. We
must turn to the *Memoirs of Scriblerus* and the "Letter of
Advice to a Young Poet" to find them in their original context. Besides being neglected old authors, Zukofsky and
Swift have something else in common: they share a cloacal
obsession. As Zukofsky observes,

> young,
> Swift had no
>
> scholaress—old, afraid
> to ease liquid— (p. 333)

3. *Satires and Personal Writings by Jonathan Swift*, ed. William Alfred
Eddy (London: Oxford University Press, 1932), p. 483.

For his part, Zukofsky repeatedly meditates on ends—all sorts of ends. This thorough approach saves him from plunging into morbidity. If a poet can enumerate his diminishing prospects in such a lively manner, he has already won the battle. Consider this wry passage, summing up the end of *"A"*, the end of life, the end of the body, and the rear end.

> No not an efficient man only an observant
> sits down with an aspirin without a prayer
> . . . .
> *"An"*: faring no cause to an unowned end:
> story of a fiddler from pogrom to program:
> Doughty: "the Semites are like to a man
> sitting in a cloaca to the eyes and
> whose brows touch heaven". . . . .   (pp. 393–94)

"Unowned end" completes a line dense with suggestion. We can dimly see Charon poling through it, and the poet scribbling on to the end of his poem, which is not yet "owned" (i.e., "possessed" and/or "admitted to"). When he wrote *"A"*-18, he could not be sure that oblivion would not overtake him before he reached *"A"*-24.

Zukofsky delicately hints at another symptom of the body's sad decline. *"A"*-9, we recall, had suggested an intimate relation between the body and the substance of verse. Now, in *"A"*-18, an enigmatic line confirms this link between *corpus* and characters: "who won't sense upper case anymore" (p. 390). All movements written after 1963 drop the custom of beginning each line with a capital letter. If we are slow to draw conclusions, there are further clues in the story of the sailor's operation (p. 390). The story teems with phallic figures and unsubtle suggestions of castration: "the surgeon operated on another wound offhand saw." Yes, "offhand saw" suggests amputation of a hand as well as "noticing by the way."

As parts of the body lose their function, the poet begins

to detect similar problems in the body politic. At times, in "A" 13–20, the whole world seems to be falling apart. To what extent Zukofsky believed this second coming of great Anarch to be true is debatable. To some extent, his despair was part of a role—that of prophet of doom. Like the Adamses and William James, he found it appropriate to play the antiquated codger. This codger seems to be the author of "A"-14. Here we find extremes screwed to a manic pitch. The world of "A"-14 is a world of unmediated opposition. Sun/moon, summer/winter, heat/cold, sound/sense, Brooklyn/Japan, 1964/1924, Jew/Gentile: all these pairings contribute to a frightening tendency toward disintegration in the movement. Furthermore, the movement lacks the emphasis on the family as center that graced "A"-13. A figure related to that lonely "Man in the Moon" appears at the beginning of "A"-14, a solitary projector "alone / in the / wilderness" (p. 317). As "Dark heart" indicates, this is Conrad's Kurtz, the man who had immense plans. Kurtz is not Zukofsky, but Zukofsky, too, had had immense plans back in 1924, "forty years gone" from 1964. Kurtz seems to function here as the figure of what a poet may become should fortune turn against him. Zukofsky did not end up as badly as Kurtz, but "A"-14 seems to open a door on an alternate universe that might have been—had Zukofsky suffered a few more setbacks.

"A"-14 keeps edging up to the pit of despair and skirting the gulf. We have to give Zukofsky credit for his courage when, for example, he peers into the future and, like Wells's Time Traveler, discovers the end of human wisdom:

> As I look at you today
> And the trouble is
> I am immortal facing
>
> Four thousand eight hundred solar cells
> Of four paddle wheels orbiting
> Only one hundred sixty thousand years

To come down, burn up in
The earth's atmosphere somewhere around
Several hundred thousand miles "altitude" —

And this whole mountain of continent under
Iced Antarctica.   (pp. 265–66)

Fire and ice dominate that inhuman future. All that lies between those polar extremes has disappeared. News from
the future turns out to be no news at all. Should we then
despair?

The problem may not be with the future, but with our
perspective. In "A"-13 Zukofsky had already criticized the
kind of thought promoted by newspapers, which turns out
to be no thought at all, but merely disconnected chunks of
data. His comment at the esplanade: "And what's in today's
ashcan / The large leaves of newspaper" (p. 275). This
variation of "what's in today's newspaper?" suggests that
the columns of the *Times* and its fellow journals are little more than repositories for junk that passes as news.
"Large leaves" hints at a wish that they would remain
trees; in that form they purified the air. "A"-14 continues
this denigration:

night of
the winter's

relieved only
by the
newspaper strike

not a
paper for
the last

17 weeks
to bring
its inanities

and horrors
home. . . .   (pp. 329–30)

We can hardly blame the publishers for the fact that the world swarms with nightmares, but a ceaseless regurgitation of them contributes to the numbing of the intelligence and an increase in public amnesia. People who insist on publicizing what lasts, and putting it in a just perspective, are generally ignored by the press. At times, though, they may rise to minor notoriety. Thus, in "A"-14:

> Ez 1962
> 1/29 in
> *The Times* crossword
>
> puzzle "Across/4
> Pound, poet" (p. 352)

"A" is not simply a refutation of the media's view of the world. The poem dissects all sorts of different approaches, and this investigation into the peculiar ways mankind sees his world is matched by a constant inquiry into how language construes the world.

As we learned early in "A", Zukofsky cannot be segregated from scrutiny; his honesty always brings him back to monitor personal fluctuations, just so we'll know who is behind "A"'s advance. We can, for example, adjust for jaundiced views by consulting the author's list of acutely felt subtractions:

> The joys of my Old World have gone
> From this new world—Ooçah—maybe the little Porto
>   Rican boy
> Still has them, waving the Flag with its
> Fiftieth star for Hawaii. (p. 279)

A hopeful speculation, this, that the joys are not dead, only transmitted to a new set of immigrants. And it is charitable of the poet to hope that the "little Porto Rican boy" might possess them. (Even here, Zukofsky seems to be tinkering with his personality, wondering what it would be like to be that boy. *"A"* contains only one cedilla, and "cedilla" means "little Z.")

But what about another recorded loss, a rather immense subtraction?

> 40 years
> gone—may
>
> ear race
> and eye
> them—I
>
> hate who
> sing them?
> while I
>
> have being?   (p. 316)

If those forty years are completely lost, the ear cannot hope to "race" them. The race would be over before it was begun. If so, the poet might as well close up shop. But another view of the situation seems possible. The living presence of the poet's ear, remaining after forty years are gone, suggests that he has won the race simply by enduring. He remains, while those years are erased ("ear race"). So the passage suspends in delicate balance two opposing conceptions of time—as thief, as illusion. A precarious equilibrium, but necessary; Zukofsky could not, in good conscience, opt for either view. He and those years come to a strange rendezvous in *"A"*. Both poet and years are "there" and "not there" in the poem, so long as it survives and is read. "Eye / them," he says, with "I / them" heard in the background, the years and the poet twining together in his art.

To maintain that double vision, that effort to remain true to the manifestations of time, was a labor of fifty years. The alternative to that wearing effort? "Past who / can recall / nothing is / / here—" (p. 328). Lethe—what a relief that would be. With the passage of time, the struggle to see the past as a living entity grows constantly more complex. The poet knows more as he grows older, that is one added burden. At an earlier time he saw things simply. Way back in 1922, he wrote a poem about time, and we find it included at the beginning of "A"-18. Celia, we learn, wanted to save this poem, "I Sent Thee Late," from oblivion. Save it, but not necessarily plug it into "A". She never told her husband how to write. Why then did Zukofsky make it part of "A"? And why insert it in "A"-18, that chronicle of public and personal disasters? The poem appears to be an early—perhaps his earliest—exercise in linking thought and image: the ocean and its waves become images for (respectively) past and future time. It was a young attempt, in short, to see time whole: as an object that, though susceptible to contradictory interpretation (how many objects are both "vast" and "tremulous"?), is perceived by the eye as a single expanse. The metaphor is simple—too simple. As the ensuing lines of "A"-18 remind us, this was a primitive stage in the development of Zukofsky's art, a time of "death not lived thru" (p. 391). The rude intrusions of death would make it increasingly difficult for the poet to render time so simply and seamlessly. One could track the progress of "A" as Zukofsky's constant pursuit of the nuances and details of elusive Chronos.

E. E. Cummings (died 1962) provides Zukofsky with a new mathematic for calculating time's subtractions:

> e.e.c. as young man saw
> *an old man 3/3 dead.* if one
> third seems wandered for 2 left alone figure
> 6/3? . . .   (p. 391)

The "one third" who has escaped the family orbit is Paul. Much has gone with him, and his father patiently totals the withdrawals. The home to which Louis and Paul returned in "A"-13 is now simply a matter of record. Louis takes note of a life's remnants in the possessions Paul has left behind:

> With the fireworks of The Fourth at the
> sill the black smudges of a child's white
> first shoes show, a tin pie plate he
> painted is Persian. . . .   (p. 404)

Paul himself sometimes seems as distant as those years. His unexpected returns provide an intermittent consolation:

> Midnight opening the door to the telephone ringing
> (the violinist's timing always right) could not believe
> the voice after two months' distance. 'P?' 'Yes
> me.' 'What is't?' 'Naturally I phone because I've
> something to ask.' What he *had*: our deep need.
>   (p. 405)

The perpetual complaint of parents that they only hear from their offspring when the latter need something is here reversed. It also serves as a proof of Louis's conviction that the uncanny intimacy of the family dialogue survives. Despite physical abysses the Zukofskyan ESP still works. But the anguish of living with the detritus of blessed years grows unbearable. They cannot remain in a home that continually reminds them that they are now only "6/3." "How unhappy," Zukofsky quietly sighs, "a place once blessed can grow" (p. 402). And so, after Louis's retirement from teaching, he and Celia move to Manhattan. As valedictory to those years in Brooklyn Heights, the last five pages of "A"-18 itemize the little agonies of their uprooting.

Loss after loss parades before our eyes in "A" 13–20. Why then are we convinced, after all is said and done, that the Zukofskys live in grace? What compensatory geometries sustain them?

In the center of "A"-13 sits section iii, displaying transformations that render it a locus of balance, with order percolating out of chaos. Are we annoyed by whining children or shouts in the street? Young Paul's perfect ear detects the rudiments of music in the clanging "Of daily garbage collectors / Storming after / 'Barrel E, Barrel A, Barrel D, Barrel G'" (p. 293). His father takes such lessons to heart.

> How mean of me ridden by words
> Always to think at first of being disturbed
> > by the dissonance
> When the years make their order.
> Order rains—Lucretius did not quite say that.
>
> > > (p. 277)

This aside (with its pun on rains/reigns) should alert us to be on the lookout for instances of unexpected orderliness in the poem. We have to be especially alert, since Zukofsky does not always bother to tag them as illuminating perceptions. What often appears as a merely ludicrous juxtaposition can suddenly snap into crystalline perfection.

> An arena divided equally by a curtain
> Into two amphitheatres,
> In the one they stage wrestling matches, in
> > the other hold concerts—
> Often together the same evening;
> In the one spectators in the smoke of the third balcony
> Are so dense they appear painted
> Like Michelangelo's hordes of the Judgment
> > in the Sistine Chapel;
> In the other perhaps the *saraband* of
> Bach's Second Partita for Violin Alone plays
> As the wrestlers thud.   (p. 297)

These odd conjunctions of life and art remind us that they cannot be separated, despite that discriminating curtain. So one theme from *"A"*-9's second half returns, altered but recognizable.

The contrapuntal symmetries of section iii reach their culmination in the dance at the close. The mutual sustenance represented by that dance takes another form as well: "Don't we become legend / Come back to read from one book" (p. 300). "Become" has both meanings: "turn into" and "ornament." "Legend" looks backs to its root, *lego*. Thus the members of the family read each other in the "one book." But what is that book? The verse does not specify, but Celia and Louis compose, at the very least, part of *"A"*. Are they therefore removed from the physical world into the world of art? Zukofsky regards those spheres as inseparable. Every time someone reads *"A"* they are drawn back into the substantial world, for a reader is never disembodied.

As we study—and breathe—the lines of *"A"*, more shapes emerge. One of these shapes seems to define most of *"A"* 13–20, and might be dubbed "parabolic." Despite his thorough detestation of missile/moon programs, Zukofsky may have thought it important for *"A"* (as it entered the Space Age) to borrow a common feature from artificial satellites, planets, and comets—their parabolic paths. It may also have been an ingenious way of knitting together his commitment to eternal principles and to the news of the day. One can't argue with the immutability of the parabola, and one can't fire one's short-lived missiles without it.

Much of *"A"* 13–20 is taken up with a series of parabolic excursions and returns. Louis's and Paul's day trip to the city overshadows *"A"*-13, and within the movement we find other, longer excursions: to Washington, D.C., where Paul's mastery of the violin creates a radius of sanity for Ezra Pound ("the mad kept way out there in a circle as he played" [p. 298]), to California, and back via Canada. (This

balancing of opposing compass points—north/south—
is another instance of section iii's equilibrial function.)
These tours are supplemented at the close of the movement; in section v, Louis contents himself with a visual
survey of the horizon as seen from a Brooklyn apartment.

Visual traveling is the preferred excursive mode in "A"
13–20. Excursion becomes identified with the grasping
eye—with apprehension. As the body succumbs to increasing immobility, the eye takes over.

> Dim eye looks
> where the lively
> mind once skipped   (p. 338)

Dim as the eye may be, years of discipline have taught it
when, where, and how to look. Zukofsky's athletic abilities are now concentrated in his eyes. This is one reason
we do not see Louis and Paul trudging through Manhattan. Instead, we are offered the scene at the esplanade,
which commences with a consideration of the intent gaze
of the poet. We look at Zukofsky looking. Even Paul remarks on his father's serious spectatorship.

> —What interests you
> In the boats out there
> Or the lights the same lights
> And boats passing evening after evening?
>   (p. 275)

This is not idle gazing; Zukofsky's eye seizes the world.
His head is no *camera obscura* into which random bursts of
data stream—that model has no validity for Zukofsky.

There is an art to seeing, though we have no name for it,
and all art requires as much patience as we can muster.

> For 17 years and for 27
> I have looked
> Towards things thru (it better be *aside*—both)

The promenade
Not to evade   (p. 275)

Not "at" but "towards," implying an endless journey toward essences. The parenthetical "aside" is necessitated by
a scrupulous concern for angles; if the eye's owner wants to
be completely honest with himself and his readers he has
to consider how, where, and under what conditions he uses
this instrument. Careful observers take elaborate precau-
tions with their narrative; Henry James spends the first
thirty pages of *The American Scene* defining the eye that he
employs to fashion the rest of the report.

The esplanade section of "A"-13 is dotted with the names
and works of a special class of visionaries: Gainsborough,
Picasso, Hopper, and Matisse. The latter is smuggled in
anonymously.

> —The afterglow in the two tallest Manhattan skyscrapers
> Has stopped glaring in my face
> They are cut of white cardboard
> On the blue   (p. 278)

This is a skyline seen with eyes attuned to the paper cut-
outs of Matisse's last years, when infirmities prevented
him from holding a brush. Louis attempts to instruct Paul
in the art of seeing, of taking in, but to no avail. Young
Paul is an "ear man." What we have here is not a generation
gap, but an organ gap. The differences born of this gap
produce a comedy of cross-purposes in the philosophical
exchange near the end of section ii.

> What your [Louis's] Ludwig probably means
> By a point in space is a place
> For an argument
> Is that no one agrees
> *This* is coal dust
> And *that* a piece of coal,
> I've the latter in my eye.

> You cannot think illogically,
> But the illogical is always logical:
> Tape recorder—tape reason—is that *my* voice,
> It is a philosophical-acoustical question
> If anyone ever hears his own voice.
>   —Now *I'm* sleepy.   (pp. 287–88)

The acquisitive eye has no interest in metaphysical ramblings, and neither does the acquisitive ear. Idle speculation by the "eye man" only lulls the young musician to sleep.

This "debate" about the ways and means of seeing and hearing foreshadows another problem for the poet. Once the eye returns home with its treasures—imprinted images—what then? Zukofsky escapes from distraction, but he pays a price: isolation. He now must decide what to do with his gathered material; like Milton, Conrad, Swift, and Montaigne (men with a common history of public careers followed by retirement to obscurity), he must create in that obscurity the artifacts by which he will be remembered. Though Zukofsky never *did* as much as those four, he clearly thinks of himself as their peer insofar as a retreat into privacy is concerned, and "A"-14, which features quotations from Milton, Conrad, Swift, and Montaigne, takes up the matter of the reclusive poet's relation to the larger world.

Can the poet strike a balance between the world (which simultaneously suggests and disturbs) and retirement (which is quiet, but lacking in suggestion)? This picture of the poet's plight is simplistic, but it carries enough truth. An event recalled in "A"-14 exemplifies the dilemma. Zukofsky ventures outside his home to what seems to be an art gallery. There he discovers, or thinks he discovers, "my / own initials" (p. 325) in a scroll by Ryokan.[4] All

---

4. Ryokan (1758–1831) was a Zen monk. His signature includes signs that might be taken for an *L* and a *Z*.

well and good—the poet has found himself in a work of art. But he, and we, are disconcerted to discover that "the / Ryokan scroll / is public / upside down" (p. 326). The phrasing could mean two things—both of which are inauspicious. Either the scroll has been mistakenly hung upside down in public, or it portrays the public as seen upside down. In either case, Zukofsky's discovery of himself suggests he is upside down in a public role: in inverse relation to the world. This seems confirmed by the play on "up" and "down" that scintillates through the page. His encounter with the scroll seems to confirm what he already knows, that he and the world are 180 degrees out of alignment. What's more, his vision does not seem to work well in public. He decides to go home, where he can see better. "Freak hard / to see / here I'll / / check when / I go / home" (p. 326). The art of seeing turns out to have troubling consequences, and though Zukofsky disdains epistemological jargon, it appears that he has chosen a course sure to carry him into epistemological difficulties.

The transformation of what one sees into words is always a dangerous leap. We might suppose that Zukofsky avoids most of this danger in "A" 13–20, simply because so much of this stretch of the poem is inventory. (The enumeration of heirlooms in "A"-13, section i; the examination of living and dead faces in section iv; the catalogue of Paul's works in "A"-20, and so on.) But Zukofsky is not content to stop there—he takes risks. Every inventory of "A" 13–20 is faceted with details that illuminate the poet's life. As he lists the contents of his world, he begins to ruminate, producing a rhetoric that is little more than simply talking to oneself. His self-involved conversation at least clears him of vanity: this kind of writing will never attain popularity. But what other virtues ensue?

Implicit in "A" from the beginning is the concept of writing as reminding. "A"-1: "Not boiling to put pen to paper / Perhaps a few things to remember — " (p. 4). And here we come to the real problem: Zukofsky's faith in his eye and his inventories leaves him vulnerable to the charge that his art is only writing as reminding, not writing as remembering. Memory and writing, as Plato observed in the *Phaedrus*, are not necessarily identical.

> But when it came to writing Theuth said, "Here, O king, is a branch of learning that will make the people of Egypt wiser and improve their memories; my discovery provides a recipe for memory and wisdom." But the king answered and said, "O man full of arts, to one it is given to create the things of art, and to another to judge what measure of harm and of profit they have for those that shall employ them. And so it is that you, by reason of your tender regard for the writing that is your offspring, have declared the very opposite of its true effect. If men learn this, it will cease to exercise memory because they rely on that which is written, calling things to remembrance no longer from within themselves, but by means of external marks. What you have discovered is a recipe not for memory, but for reminder. And it is no true wisdom that you offer your disciples, but only its semblance, for by telling them of many things without teaching them you will make them seem to know much, while for the most part they know nothing, and as men filled, not with wisdom, but with the conceit of wisdom, they will be a burden to their fellows.[5]

Zukofsky knows there is a distinction between telling and teaching, and Thoth makes two brief appearances in *"A"*-13 (pp. 267, 308) to assure us that Zukofsky's approach to writing is the reverse of naive.

Just as the Platonic dialogues are ways of circumventing the king's objections, Zukofsky's cryptographic style, "talking to himself," is an analogous method for making

---

5. *Plato: The Collected Dialogues*, ed. Edith Hamilton and Huntington Cairns (Princeton, N.J.: Princeton University Press, Bollingen Series LXXI, 1961), p. 520.

sure that writing produces wisdom rather than stifling it. By working to recover Zukofsky's ingredients and methods, we are compelled to augment and utilize what wisdom we have. So the poem is closed to any casual reader.

If the design works correctly, "A" should steadily disclose itself to the reader who meets its tough criteria. There are revelations on every page of the poem, and, in a broad hint to the reader, Zukofsky introduces the theme of revelation into "A" 13–20. These revelations are not the rewards of the poem, but examples of the kind of insight the reader may, if he chooses, emulate. A great deal of patience may be required. Some of the connections Zukofsky brings to our attention took him forty years to see. There are no "immediate" revelations, he implies. But the prepared eye will be ready when the time is right. In "A"-19 a momentary spark—a shock of recognition—leaps across the gap between Old World and New, between Ancient and Modern.

> (West of
> Vatican Belvedere
> Apollo "By
> God a Mohawk")   (p. 430)

Benjamin West, that is, the expatriate whose painter's eye detects the noble lineaments of the savage form divine.

Revelations of all kinds of secrets occur in "A" 13–20, and there are as many different kinds of seekers as there are secrets. The poem acknowledges this in "A"-13 by contrasting the kind of hermetic wisdom pursued by devotees of Hermes Trismegistus (Thoth) and international intrigue. Nikita Khrushchev jokes during his 1959 American tour:

> "By pooling intelligence nets (laughing)
> So we don't have to pay twice
> For spying the same information. . . ."   (p. 284)

Family secrets, personal secrets, these too come to the surface in "A" 13–20. We are told, among other things, where Zukofsky first saw the light of day ("seminarian briefed chrystie street where I was born" [p. 399]), and, as we have already seen, personal ailments are diagnosed in print.

One test of poetry, and of a poet, is whether all his ruminations and revelations can be made to fluoresce into a language sufficiently faithful. Perhaps the most explicit example of this contest appears at the beginning of "A"-18. Here Zukofsky is trying to tell Celia that he loves her, and seems to be fumbling the ball. We can easily identify with his problem. Finding an appropriate phrase to speak our love is a responsibility everyone feels at one time or another. The best ways of saying it, however, seem to have been said before, so if we borrow something Shakespearian we may feel we've got the goods. But they aren't *our* goods, are they? We want to give our love the best—the best from our own heart (which presumably speaks a unique language). So we generally fall back on a compromise, employing something common that is sanctioned by tradition as an appropriate message. This is one reason children and lovers on St. Valentine's Day exchange heart-shaped candies bearing brief messages such as "my valentine" and "thinking of you." These are the phrases we find embedded on the first page of "A"-18. The whole movement can be considered a lengthy elaboration of those hackneyed expressions, just as "A"-13 can be seen as a backdrop that renders sufficiently significant its last two words: "love you." Zukofsky goes to extremes to invest cliché with its original power, to put spirits back into a moribund language.

"A"-19 begins with a threat of extinction. Not our extinction, but the poem's. An unspecified someone has demanded of Zukofsky "another encore." As so often happens in *"A"* 13–20, however, he presents himself as a has-been. Not only is he tuckered out, but he is also constrained by still another figure to quit the field. "I / / hear back / stage the / stagehand's *late*" he remarks, with an obvious echo of Andrew Marvell's "but at my back I always hear / Time's winged chariot hurrying near." So he suffers under two conflicting obligations: to continue his song, but to hurry its completion. This double pressure repeats the pattern, so common to *"A"* 13–20, of fracture bordering on disintegration.

"A"-19 does not, however, point to the end of writing. Rather, it introduces new possibilities for *"A"*. Though the movement begins as a farewell performance, it soon becomes a rehearsal for subsequent performances. The rehearsal begins with four pages of deliberate obscurity. Its leaps and fleeting references apparently represent the artist showing what he can do with his material, demonstrating his virtuosity. Reading these lines becomes a matter of simply picking out words and phrases that can be related to other portions of the Zukofsky canon. By themselves they seem mere gibberish, but when we observe "bonding" followed at a distance of thirty lines by "anti-matter," we may deduce that Zukofsky's interest in physics is keeping up with new developments. Making sense of that interest in relation to *"A"*-19 leads us to further imaginative leaps.

Physics describes the mechanics of the universe, and therefore aids astronomy when scientists puzzle over the origin of the cosmos. At the beginning of *"A"*-19, Zukofsky appears to be trying to investigate cosmogenesis all by himself. His interest in the subject here is only preliminary; it will come to fruition in *"A"*-22. (Another instance of the author's contrariness: he shows more interest in ultimate origins the closer his poem gets to completion.) "Tohu bohu" (p. 409) is the primeval chaos from which God extracted form. "Benign day's / first kiss" (p. 409) celebrates the new beginning of every day. Interspersed with chaotic grammar and syntax in those four pages are brief references to music. Pythagorean material appears in the middle of the movement, indicating that Zukofsky's concern in "A"-19 is with music as the prime paradigm for the production of form out of mere anarchy.

As he plunges into musical problems, he questions a musician:

> Asked him
> 4-year old
> 'why the
> violin?' responded
> "Individually I
> love it"
> Finally—"you
> don't understand
> you're like
> a sleeping frog."   (p. 412)

Paul's rebuke shows that the direct approach misses the point. Those subtle, eternal principles forming all things will not appear unless coaxed into being by art. And it is not the poet's fault if we can't keep up with him as his art ascends into unchartered territory.

From "A"-19 onwards, the poem looks increasingly like an experiment in English as a foreign language. We should recall that no poet worthy of the name knows enough about the language we call English, a language so thoroughly an amalgam of other tongues. Mallarmé, one of the guiding lights of "A"-19, taught English for a living— as did Zukofsky. So when Zukofsky begins to exploit resources of English that were hitherto unsuspected, it is no wonder that we begin to feel like novices in a Berlitz course.

The longest quotation lacking a literary halo in "A" appears in "A"-19. It is an Italian prospectus for the Paganini

Prize competition, and it is written in less than perfect English. (And what is perfect English?) Its strange lurches of idiom and vocabulary remind us, as "A"-18 did, that dictionaries are poor guides to a language. "Overcome" in "have not / overcome the / age of / 35. . . ." (p. 412) probably seemed a logical synonym for "attained." As a non-literary, almost non-literate, tussle with English, the prospectus stands at the other extreme from Milton, Gibbon, and other giants found in neighboring movements—not to mention Mallarmé. If we look ahead to "A"-22 and "A"-23, however, the prospectus appears to be a benchmark. It represents the kind of English that Zukofsky might have composed when first encountering the language at P. S. 7. At the time he wrote "A"-19, he was presumably too far advanced to be able to duplicate his aboriginal attempts at English, but he discovers something similar in the prospectus.

The tacit measurement along a linguistic line—from those harsh and crude attempts to the innovations of the last movements of "A"—are paralleled by an Old/New World trail of immigration. The Paganini Competition, we learn, is held on Columbus Day. Thanks to Columbus, millions of school children have ended up chanting the Pledge of Allegiance on a new continent. By happy accident we (and Zukofsky) discover stuck in the middle of the prospectus the words "indivisible" and "liberty," words also found in the Pledge. So "A"-19 quietly coordinates the course of European and American history with successively more sophisticated assortments of English. As Zukofsky directs our attention to felicities in what seem at first mere botches of language, losses become riches. Job had his reward in the end, too.

FIVE

Rich and Strange: "*A*" 21–24

These lines, therefore, will probably blend the weft
of first purposes and speculations, with the warp of
that experience afterwards, always bringing strange
developments.

Walt Whitman,
"A Backward Glance O'er Travel'd Roads"

To FINISH "*A*" would be no easy matter. Readers familiar with "*A*" 1–21 (what few of them there were) must
have wondered how he would go about topping himself.
Zukofsky sidestepped this challenge, for Celia solved the
problem well in advance. How this came to pass requires
some explaining.

Intimate as the family Zukofsky was, they did not insist
on extracting the last full measure of privacy from one another. There existed clearly defined spaces—physical and
mental—into which each member could retreat. It was
Louis's privilege, for example, to shut the door of his study
when reading and writing. From one such family cocoon
there emerged Celia's *L. Z. Masque*, a digest of her husband's work set to Handel's music. It was composed without his knowledge, and she was able to present this gift
as a complete surprise. He then decided upon a counter-
surprise. The masque was pressed into service as the final
movement of "*A*". This maneuver raises manifold aesthetic complications, but one in particular applies to the
problem of ending "*A*". Since Celia never intended her

masque for *"A"*-24, it could be said that she composed the final movement without knowing it. And though her husband was responsible for the content of *"A"*-24 (those are his words, after all), he was not responsible for the arrangement. Since no one was completely in charge of *"A"*-24, the onus of ending the poem was lifted from the poet's shoulders. In a sense, *"A"*-24 wrote itself. Celia's response to his work undoubtedly meant a great deal; his life's work was validated by the person he most loved. It was validated, moreover, as music. The masque also showed his canon to be—as he thought it was—apprehensible as a unit. His work and the masque are an integrity: the masque's five voices are separate, but (as Celia's prefatory note affirms) their effect is one. It also pleased Zukofsky that the masque was a paring down to essentials: the art of Louis and Celia Zukofsky presented in only seventy minutes. Essentials, though, as he was constantly reminding us, are not necessarily simple. And *"A"*-24 is the reverse of simple.

Act I, scene I of *"A"*-24, the "Lesson," is, as its title suggests, a reading aloud. It is also a lesson in how to listen clearly to what seem to be chaotic words and phrases. We must practice, as it advises, that art of "blending views a little way apart into a solid": an art practiced by Celia throughout the masque, and practiced by Zukofsky throughout his career. We, their readers and auditors, have little choice but to master the divergences, coordinations, and unexpected conjunctions arrayed in the masque. The first promise made to us is that "Blest / Infinite things . . . Which confuse imagination / Thru its weakness" are actually heavenly harmonies. We saw that possible payoff before, near the close of *"A"*-12 (p. 231). So far as the Zukofskys are concerned, it doesn't really matter that Spinoza said it first, since the poem assumes that Baruch, Louis, and Celia work on the same wavelength. If we want to understand the masque, we must at least make the effort to tune in on that band. The difficulties that ensue are re-flected in the poem's selection from *Arise, Arise*. Here we find the son bereft of his mother, trying to ferret out infor-mation about her—and, by extension, about himself. The search may be fruitless ("How do you catch such a bird," he cries), but it's no use telling him. Of course, the poet's and the composer's mission is equally taxing. How does one catch Louis Zukofsky over the course of seventy years—or seventy minutes?

Time is the great adversary. How can it be circum-vented? One strategy the Zukofskys use consists of multi-ple shafts of attention presented simultaneously: a syn-chronous approach. One had better be sure, however, that the subject under examination is well integrated to begin with, that it can withstand such dissection. So the poem's extract from *Prepositions* speaks of information "developed among the sounds of natural things" that escapes "the con-fines of time and place."

Learning to follow the dance of Thought, Drama, Story, and Poem—which, with Handel's music, comprise the five voices of the masque—requires more than practice and patience. We also need some familiarity with the whole of Zukofsky's work. If we are unaware that he com-monly approaches deeply felt emotional zones by indirec-tion, we are going to miss part of scene 2's delicacy. In the extract taken from *"A"*, William Carlos Williams visits Louis's classroom at Brooklyn Polytechnic "shortly after / his mother died." For "his" it would not be inappropriate to momentarily substitute "Zukofsky's." Zukofsky's tech-nique is not simply a way of considering matters too pain-ful for direct treatment. It also permits him to put his emo-tions in context. Williams's deportment helps Zukofsky to understand his own. His excursive imagination would not be content with merely its own viewpoint.

The poem's quotation from "Ferdinand" leads us in

the same roundabout direction. Urgency and tension are evoked by a sedulous concentration on trivial images (irises, a mirror). Painful thoughts are being curtained off by that concentration. Displacement again, and not only visual displacement. Since "Ferdinand" is a tale of the upper classes, Zukofsky's own wretchedly impoverished background inevitably comes to mind. In this story he is invading the territory of James and Fitzgerald, who at least had some acquaintance with the so different rich. But he is not merely being an interloper, he is imagining in the most fruitful sense, collecting pieces of different lives to put on the map with his own. Little wonder that he puts himself into the story, thinly veiled as one of the minor characters. And no wonder "imagined" and "imagination" are the key words in scenes 1 and 2.

This assembly of clusters of images, suggesting as it does an adventurous, liberal, cosmopolitan approach by the poet, speaks well for his courage. But then comes the problem of connection. How are the connecting lines cast out to other lives to be knit together? Zukofsky's lasting ambition to bridge abysses comes through strongly in scene 3, a suite whose theme is the striving for unification. "A"-11, the most moving example of the poet laboring for contact with Celia and Paul, is quoted in its entirety. The river that figures in "A"-11 also meanders through "Ferdinand." As he walks near its shores, Ferdinand moves from the anxieties associated with solitude to a reunion with his aunt and uncle after a long separation. Setting the tone for the entire scene is a selection from *Arise, Arise* that emphasizes the gulf between the dead and the living. Each of these three strands—Poem, Story, Drama—moves from rupture to reconciliation. Each, however, encounters a momentary crisis before reaching that serenity. At precisely that moment, a brief passage from *Prepositions* enters, speaking of the necessity of beginning with "a portrait of what is closest to oneself" for the sake of "honesty." Last to enter the scene, it is the first to leave, but its self-assured and accurate advice seems the necessary catalyst for the resolution of the crisis in the other texts.

"Know thyself," in other words, before presuming to know others. Then, perhaps, one can discover what one truly values, and begin to move toward what is valuable in the outer world. The status of "self," as we might have feared, raises a host of problems. We all esteem that slippery character, yet all agree it is sinful to be "selfish." So we pass into the realm of moral entanglements. Scene 4 shows us the self emerging from self-involvement, taking faltering steps toward contact. Passages from "A" return us to the earliest movements, where young "Zukofsky" first ventured out of his shell. This excursion takes the form of early love affairs in the extracts comprising the voices of Story and Drama. These are adolescent adventures, immature and troubled. The "benign" girl drawing the shy boy out of himself seems a deliberate echo of the bird-girl who enchanted Stephen Dedalus. But that impulse only bent back on itself, like a hoop, and was hardly a good model for young lovers. The situation in *Arise, Arise* seems almost as bad: the girl does not seem to be communicating with her lover. She tactlessly probes for information about his dead mother, apparently oblivious to a reserve that is not the withholding of love, but the conservation of the soul that loves. So these early adventures of the self only raise questions about self-identity again. Excerpts from Zukofsky's review of *Him* complete the structure of the scene; the penetrating intellect of the artist seems to find relationships extremely shaky; the integrity of personality withers under questioning. How insubstantial we must be if we cannot stand a few pointed questions. Or is it merely that the wrong sorts of questions are being put?

Since man is the interrogating animal, our quest for answers continues without remission. The dividend? We end up with analytic skills nicely sharpened. With luck these skills can be put to other uses, such as making poetry or music. Scene 5's music consists of sixty-two variations on a single theme—a remarkable instance of artistry renewing itself within a strictly confined space.

A theme exists as the sum of its variants. Some themes the Western mind is fond of are still in the process of construction and may never come to an end. The theme of the "self" on the other hand can be worked out in an individual's lifetime. One way poets have of working it out depends on the creation of characters whose traits and adventures seem a more or less distorted version of the author's. So we find Zukofsky, through Ferdinand, magnifying bits of his own life. Did Zukofsky suffer from an identity problem? Ferdinand, the European/American without roots, has it worse. Was Zukofsky the son of immigrants? Ferdinand *is* an immigrant. Zukofsky's mother died slowly from tuberculosis; Ferdinand's mother is blown to pieces before his eyes. Zukofsky, somewhat dilatory in making it to the altar, makes Ferdinand a loner who will probably remain that way. The exaggeration can be read backwards, too. The aristocratic inclination of Ferdinand tips us off to a similar bent in Zukofsky. Raised among the poorest of the poor, and completely sympathetic to their plight, Zukofsky had an ineradicably elitist streak. In scene 5, the attendants from *Arise, Arise* appear, speaking on behalf of the oppressed, but their comments are balanced by selections from Yeats. The material from *Prepositions* included here—the essay on Charlie Chaplin—also exhibits this two-way split. The grace of Chaplin's art, demonstrating allegiance to the aspirations of the poor, does not come from an impoverished man. Chaplin's deportment shows he has mastered completely the better traits of the aristocracy: sensitivity, education, refinement, and discipline. Zukofsky would not count poverty against anyone, but would not excuse anyone for using it as a reason for acting and thinking poorly.

Act 1 bears a resemblance to the first half of "A", especially in its creation of "Zukofsky" by the building up of a composite portrait. We presume that portrait is a fair approximation of him, seen this time from the perspective of another mind. Act 2 follows the general course of "A" 13–20: three scenes of private disasters followed by a fourth, more hopeful, scene.

In scene 1, Drama, Story, and Poem take stock of dispossessions and losses. A daughter leaves home, an elderly couple (the Zukofskys) are once more on the move, crazy fragments of the past are thrown at Ferdinand, and a mother speaks to her son from that shadowy region that the dead inhabit in dreams. The touch of grace in this scene is provided by Zukofsky's essay on Blake, whose words specify the wealth remaining within oneself after all deductions are accounted for.

As we advance toward the bright horizon promised by Blake, however, our bodies grow increasingly decrepit. Scene 2 is forebodingly entitled "Doctor." It gradually becomes clear that Zukofsky thinks most M.D.'s are frauds. And his animus is not limited to medical doctors. We find him railing against "abstract" thinkers. Providing a backdrop for this attack are incidents from "Ferdinand": a gramophone that plays backward, Ferdinand forced to the curb on the wrong side of the street (in a car with its steering wheel on the wrong side), and time out of joint— "twenty years as one day." Some doctors, though, are genuine healers. In the selection from *Prepositions*, Zukofsky twice cites Spinoza as the doctor who cures erratic thought. Sextus Empiricus also has good advice to offer: "the art of letters" as sovereign remedy against forgetfulness.

However much we subdue our internal storms, public

issues have a way of filtering down to individuals and making life difficult. Quotations from "A"-6 appear in scene 5, mournfully relating the difficulty of maintaining dignity in this hard world. Families in *Arise, Arise* argue about class warfare and other unhappy topics of our century. Finally, the shy and unworldly author Lewis Carroll is revealed as an observer of Czarist tyranny. No one, it seems, can be blind to arrant injustice, painful as it may be.

The masque concludes with a calm synopsis of art's renovating power. "A"-6, "A"-7, and "A"-20 appear in turn, with "A"-6 suggesting possible formulas for revitalization in art, "A"-7 performing its resurrection dance, and "A"-20 demonstrating art continuing in the next generation. Also threading through that last scene is a quiet reminiscence of Celia and Louis's early romance. Selections from "It Was" recall their first married years in the Bronx. Intertwined with the connubial bond is the tie between mother and son. Passages from *Arise, Arise* continue the monologue of the son addressing his mother in a language that she could not understand, but that was the best gift he had to offer. Pieces of his essay on Henry Adams, written when his mother was still alive, return us to his origins. We are reminded that there were two women in Zukofsky's life: by her selection for the masque's conclusion, the second pays tribute to the memory of the first.

It could be that the "A"-24 we hold in our hands, for all its richness of suggestion, has only a shadowy existence. What we see on the page are directions for musicians and vocalists. Perhaps it only comes to life when performed. It would make sense to include a recording of "A"-24 with all future editions of the poem. Such a bonus lies implicit in the earliest movements, where competing voices seem to beg for spoken transcription (as in *291*'s "Simultanism"). Zukofsky himself took the trouble to make performing versions of selected portions of "A"—some of which were duly performed.

The poem began with memories of the Carnegie Hall *St. Matthew's Passion*, and its musical ambitions, straining to escape the bound volume, aim for release in actual performance. Had Zukofsky possessed Celia's musical talent and training, he might well have produced an "A"-24 similar to her masque. Within the poet there lurked a frustrated dramatist, anxious to hear his words uttered and in motion. "A"-12's listing of aborted projects includes "notes for different plays / I'd have done in my twenties / At the slightest encouragement" (p. 252). Celia's masque at least satisfied the poem's tacit striving toward public performance. The immediate spark that moved her to composition, however, may have been "A"-21. This movement has all the trappings of a play, but it is clearly not intended for the stage. It is, rather, one of those dramas—such as *Prometheus Unbound* and *Pippa Passes*—meant to be read. But "A"-21, thanks to its contorted style, is terribly obscure. The question often raised in "A"—how to read it—comes back to plague us.

We can begin by noting that "A"-21, though based on Plautus's comedy *Rudens*, is not a translation. To call it a translation expands that term beyond recognizable bounds. We can more easily approach the problem from the other direction, by thinking of Plautus's drama as a template. Zukofsky works from that mode, manufacturing variations, arabesques, jokes, and strained readings not present in the Latin—but extractable from it. Zukofsky relied on a particular edition (the Loeb) but "relied" in a strange fashion.[1] He treated the text as a frozen language on which he could play variations. This results in some "translations"

---

1. *Plautus: Poenulus, Pseudolus, and Rudens*, trans. Paul Nixon (Cambridge, Mass.: Harvard University Press, 1965).

that professional translators would (and do) regard with disdain. Thus, *edepol* is variously rendered as "edible" (p. 454), "polled" (p. 457), "eddy-polled" (p. 458), "a pole" (p. 463), "a pool" (p. 469), and "O deep pool" (p. 470). Even while treating the Latin with apparent abandon, Zukofsky sticks so close to the Loeb edition that the number of lines in his *Rudens* and Plautus's *Rudens* are equal. It seems that Zukofsky has deliberately flouted the cardinal rule of good translation; he has tortured the spirit of the original on the rack of the letter. No reasonable definition of translation has room for such manipulations as the cobbling of "sed ad prandiam uxor me vocat. redeo domum. / iam meas opplebit aures vaniloquentia" to produce "My wife's crowing prandial. *Ready!* / Prattle, my ears, vain eloquence" (p. 475).

What is Zukofsky up to in *"A"*-21? Why make a version of *Rudens* and limit the line length to five words? Since he has restricted himself to the same number of lines as the Loeb edition, and the Latin has no such cramping in its line length, *"A"*-21 has to pack its meaning into fewer words. As a result, we often have trouble following the action. Again and again we are forced to consult the Loeb text to discover what is "going on." This may have been one of Zukofsky's intentions. Anyone willing to take the necessary trouble with *"A"*-21 must detour to Plautus. Nor do we stop there. Other dramas about the recovery of things lost—*Pericles* and *The Tempest*—echo in the movement. *"A"*-21 has to be considered as the latest mutation in a series that stretches back to 300 B.C. (the presumed date of a lost play by Diphilus, on which Plautus's *Rudens* is based). Zukofsky's version can be said to sum up that continuum, just as *Ulysses* sums up the Ulysses theme. Of course it is not the final or "definitive" version, for each separate appearance of the myth is part of a construction that will never be completed. There is no lost "original" tale recoverable, only elements commonly shared and slightly altered in each telling.

Between the second and third scenes of "*A*"-21's act 1 appears the first authorial interruption:

> *nine*
> *men's*
> *morris*
>
> this
> is
> my
> form
>
> a
> voice
> blown   (p. 445)

—three distinct phrases, the third returning from "*A*"-8 (p. 104), the second from "*A*"-2 (p. 8), and the first somewhat more ancient:

> The nine men's morris is filled up with mud;
> And the quaint mazes in the wanton green
> For lack of tread are undistinguishable.[2]

Nine men's morris, a game for two that is older than human memory, could be an analog for the myth that powers *Rudens* and "*A*"-21. Both are millennia old, and both have survived variation—perhaps because of variation. The game's rules are also applicable to "*A*"-21. Pieces are moved, one at a time, on a small grid. This conforms to the reduction in "*A*"'s line length and the consequently corseted style. The game ends when one of the players no longer has enough counters to arrange three in a row, a termination fit for the lessening number of movements that remain to "*A*". (Only three are left after "*A*"-21.) If

---

2. *A Midsummer Night's Dream* 2.1. 98–100.

"blown" suggests "past its prime," we are once again faced with terminations.

But, at the end of *"A"*-21, there is a sudden flashback to earliest stages.

> Saturday
> matinee and night and Sunday
> matinee and night child in
> the morris harp   (p. 507)

"A"-8 told us that Louis's older brother regularly took him to the Thalia, back in the days of Roosevelt and Taft. There they could witness such offerings as a Yiddish *Lear*, and one day Louis would read Shakespeare's *Lear* and other versions, such as *A King Lear of the Steppes*. He learned at an early age that no author has a monopoly on myth, and in *"A"*-21 he taps the enduring, expansive power of an immortal story. Voices dead for thousands, perhaps tens of thousands of years, come back to fill a twentieth-century dream.

Our dreams habitually surprise us with strange conflations. The word "morris" and the name "Morris" (that older brother, co-dedicatee of *"A"*-21) merge in this dramatic game. Zukofsky valued dreams, and if this seems at odds with other elements of his character, we must remember that Einstein slept twelve hours each night, and that the shape of the benzene molecule was discovered in a dream. The myth that *"A"*-21 adopts treats dreams as truthful oracles. In *Rudens* a dream shows Daemones a cryptic vision of his daughter's plight. The importance of sleep and dreams in *The Tempest* needs no elaboration, and *Pericles*, too, invests dreams with deep significance. In his only play, *Arise, Arise*, Zukofsky specifies that much of the action takes place behind a "dream curtain." The final words of *"A"*-21 suggest that his *Rudens*, like *Finnegans Wake*, has all been a dream; we hear someone asking his (or her) spouse to make more room in the bed. Late in "A"-21 these lines explicitly broach the subject.

> *for no man is so*
> *watchful he never falls asleep.*
> Dreams guard sleep, eyelids motion
> sometimes *reason's monsters*, or
> a dream unexplained *like an*
> *unopened letter.*   (p. 473)

The sleeping mind, writing poems and stories, lards them with golden words. On waking, we usually find them to be sadly lacking in sense. So the tortuous diction of "A"- 21's *Rudens* seems to be a dream of Plautus's Latin. If we know the source, we can interpret the dream. Without it, reading "A"-21 is like listening in on a stranger who talks in his sleep. All seems confused, and principles of organization elude our grasp.

"A"-22 and "A"-23 present problems that hope may well break before. Their density and intricacy baffle us at every turn, and the search for meaning becomes largely a matter of guesswork. This, of course, is not new in "A". What makes these movements especially vexing has nothing to do with cracking codes. The new difficulty, in fact, teases us away from intellectual problems.

Zukofsky has fashioned a rhythm that flows beautifully from one gemlike phrase to the next, an insidious music that puts the intellect to sleep. No matter how hard we try to stick to "thinking" about these puzzling passages, the music eventually carries us away. With other poets, such as Poe, this causes no distress. "Ulalume," for example, does not offer the impression of a multitude of significant details passed a bit too quickly before our eyes. The closest approximation to "A" 22–23 in English verse appears to be the poetry of Gerard Manley Hopkins. His combination of bewildering variety and melody would, given sufficient scope, operate much like Zukofsky's verse. Imagine "sheer plod makes plough down sillion" followed by a thousand similar lines; we could have had something like *"A"*-22 a century before its time.

One way of approaching these movements is to follow the music, reading straight through for the dip and sway of the accents, the chiming of vocal clusters, the echoes that leap from one page to the next. This may, in fact, be the most enjoyable way of dealing with it. Nevertheless, *"A"*-22 and *"A"*-23 are made up of words, and, unlike the "Iyyob" section of *"A"*-15, these words work together to generate meaning. Despite the allure of the music, it is possible to sift content from the jumble. Prospectors should be warned, however, that intellectual fatigue soon sets in. Then the mind slips into the soothing care of that anesthetic cadence. Zukofsky may well have planned this brain-frustrating strategy to insure that a single reading of the movements could only be carried on at the musical level. Those merely intellectual faculties would have to be content with a piecemeal apprehension. Zukofsky was always careful to differentiate among his audiences, letting some groups (such as his family) into more of *"A"*'s secrets than other groups. It would not be surprising if he extended this discrimination to a single reader—allowing some parts of the reader's psyche more privileges than others.

His awareness that poetry is absorbed through various portals led him to make an announcement at the beginning of *"A"*-22.

AN	ERA	
ANY	TIME	
OF	YEAR	(p. 508)

On the left-hand column: three little words that humbly cement sentences. On the right: three nouns drawn from man's eternal obsession with time. But the heading is not a sentence, and those imposing nouns have nothing to bully. When those lines are read aloud, however, two "ears" appear, a covert direction indicating that we should speak as well as see the lines that follow.

Others letters a sum owed
ages account years each year
out of old fields, permute
blow blue up against yellow
—scapes welcome young birds—initial

transmutes itself, swim near and
read a weed's reward—grain
an omen a good omen
the chill mists greet woods
ice, flowers—their soul's return

let me live here ever,
sweet now, silence foison to
on top of the weather
it has said it before
why that was you that

is how you weather division
a peacocks grammar perching—and
perhaps think that they see
or they fly thru a
window not knowing it there

the window could they sing
it broken need not bleed
one proof of its strength
a need birds cannot feign
persisting for flight as when

they began to exist—error
if error vertigo their sun
eyes delirium—both initial together
rove into the blue initial
surely it carves a breath   (pp. 508–9)

If we take the hint, the first line's single open vowel—
o—stands out audibly. And it has a visual counterpart in
the first letter of the line, a capital O. These two *o*'s, balanced in the line, attract eye and ear. Zukofsky remembered that a single reader is made up of a bundle of competing faculties.

The dalliance between the two organs continues in the
first page of "A"-22. The long *o* repeats quickly in "old,"
"blow," "yellow," the double use of "omen," and "soul's."
With the importance of the sound established, the verse
begins to play with images based on the letter's contours.
O can be thought of as egg-shaped, and thus the status of *o*
as the initial letter of the movement supplies meaning
to the mysterious phrase "initial // transmutes itself"
(p. 508). Eggs turn into birds, given the opportunity, and
in line 17 a bird does appear: the peacock, whose tail unfolds a hundred eyes. Eggs, now eyes; the more we search,
the more round objects we find cluttering the beginning of
"A"-22. "Rove" (line 29) sounds the long *o* again, but it
also has as one of its meanings the passing of a thread or
rope through an eyelet or hole. A reasonably fanciful de-
coding of the passage allows us to watch chicks roving into
"the blue initial," i.e., passing from the egg to the great
round bowl of the sky. We wish them well, but ominous
undercurrents appear. O as a numeral signifies emptiness.
A few lines after the young birds fly away, the phrase "an
assemblage of nought" (p. 509) appears. A little later, the
movement mentions "an affair with the moon," and we recall that in "A"'s cosmology the moon is a sterile rotundity.
Opposed to eggs, suns, cells, and sky, we find moons and
noughts. It appears that the careful balancing of vitality
and void has never left "A". It constantly returns in different forms.

By now it should be evident that "A"-22 is obsessed
with metamorphosis. This ancient and honorable poetic

preoccupation includes among its forms the sub-topics of genesis and death. So *o* serves Zukofsky as a convenient shape through which both of these can be threaded. This is only the beginning. Not content with alterations latent in a single shape, or changes observable in the natural world, Zukofsky considers more abstract changes. For example, the way man's best friend moves from the front porch to speech and print.

> dog's letter growled dog-ear marked.
> Dog his luck. . . .   (p. 514)

Translation considered liberally is a type of metamorphosis. Without it, "A" would have been impossible. Thanks to such monuments of scholarship as the Loeb series, Zukofsky has in his library the thoughts of the Greeks on the subject of change.

> Pith or gore has 4
> seasons, 20 yet boy, 40
> young, 60 ripe, 80 aged   (p. 517)

In a remote age, in a world unknown to Pythagoras, his thought returns. The previous step before Zukofsky's version can be found in the Loeb edition of Diogenes Laertius. "He divides man's life into four quarters thus: 'Twenty years a boy, twenty years a youth, twenty years a young man, twenty years an old man.'"[3] If Pythagoras sees four ages in a man's life, others find seven. Shakespeare, whose presence charges all of Zukofsky's late work, had a good deal to say about metamorphosis. The play that immediately comes to mind, *A Midsummer Night's Dream*, contributes slightly to the movement, but another drama of transformation gets top billing: *The Tempest*.

---

3. *Diogenes Laertius: Lives of Eminent Philosophers*, trans. R. D. Hicks (Cambridge, Mass.: Harvard University Press, 1970), II, 329.

The beginning of "A"-22, concerned with the birth of things, operates near the ocean. Zukofsky is following one of man's oldest insights: that the meeting of sea and shore is the theater of birth. On Prospero's island, all kinds of new felicities are distilled from an old injustice. The best of these felicities is the union of Ferdinand and Miranda. The words of lines 9 and 10 of "A"-22, "let me live here ever, / sweet now, silence foison to," are lifted *passim* from the betrothal scene in act 4, scene 1, where the two lovers are joined under Prospero's blessing. (More bits from *The Tempest* conclude "A"-22.) There are personal reasons, too, for emphasizing the seashore in "A"-22. Zukofsky spent his last years in Port Jefferson, a small town on Long Island Sound. Though the ocean was not visible from his house, it was not far away. So seascape mingles with landscape at the start of "A"-22. "Out of old fields, permute / blow blue up against yellow." These lines describe waves crashing on a shore and blossoms tossing in the wind equally well. The ocean and a Long Island garden are both "old fields" were life can begin. If we prefer to stroll on the beach in those lines, we might observe that immediately west of Port Jefferson is the hamlet of Old Field, where one can stand on Old Field Point jutting into the sound. Those who like solid ground can remind themselves that since Dylan Thomas once saw a flower as a slow explosion ("green fuse") it is no novelty to consider "blow blue up" as an iris zooming sunward.

Far above land and sea, metamorphosis even permits Zukofsky to come to terms with the space race:

> spine follows path once born,
>
> to arrogate it small eloquence,
> an affair with the moon
> it looked as if it
> looked up someway above earth
> a hectic of an instant

                    until computed in the metal—
                    tidal waves also timing it   (pp. 509–10)

Man's spine, after millions of years, turns into a Saturn V,
and we view a launching. The rocket slowly rises from its
pad and hesitantly noses to the right trajectory. Nature, we
might say, is forever bringing its various segments together, and man's hankering for the stars may be a form of
nature's weaving. The moon has its part in the cosmic syn-
thesis, since its "tidal waves" call to the spine and the
spaceship. No longer seen as a dead world, the moon of
"A"-22 reminds us that nothing is completely lifeless. Before the astronauts landed with their shiny debris, a man
carrying a bundle of thorns was in residence.

    The advance from spine to rocket can be run in reverse,
if we wish. After this moon voyage, the movement begins
to turn back the clock of Western progress. ("A"-8 did so
on a lesser scale.)

                         unearthing
                always only their past futures

                hearing iron horse scrape me

                . . . .
                    painting a standpipe
                seeing it swan or stork—

                fish purl in the weir:
                we are caught by our
                own knowing . . .

                . . . .

                a pan plinth table of
                law   (p. 510)

Elements of the nineteenth century hover over these passages. The "iron horse" was that century's last word in
transportion. Zukofsky seems to be honoring that period
as the one that discovered anew the intermingling of man

and nature. That century produced Apollinaire, who taught Zukofsky to let go of the all-pervading ego in favor of the intermittent self. Perhaps Yeats's theory of "masks" sprang from the same insight. And Yeats ruminated about "The Fish" and "The Tables of the Law"—regions beyond the ego's purview.

The style of "A"-22, considered apart from its alluring music, presents no greater difficulties than the most obscure portions of "A"-19 and "A"-21, though its uniform density makes it appear more puzzling. Ever since "A"-3, Zukofsky has been arranging syntax to allow for two equally valid readings of the same passages; by now we should be used to that. The movement's first line works this way, casually dropping personal pronouns to achieve ambiguity. "Others letters a sum owed" (p. 508) means nothing as a statement of fact; it is only a semi-sentence. If we want to complete it (and Zukofsky probably expects us to), we must provide pronouns that are only implied. We can construct at least two orderly sentences: "I owed others a sum of letters" and "Others owed me a sum of letters."

This ambiguous language constantly frustrates attempts to pin "A" down to a single meaning. It is especially vexing to the reader bent on quarrying consolation from the poem, since "A"-22 appears to be offering wisdom in garbled form, as if the Cumaean sibyl had crept into the poem. Even those passages that seem to be lucid and straightforward turn devious after close inspection.

> old in
> a greenhouse the stabled horse
> sings sometimes, thoughts' template
> somehow furthers a cento reading   (p. 535)

We tend to identify the poet with that "stabled horse." But what does "stabled" mean? If we define it as "confined" that conjures up unpleasant visions of the glue factory.

"Balanced" seems better, suggesting solid wisdom. Zukofsky could have written "stalled," which, being pre-
dominantly negative, would have missed the tension inherent in "stabled." The phrase "thoughts' template" looks
and sounds noble, but what does it mean? Is it a pattern
that guides thought, or is thought the pattern guiding
something else? Another possibility: *"A"* 1–21 and 24
might be templates forming the thought of Zukofsky as he
composes *"A"* 22–23. This could be the way the poem extends itself through the medium of Zukofsky. But where
does the reader fit in? And what does "thoughts' template"
have to do with "a cento reading"? What, indeed, is "a
cento reading"? Zukofsky's favorite dictionary—the *Century*[4]—offers this definition:

> cento: 1. A patchwork
>
>   2. In *music* and *literature* a composition made up of
> selections from the works of various authors or
> composers; a pasticcio; a medley.

But even this doesn't provide a single meaning for "a cento
reading." Is this the way we are supposed to read *"A"*—as
patchwork writing? Or is this how the poet reads other authors? Faced with the endless duplicity of such a style, we
have no recourse but to read "in pieces." Our minds cannot hold all the meanings in any one of the movement's
forking lines as a single conception, any more than the eye
can see duck and rabbit simultaneously in the famous opti-
cal illusion.

    Though Zukofsky's style did not change radically over

---

4. Zukofsky's appreciation of the *Century* can be found in "For Wallace Stevens," in *Prepositions: The Collected Critical Essays of Louis Zukofsky* (Berkeley and Los Angeles: University of California Press, 1981),
p. 35. He also liked it because Charles Sanders Peirce, one of his intellectual heroes, was an editor of the *Century*.

fifty years, his use of it did grow increasingly ambitious. In "Poem Beginning 'The'," double writing was useful for grasping the contradictions in his life. Now, in *"A"*-22, that method presses against the bounds of language's ability to convey meaning. The movement, as its interest in metamorphosis suggests, is concerned with one sort of meaning in particular—that which passes from nature through man into words. We could go back to Hesiod in tracing poets' fascination with such transactions, but a much shorter view seems sufficient.

In quite respectable English, Tennyson once pretended to talk to a plant:

> Flower in the crannied wall,
> I pluck you out of the crannies,
> I hold you here, root and all, in my hand,
> Little flower—but *if* I could understand
> What you are, root and all, and all in all,
> I should know what God and man is.[5]

The flower addressed is hardly an individual. We don't even know if it is a streaked tulip. Plucking it was an idle gesture, since the poet knows beforehand that he will not be any the wiser. The blossom only serves as a prop, there as part of a tableau, and we are permitted to overhear the poet talking to himself. How did the flower feel about being uprooted to serve as a brief focus for philosophical velleity? Hopkins, for one, was capable of asking that sort of question. His attempts to match nature's amplitude with words and rhythm seem more genuinely inquisitive. A century later, *"A"*-22 seems nothing less than Zukofsky's attempt to translate nature into English.

Certain passages suggest that he is only assisting in

---

5. *The Poetic and Dramatic Works of Alfred Lord Tennyson*, ed. Horace E. Scudder (Boston: Houghton, Mifflin, 1898), p. 274.

an effort as old as language. Consider this catalogue of attempts to transform cave formations into domestic furniture:

> rocks avulsed from their beds
> water long percolating dripped caves'
> massive columns, incrusted elegant drapery. (p. 514)

The unsettling thought that mankind exists only to implement the transmutation of nature into words may come to anyone familiar with the pervasive and powerful dominion of language. This possibility seems to have occurred to Zukofsky:

> Races endure more
> slowly than languages unconsciously sounding
> skills as of bees in
> a hive. . . .   (p. 512)

After the creation of the earth, amoebas, plants, the higher animals, and featherless bipeds, what comes next? Nature's efforts, the passage suggests, are now concentrated on genetic experiments with words and grammar. Each succeeding stage of ongoing creation requires less time. The creation of the solar system took many billions of years, whereas the last experiment—man—was completed in only a few million. So the most advanced form at present (language)·alters faster than the form that bears it (humanity). This disturbing view of evolutionary history would have delighted Henry Adams. And this, in fact, is one argument against its truth; it smacks of the kind of thinking about evolution that was popular at the end of the last century.

Let us assume that language exists as man's servant, rather than vice versa. "A"-22 explores a spectrum stretching between man and nature, with language as mediator.

In this movement, Zukofsky turns to the myth of Orpheus, the old dream that a natural language exists. This is probably why *The Tempest* surrounds the movement; Prospero's book yielded such a language, a language consonant with the forces of nature. Zukofsky doesn't have Prospero's power, but he does seem intent on interpreting what seaweed has to say ("read the kelp" [p. 510]), even if it is only a rudimentary transmission of signs ("kelp waves arms" [p. 533]).

The road from Old Field leads eastward to Port Jefferson, then turns north to Paul's residence—Arbutus Road. *"A"* 22–23's movement from third line ("out of old fields") to last ("z-sited path are but us") projects a journey both spatial and temporal: from the past to the future of the family Zukofsky. Plotted on a private axis of reference, the journey is visible only to family members. Modesty, not snobbishness, produces such hermeticism.

Halfway on that tour, we pass through the home of Louis and Celia. Halfway through *"A"* 22–23, we find Celia—the center. She, too, is concealed from the public eye, but recoverable. At the end of *"A"*-22, "*she's hid*" both describes the act of concealment and hides the "she" signified in the impersonal personal pronoun. Once our curiosity is piqued, however, the beginning of *"A"*-23 offers satisfaction, if we can solve a puzzle. If we are devoted readers of *"A"*, we will find these words: "blest," "ardent," and "happiest." These, of course, are three of the four notes that completed *"A"*-12's *B*, *A*, *C*, *H*, theme (see page 125). But the capstone—Celia—is missing. She has been smuggled off seventy lines distant and hidden again: "what / submerged name in coldenia" (p. 538). Quite clearly (or unclearly) this movement is concerned with wrapping things up, with putting *"A"* together once and for all. "A"-23's first lines not only recall the mid-point of the poem, they also look back to the poem's earliest movements:

> An unforeseen delight a round
> beginning ardent; to end blest
> presence less than nothing thrives   (p. 536)

"A round"—words that launched "A". The poet of 1928 was ardent to end blest, and so implied in the first words of the poem a promise that the circle would be completed. The "foreseen curve where many / loci would disperse" (p. 536) now extends the final segment. The end is even closer than we think; it appears in the opening lines of "A"-23, close to memories of "A"-1. "Four," heard in "unforeseen" becomes "two" in "to," and winds down to zero in "nothing." 4, 2, 0 . . . From burning desire we have come to ashes in whose "presence less than nothing thrives." So double writing ascends to a new pitch of contradiction in this movement, as the triumph of "A"'s completion coincides with its expiration.

In "A"-23 we seem to hear a commentator on stage (*Pericles*'s Gower redivivus?), but the action escapes us, as it did in "A"-21. Most of "A"-23 sounds very familiar, and it should, for much of the movement consists of phrases recycled from earlier parts of "A". "Day's eyes averted—look her / lamp brightens, he sleeps. . . ." (p. 555) remembers the second half of "A"-9: "averted / Loss seize the hurt head Apollo's eyes point to" (p. 110). Even the floral aspect of that section returns. "Day's eyes" are simply daisies, since "daisy" stems from "daeges eage," Old English for "day's eye." Everywhere we touch "A"-23 we feel the pulse of the whole of "A".

The poem has long since had enough of world history— "A"-18 saw the last of that. "A"-22 covered natural history. What sort of history remains for "A"-23? These lines covertly announce the topic to be pursued.

> words earth—the saving history
> not to deny the gifts
> of time where those who
> never met together may hear
> this other time sound *one*.   (p. 539)

Human history, natural history, and now this mysterious "saving history." What is it? We could probably guess, had not Zukofsky already told us in his essay on Wallace Stevens, where he speaks of the "impersonal friendship when one poet reads another . . . a reading removed from yet out of time. . . ." The saving history is poetry: "saving" as in "remembering" and "salvation." As the hundredth line of "A"-22 began an account of archaic geological turbulence, so the hundredth line of "A"-23 offers a sampling of primitive song. This is followed by a long "condensed" version of the Gilgamesh epic, one of the oldest narratives extant. "A"-23 is partly oriented toward the East, where the story of Gilgamesh was born. Hebrew had its origins there, and in "A"-23 we discover English serving up Hebraic sounds in brief spurts:

> near
> him, sap pay rue if
> near him, live near him
> if near him, low door
> a har. . . .   (p. 544)

In its survey of poetry the movement has as one of its objects the cataloguing of tongues, not forgetting the aboriginal inhabitants of America:

> West redskins' talk grammars older
> than East's. Tongues: lark's wings:

> '*hi!*' requires a serious answer
> agglutinative questions when no redskins
> lust white gospel in red-tongue.   (p. 561)

After the primeval sallies of poetry, we eventually reach the Romantic age. References to Wordsworth ("skiddaw" and "words earth"), the appearance of a figure resembling *Alastor*'s young hero who "strayed to seacoast" near "a veiled girl" (p. 542), and traces of Keats, especially *Endymion*, color the scene. Why this return to Romanticism, which had apparently been dismissed for good in *"A"*-6? The Romantics were Zukofsky's early idols, the patterns behind his first attempts at making poems. *"A"* bends back. The "foreseen" (four scene) curve of childhood, youth, maturity, and old age rounds out to a full circle.

SIX

"A"'s Unities: A Survey

In 1814 Wordsworth released *The Excursion* with a prefatory note advising his public that it was only part of a "long and laborious work," *The Recluse*. The projected opus, had it ever been completed, would have consisted of *The Prelude*, *The Excursion*, and a concluding section. Apologizing for the publication of only one-third of the work, he offered an analogy to appease disappointment:

> The two works [*Prelude* and *Excursion*] have the same kind of relation to each other, if he may so express himself, as the ante-chapel has to the body of a gothic church. Continuing this allusion, he may be permitted to add, that his minor pieces, which have been long before the Public, when they shall be properly arranged, will be found by the attentive reader to have such connection with the main work as may give them claim to be likened to the little cells, oratories, and sepulchral recesses, ordinarily included in these edifices.[1]

1. *Wordsworth: Poetical Works*, ed. Thomas Hutchinson and Ernest De Selincourt (1936; rpt. London: Oxford University Press, 1969), p. 589.

Wordsworth's emphasis on the details of cells, oratories, and recesses suggests that he knew very well that his great work would never amount to anything more than a ruined abbey. It was his misfortune—and opportunity—to live at a time when the problem of completing a long poem had become an imposing one. After Milton, poets seemed to lose faith in the efficacy of grand designs as vital and vitalizing structures.

Up until the eighteenth century, the long poem had functioned as a cultural memory bank. It was, in effect, only reminding the audience of something already known. Homer could take it for granted that his auditors were familiar with the history of the Trojan War and the wanderings of Odysseus. Virgil altered some of the details in the story of Aeneas, but the general train of events was true to ancient tradition. Dante's itinerary had novel elements, but the basic terrain and cast of characters were familiar to his contemporaries. Milton's version of primal events had the Bible backing it up (more or less), and what better authority was there? From Homer to Milton, bards could easily begin *in medias res* because the public knew what went before and after. Though invention flourished, prior narrative or narratives supplied foundations for stories with a beginning, middle, and end. Poets could drape their poem on the convenient rack of preordained structure.

During the seventeenth and eighteenth centuries, however, formidable competitors challenged the poet. Institutions such as the Royal Society and publications like the *Encyclopédie* proffered a new kind of cultural memory, a memory based on the assembly and publication of collective knowledge. Furthermore, this kind of information bank purported to be independent of *a priori* structures. For the enlightened, the story of nature tells itself, and, in the telling, reveals what unity it may have. Transmitted knowledge was no longer good enough for the Western mind. Henceforth anyone who wanted to be taken seriously had to produce discoveries. This seemed to put epic poets out of a job.

But Wordsworth realized that though the outer world seemed to have been appropriated by scientists and engineers, there remained a territory on which no collection of Newtons could trespass—the poet's mind. Wordsworth's retreat into himself actually opens up new possibilities for the long poem. His ambitions for *The Prelude* were egotistical in two senses. First, he was reinventing the long poem. Second, he was taking himself as his theme. But autobiographies had been written before. In examining his "self," Wordsworth aimed higher; he attempted to recover the course of memory. This is what is involved in charting "the growth of the poet's mind."

Memory, though multitudinous and various, exists in each of us as a most intimate possession. Hume went so far as to suggest that it was "the source of personal identity."[2] But the conscious mind exists only in the present moment and taps only a fraction of memory. Somewhere within us, we presume, exists the entire body of memory—yet we can only recover it in bits and pieces. So the poet who takes himself for his subject is in trouble before he starts; his subject is apprehensible only in fragments. Memory is, however, always "there" to be drawn on, and the poet may fondly dream that a serious, systematic labor of recall (such as an autobiographical poem) might make it explicit in print. Perhaps Wordsworth hoped that *The Prelude* would be memory transposed to a concrete medium. And, if memory equals self, the finished work might claim to be more the poet than that flesh-and-blood creature who called himself Wordsworth.

2. David Hume, *A Treatise of Human Nature*, ed. L. A. Selby-Bigge (1888; rpt. London: Oxford University Press, 1973), p. 261.

The equation of identity with memory produces another curious problem: each individual's autobiographical long poem must assume a different form. The "tracks of my memory" that guided Rousseau in writing his *Confessions* are, like Wordsworth's "spots of time," unique guideposts not amenable to prefabricated design. The poet must trust to his memory to take him safely through the poem. Construction of a long poem becomes a joint enterprise on the part of the poet and his unpredictable recollections.

The Prelude's break with traditional ways of unifying a poem and its exploration of the coils of memory lead inevitably and unfortunately to obscurity. Though we all have memories, they are not all the same, nor do we treat them similarly. What's worse, many of our most tenacious and interesting memories are as mysterious to the author as they are to the reader. Why, for example, does Wordsworth feel tip-top when he reaches the summit of Snowdon and beholds the moon flooding the clouds with light?

The account Wordsworth appends to his vision is a product—as such accounts always are—of reflection. His attempt to divine the significance of the scene suggests that we have almost as much right to make an interpretation. So meaning has to be constructed, with attendant doubts, gaps, and hesitancies. Wordsworth staked all on the latent significance of his spots of time, but his very reliance on them as, energizing loci, depending as it does on their *not* being fully explicable, leaves us a step removed. We are entitled to match interpretations with the poet, yet we are always at a disadvantage. He feels their power; we feel it only through his mediation. Wordsworth is being as plain as his methods allow, but those methods inevitably leave the reader a distant second.

The Prelude continually offers truths that the author discovers, but they are truths that are not necessarily communicable—either to the reader or to himself. This is what happens when poetry drops patterns with social currency in favor of personal design. Memory, that absentminded and inarticulate guide, has assumed the task of leading the inquiring spirit on its pilgrimage, and henceforth the long poem wanders into territory where common knowledge has very limited usefulness.

The provisional nature of the long poem becomes one of its hallmarks, even for those poets who did not rely so much on memory. Williams remarked, when he found it necessary to continue *Paterson*, "It called for poetry such as I did not know, it was my duty to discover or make such a context on the 'thought.'"[3] The context that might supply unity can hardly do so while still undiscovered or unmade. How can we know when we have uncovered all our important memories, and how do we shuffle them into a unity once we have?

Two poets of our century, David Jones and William Carlos Williams, tended to deemphasize the importance of unity.[4] They seemed to consider it desirable, but hardly necessary. Of *Paterson* Williams remarked, "As I mulled the thing over in my mind, the composition began to assume a form which you see in the present poem, keeping, I fondly hope, a unity directly continuous with the Paterson of *Pat. 1* to *4*. Let's hope I have succeeded in doing so."[5] His curious estrangement from the poem, suggested by "the composition began to assume a form," bears a resemblance to Zukofsky's withdrawal from full responsibility for his poem. Both men saw their work developing a life of its

3. William Carlos Williams, *The Autobiography of William Carlos Williams* (New York: New Directions, 1967), p. 392.
4. David Jones (1895–1974) was an English-Welsh poet and painter. Of his works, *In Parenthesis* and *The Anathemata* are the ones best known in America.
5. William Carlos Williams, "Author's Note," in *Paterson* (New York: New Directions, 1963), p. i.

own, a life not necessarily amenable to unity imposed by the author.

Jones's conception of unity in *The Anathemata* was even more nebulous. "What I have written has no plan, or at least is not planned. If it has a shape it is chiefly that it returns to its beginning. It has themes and a theme even if it wanders far. If it has a unity it is that what goes before conditions what comes after and *vice versa.*"[6] For Jones, discovery is mostly a matter of collecting what is already at hand. Therefore the chief operation in *The Anathemata* is one of arrangement. To have started with a preestablished unity would have been to assume that the materials would sort themselves out according to a plan fashioned by Jones. But this is precisely what Jones wanted to escape.

Furthermore, Jones's materials, like Wordsworth's, are fundamentally mysterious. They can only be presented, not explained. The poet works to explore, elaborate, and celebrate them—not bring them down to his measure. Charles Olson once attempted to grapple with this process: "Energy is larger than man, but therefore, if he taps it as it is in himself, his uses of himself are EXTENSIBLE in human directions & degree not recently granted."[7] Since Wordsworth, poets have been seeking that "something" larger than man, whether we call it memory, divinity, energy, the imagination, or paradise. Unity becomes a useful way of channeling that larger dimension into the poem. If the manifestations of that larger entity can only be perceived multiply, unity is fractured into a collection of unities. Pound, Williams, Jones, Olson, and Zukofsky were attuned to a wider spectrum than is tidily manageable.

Though Zukofsky insisted that *"A"* (and his entire body of work, for that matter) was a unit, we can detect differ-

6. David Jones, *The Anathemata* (New York: Viking, 1965), p. 33.
7. Charles Olson, "The Gate and the Center," in *Human Universe and Other Essays,* ed. Donald Allen (New York: Grove Press, 1967), p. 22.

ent principles of unification operating in different parts of the poem. "A" 1–12, for example, organizes itself around a principle that is missing from the second half of "A".

We might start our orientation for the first half with Zukofsky himself. As we have already seen, he began "A" at a time when "impersonality"—the poet's discreet withdrawal from his work—was all the rage. Zukofsky endorsed that strategy, praising Apollinaire for hitting on just the right blend of objectivity and subjectivity:

> With intelligence there is the handling of, and absorption by, a matter and a time for a creation which moves: intelligence as writing which to the concerned or observant never becomes an attitude, the subjective grease in the cracks of brilliance. . . . For the intimacy revealed is not Apollinaire's, a reflection's, but that of an intelligence, the fact and a life.[8]

Apollinaire served as a model for the retention of "intelligence" in the work and the purging away of the dross of "attitudes." Though Zukofsky does not pause to define these terms, he clearly has in mind some mysterious process by which the writing speaks for itself while the artist (burdened with "attitudes") stands out of the way. The talent, not the artist, creates the work.

The early movements of "A" reveal an author obsessed with the self and the self's unmediated confrontation with the world. In "A" 1–12 Zukofsky is careful to treat himself as subject matter. "A" rotates the author, now showing him as formulator (as ego presiding over and constructing the poem), and alternately as character and inmate. The framework of this dual approach is simple. The odd-numbered movements of "A" 1–12 are short, lyrical, and tightly knit. They are "subjective" in the sense that the poet's personal concerns dominate: family, friends, his art, his psychology, and so on. Even-numbered movements, however, tend to

8. "The Writing of Guillaume Apollinaire," holograph MS, HRC.

lengthy, prolix, and concerned with larger issues and public events. We can call them "objective," since they generally cast Zukofsky in a minor role, as participant in, and observer of, matters larger than himself: the Depression, wars, class struggle. (These categories are not absolute. The first half of "A"-9 does not entirely conform to the pattern.) For the most part the movements follow this plan. In "A"-4 we come upon what amounts to an elegy for Yehoash, and in "A"-5 we encounter bits of veiled information about Zukofsky's recently deceased mother. Yehoash lands in an "objective" movement because he was a public figure. Mrs. Zukofsky is put in a "subjective" movement because she was known only to her family. Exact discrimination determines the placement of material that, at first glance, seems thrown in helter-skelter.

Zukofsky aimed to have it both ways. He could introduce his private concerns to the reader, and he had a platform from which to inform us about the issues of the day. "A"-6 briefly acknowledges this two-legged stance:

> Natura Naturans —
> Nature as creator,
>
> Natura Naturata —
> Nature as created.
>
> He who creates
> Is a mode of these inertial systems —   (pp. 22–23)

If the author thinks of himself as such a "mode," it relieves him of the responsibility to be "original" all the time. It would, in fact, be an impossibility. Nature includes Zukofsky, the Adamses, Marx, Spinoza, and the reader; none of them have privileged access to the truth. We are all in this together, Zukofsky would say, and anyone who reads "A" has the right to participate in the process of creation and re-creation. Readers conscious of their exalted position might exercise their rights and object to Zukofsky's selective use of quotation. How can he be faithful to the nature that created him if he is always loading quotations with meanings the originator never intended? "Natura Naturans, Natura Naturata," for example, is Zukofsky's free adaptation of a passage in Spinoza:

> Before proceeding, I would wish to explain, or rather to remind you, what we must understand by active and passive nature (*natura naturans*, and *natura naturata*), for I think from the past propositions we shall be agreed that by nature active we understand that which is in itself and through itself is conceived, or such attributes of substance as express eternal and infinite essence, that is . . . God, in so far as he is considered a free cause. But by nature passive I understand all that follows from the necessity of the nature of God.[9]

It would be hard for Zukofsky to defend himself against the charge that he has rewritten Spinoza. Prosecutors might begin by pointing out his deletion of God from the passage. Zukofsky in turn could reply by simply noting that Spinoza adapted these phrases from an earlier source..

By refusing to be the god of his poem, Zukofsky invites participation by the reader. We are pressed into service, whether we like it or not, and asked to complete the poem with our interpretations. These interpretations often demand a judgmental leap of faith. As often as not, the poem offers insufficient data for interpretation; the poem becomes a process to be completed, not a code to be deciphered. We can either make that jump or shut the book—there is no middle course.

Zukofsky, too, is faced with difficulties. He sometimes veers dangerously close to solipsism, or, on the other hand, sometimes seems to lose his identity. The poetry walks

9. Baruch Spinoza, *Ethics and On the Correction of the Understanding*, trans. Andrew Boyle (1910; rpt. New York: Dutton, Everyman's Library, 1970), p. 24.

between language that cannot communicate (as in "A"-7) and language that would be communication from no one ("A"-8). We have to take risks in reading "A", but so did Zukofsky when he wrote it.

The objective/subjective stride of the poem serves as a frame for further dichotomies. A mathematical pattern, for example, is dimly discernible in the early movements. The word "one" seems generally to be associated with the individual, sometimes with the individual as solipsist. Its first use in the poem occurs at the beginning of the fantasy of the self-centered "Zukofsky" in "A"-1: "as one who under stars" (p. 2). In "A"-2, where Zukofsky recognizes himself as part of a wider natural and social order, "two" enters. The second movement abounds with doubles: "twice," "two," "half-hours," "half-human, half-equestrian." "One" appears in "A"-2 in connection with subjectivism: "in one's own head" (p. 7). Of course, the titles of the movements themselves contribute to the distinction. No sooner is the sequence begun, however, than Zukofsky abandons it. "A"-3 mentions "two dark heads" (p. 10) and "A"-4 speaks of "one shadow of your light" (p. 13). "One" returns strongly in "A"-5 and "A"-6. "Two" seems an aberration occurring only in movements 2 and 3, an appeal to otherness that cannot be sustained. It may simply reflect Zukofsky's solitary state in the years between 1925 and 1935. "Two" makes a comeback in "A"-8, by which time Celia had entered his life.

A more consistent dichotomy than this numerological split is submerged in the first half of the poem. The odd-numbered movements, where the ego presides, tend to support fixed forms and dry imagery; "A"-1 has a desert, flaming pits, streets, subways, and so forth. Even-numbered movements are damp and freely flowing. "A"-2 contains an ocean, sailors (ancient Greeks as well as modern gobs), sea-horses, and lovers who "impinged upon

field as an ocean" (p. 8). The odd movements are not totally devoid of marine imagery, but the majority of oceanic/
watery references do cluster in the even movements. "*A*"-
6's cross-country jaunt might be expected to be arid, but
not so. As a "wet" movement, it reveals liquid lines:

> A roof, like a green sea, of a desert shack in Nevada
> (p. 32)

> While in the sea
> The seals pearled for a minute
> In the sun as they sank.

> Returned,
> Three thousand miles, over rails,
> To adequate distribution of "Camels";
> New York — Staten Island —
> Bay water viscous
> where the waves mesh   (pp. 35–36)

In "*A*"-8 the watery slant of the "objective" movements
continues. "Or when glass harmonica or dining table /
Tuned their glass (plunged tones)" (p. 49). The glass harmonica, perfected by that great republican Benjamin Franklin, basically consisted of glass vessels filled with water.
"*A*" seems to associate it with social, political, and scientific change late in the eighteenth century. The aristocracy
amused itself with the glass harmonica, but upheavals ush-
ering in the nineteenth century mark the end of their
power.

> I saw my lady weep, the glass harmonica
> Stilled — society splitting into two camps, two
> Classes. . . .   (p. 50)

"Two" again, and other doubles are associated with the
glass harmonica; "who had whistled? The scale fell as the
pail emptied" (p. 51)—referring simultaneously to the
change in pitch as water gradually decreases in a container

and the decline in the standard of living as the workers' lunch-pails empty.

Binary structures force the reader to see and think stereoscopically. "A"-8 briefly touches on one instance of the "physics" theme that deals with such a problem.

> Light-wave and quantum, we have good proof both exist:
> Our present effort is to see how this is: to
> Perfect the composition of a two-point view (p. 49)

> Build it. Designate by Ψ that "something," changes
> In which trident stay responsible for the waves,
> Thought has assumed what thought is compelled to
> assume!
> (p. 50)

Neptune's trident is the watery motif intruding again (via the Greek alphabet), vying for attention with the solid quanta. The nature of light, perceptible only *as* double, summarizes the watery/dry and solid/chaotic polarities suffusing "A" 1–12. It also launched Zukofsky on some metaphysical ponderings in a letter to Niedecker many years after "A"-8.

> But the point is the human mind can think of *something* & *nothing*. . . . So while *waves* explain some things and *quanta* others—all S & N can never be explained only presented like a poem for instance, wave-particles, which was one explanation (as per "A"-8).[10]

Science's inability to reduce light to one category or the other looms as another reason for the binary thrust of "A" 1–12. Not only is the author compelled to recognize his status as created and creator, he (and we) must abandon the notion that a single vision adequately mirrors experience.

10. Letter of September 11, 1959, HRC.

This binocular approach is hardly Zukofsky's invention, but few poets have gone to so much trouble in executing the design.

We suggested in chapter 3 that the discovery of the family as a mediating ground rescued Zukofsky from imprisonment in patterns based on the solitary self. No longer would he have to think in terms of such oppositions as self/world or created/creator. And indeed the objective/subjective rotation of "*A*"'s first half does not carry through to the second half. "*A*"-11 and "*A*"-12, the final steps in that advance, bridge the gap between self and family, and between family and world. "*A*"-11's double axis of reference (familial/literary), for example, represents in miniature the transformation of "Zukofsky the loner" into Zukofsky the family man. Though "*A*" 13–24 shows no loss of poetic power, its growth follows different, freer patterns.

These patterns, which are also observable in "*A*" 1–12, do most of the work of tying the poem together. Less rigid than the objective/subjective dichotomy, they provide the flexibility the poem needs. We find botanical, physiological, ornithological, zoological, and mineralogical details guiding "*A*"'s formation. Consider this dense passage:

> human cranium's dendritical crystallizations offer
> no sure estimate of antiquity
> only archaic time unchanged unchangeable:
> aeolian loess, glacier carrying *graywether*—
> chipped and rubbed contorted drift—
> concentric bed blue clay—white,
> yellow sand, striped loam—blue
> laminated. Laminated marl—fret changes
> only himself, to prove peach
> blooms, cherry blossoms, dogwood: seen
> seeded flower. . . .   (p. 512)

The passage notes that "dendritical" ("treelike") has been applied to nerve cells in the brain. The *OED* informs us that it has also been used to describe crystallizations in stone, by, among others, S. T. Coleridge. The word is a kind of floating spark, lighting up geology, the human brain, and vegetation; though it is a product of human brains, it helps show how the body shares form with natural objects. Our intimate connection with nature received explicit attention earlier in the poem:

> His innocence his blood is water, his
> Tears salt, his seed like the
> Cells of seaweed, his
>
> Bones the matter of coral
> So that his God
> Does not need advertisement   (p. 271)

The passage concludes a long section relating the different forms in nature and inviting us to see them as variations on one another. "The elephant clasps with / Nostril as a hand" (p. 270). If the forms of nature flow into one another, such a mixing suggests a seamless world, both in *"A"* as an artifact and the world it mirrors. So in *"A"*-14 artistic activity is described as a series of related steps:

> "history" integrates
>
> lower limit body
> upper limit dance,
> lower limit dance
>
> upper limit speech,
> lower limit speech
> upper limit music,
>
> lower limit music
> upper limit *mathémata*
> *swank* for *things*
>
> *learned.* . . .   (p. 349)

No priorities can be established in such a schema. Note also that the transitions are couched in terms of a calculus.

The continuities that a calculus tracks must have similar form. Devious connections based on similar form can be found everywhere in "A". In a passage from "A"-10, we must observe a denunciation of certain political leaders through ornithological glasses. The two men in question bear Teutonic and Mediterranean names:

> Henri Philippe Pétain and Herr Hitler
>   have made peace
> One name is spit
> The other is hawked from the throat
>
> French people, Spain's dead asked you to help
> Now you cannot ask them for help
> Do you still ask us gullible people for help   (p. 114)

"Hitler" is undeniably guttural, and "Pétain" forms on the lips in almost the same fashion as spitting, but there are other reasons for Zukofsky's choice of birds. Hitler is "hawked" because hawks prey on small animals. "Gullible" suggests a victimized bird; the world seems divided into hawks and gulls. Birds—ubiquitous in "A"—act here to help diagnose and identify the battle-lines of 1940.

Zoology also helps "A"-10. Zukofsky equates fascism and the rhinoceros in a bit of doggerel ridiculing fascist pomposity:

> The Rhino is a lovely beast
> He has two horns or one at least
> And neither horn is just a horn
> Provoking a dictator's scorn
> His surest backside venting scorn
> He sits upon the Rhino's horn
> And corporate spumes up a yeast
> The Rhino such a lovely beast   (p. 120)

This seems a hit at Mussolini's African adventures, but why pick on the rhino? The rhinoceros happens to be a member of *Perissocactylic ungulate*, "the group which includes the rhinoceros . . . and the horse."[11] So the horse, example of vitality and right action in the poem, has a cousin of ungainly form. The theory of evil as a deviation from a norm is consistent with Zukofsky's synthetic approach; the world, far from being a Manichaean battleground, is plagued with forms slightly out of whack, forms similar enough to be associated.

Botany helps Zukofsky comment on the national scene. The closing lines of "A"-15, as we saw in chapter 5, take up the problem of race relations in floral language.

> *negritude* no nearer or further
> than the African violet
> not deferred to
> or if white, Job
> white pods of *honesty*
> satinflower
>
> (p. 375)

Zukofsky's unusual approach to the structuring of his poem is apparent from the very beginning. Mineralogy comes into play in "A"-1. The diamonds adorning the wives of New York's elite are a form of carbon. The presence of a molecular spectrum is clinched by the name of one of the demonstrating radicals—"Carat"—and the reference to striking coal miners. A mineral contrast (coal/diamond) parallels the social split (miners/exploiters). "Carat" is, no doubt, a diamond in the rough.

From the physical sciences to the empyrean of philosophy may seem like a giant leap, but if the former can serve as unifying material, why not the latter? We have already

---

11. D'Arcy Wentworth Thompson, *On Growth and Form*, abridged and ed. John Tyler Bonner (Cambridge: Cambridge University Press, 1961), p. 309.

seen how Zukofsky wove philosophy into "*A*"-12 (Empedocles and his four elements), and we touched on the meaning of discord and harmony in that movement. It could, however, stand further investigation.

At the beginning of "*A*"-24, the most prominent voice reads part of a quotation from "*A*"-12:

> Blest
> Infinite things
> So many
> Which confuse imagination
> Thru its weakness,
> To the ear
> Noises.
> Or harmony
> Delights
> Men to madness —   (p. 231)

The passage describes a condition existing when we listen to "*A*"-24, read "*A*", or, for that matter, meditate on the world. It describes Zukofsky's problems as fabricator and our problems as readers. The passage is from Spinoza's *Ethics*:

> Nor would they then find it perhaps a stumbling block to their theory that infinite things are found which are far beyond the reach of our imagination, and many which confuse it through its weakness. . . . And such things as affect the ear are called noises, and form discord or harmony, the last of which has delighted men to madness.[12]

The harmonies of "*A*"-24, and the harmonies of "*A*", may strike us as discordant, especially since they are initially "beyond the reach of our understanding." Discord and harmony, the problem perplexing us as we face the world,

---

12. *Ethics*, pp. 34–35.

and plaguing any artist, is a binary motif permitting access to one of the most intricate of the poem's large-scale harmonies, for Zukofsky consciously weaves the strife between these two into "A"-12. He writes in a letter to Niedecker: "I bought C. the 8 Concertos that followed *The Four Seasons* . . . the trial of Harmony and Invention—which I called Battle of Discord and Harmony in 'A'-12."[13] This crucial fragment suggests several important matters. First, there must be some kind of binary theme (discord and harmony) present in the movement. Second, the musical influence is there, but exactly how is difficult to say. We find Bach and Vivaldi mentioned in the movement, but if there is a specific model for "A"-12, such as the concerto form, it is well hidden.

The binary structure posited in Zukofsky's letter accompanies the numbers 8 and 4, which add up to 12, the number of the movement. So there appears to be a numerological pattern built around the number 4 (the number of letters in Bach's name). It débuts with a frequency that calls attention to itself in the first few pages of "A"-12. After noting this, we might begin to hunt for other quartets, such as the four elements: earth, air, fire, and water. They happen to be present in the movement's opening lines.

> *Out of deep need*
> Four trombones and the organ in the nave
> A torch surged —
> Timed the theme Bach's name,
> Dark, larch and ridge, night:
> From my body to other bodies
> Angels and bastards interchangeably
> Who had better sing and tell stories
> Before all will be abstracted.

13. Undated letter, HRC.

So goes: first, *shape*
The creation —
A mist from the earth,
The whole face of the ground;
Then *rhythm* —
And breathed breath of life   (p. 126)

Fire comes first, in the torch; water rises from the earth in the form of mist, and a particular kind of air—"breath of life"—brings up the rear. The genesis theme and the references to fundamental constituents stand opposed to the danger that "all will be abstracted," and the void (which creeps into line 24). The void merits two mentions in the first thirty-three lines of the movement.

With some difficulty, the reader gradually understands that the genesis at the start of "*A*"-12 centers on Paul, who enters as an infant. Fire and light are associated with Paul *ab ovo*. At the age of four, he is quoted as perceiving a floating seed as a star. Zukofsky persistently puns on sun/son through the rest of "*A*", and some of Paul's drawings catalogued later in "*A*"-12 have blazing titles: "O Pad Fire," "Suddenly a fire," and "Putting Out the Fires in the Old Days" (p. 243). Fires seem to be creative forces in the movement; even its destructive manifestations allow for invention; Richard Brinsley Sheridan makes "almost a verse" (p. 210) as his theater goes up in flames.

The presence of the four elements along with a "Battle of Discord and Harmony" suggests that "*A*"-12 aspires to be the central cosmological section of the poem, bestowing on the work a dignity and purpose as ancient as Hesiod and the author of Genesis. Empedocles taught that his four elements mixed and separated under the influence of two contending powers: love and strife. The simplicity of the scheme makes it similar to mathematical and musical structure, as Zukofsky suggests in his letter equating the "Battle of Discord and Harmony" with "the trial of Harmony and

214 | Zukofsky's "A"

Invention." Being a cosmological design, it serves as an excellent vehicle for aligning the Zukofskys' history with world events; the four elements apply as much to them as to anyone else, past or present, high or low. The fire, for example, can suggest young Paul's excess vitality and the inspiration Homer drew from the fall of Troy. Grandfather Pinchos is associated with water, indicating his imminent return to the formlessness of the grave. Water also surrounds Odysseus and Jackie, the young Pfc., since both face death.

By drawing on the collective wisdom of the past two thousand years, Zukofsky has not only furthered the integrity of "A", he has also advanced his method of shared authorship. We can take issue with the uses Zukofsky makes of botany, philosophy, and so on (though our objections may seem petty), but how can we argue with Spinoza, Linnaeus, Vivaldi, and Homer?

There are, however, unifying elements in the poem for which Zukofsky is solely responsible. And these are the materials that do most of the work in providing "A" with what unity it has. To begin with, we should note that no all-embracing design serves to unify the poem. A few characteristics of the poem's history, such as the fact that Zukofsky knew from the beginning that it would eventually reach twenty-four movements and stop, hint that a skeletal plan lies hidden. Even if a grand design exists, however, its principles must be so rarefied as to form only the sketchiest of frameworks. For all we know, Zukofsky might have decided on twenty-four parts simply because twenty-four inches equal two feet (so emphasizing the reciprocal aspects of the poem). Whatever the reason, generalization was never Zukofsky's forte.

The unifying elements that do most of the work for the poem are intertwined structural, thematic, imagistic, and verbal similitudes. This network of form is not a lack of form; if anything, it can be argued that "A" is too orderly.

A form, an order, is useful insofar as it does what it is designed to do. "*A*"'s unities function as planned. They permit the creation of a poem that is both inclusive and repetitious, in which new themes can be introduced to harmonize with the old.

Zukofsky is always interested in discovering hidden laws (as were Marx and Adams), but more interested in using them. He is also acutely aware that the material forming an artifact partly determines that artifact's shape. By funneling a multitude of complex forms into the poem, he throws light not only on them, but on himself as the alembic that transmutes materials according to laws that are partly his invention and partly inherent in the materials themselves. "*A*" might be dubbed a "symbiotic" poem. To borrow Pound's Vortex for a moment, we can see both Zukofsky and his materials as part of the patterned energy that is "*A*". Trying to discern where one leaves off and the other begins can be difficult and unprofitable.

"*A*"-12 offers part of a letter to Niedecker describing one way Zukofsky furthers his poem.

> I have to reread several times
> to find out what I meant. Only
> after a while, with no pen in hand,
> does the "fact" I wanted come
> back — a sort of perennial-annual.   (p. 215)

"*A*" seems to recur as naturally as leaves on a tree. Time and again, Zukofsky's gloss on the whole poem and his method of long-term composition amounted to its being "in the blood," that is, exuding from the author like sap. These "habitual" arrangements are noted in the same letter.

> Each writer writes
> one long work whose beat he cannot
> entirely be aware of. Recurrences

follow him, crib and drink from a
well that's his cadence — after
he's gone.   (p. 214)

The unplanned recurrences of "A" are pointedly not the products of chance. Even the brief accounts Zukofsky provides analyze the act of writing in terms of ritual. As if it were a shy animal, the "fact" becomes available only when he has "no pen in hand." In some way, he insists, the work is other than the author, and it resists his attempts to take too much control. As the term "perennial-annual" implies, "A" has a life of its own.

His relationship to the poem is reciprocal. He writes the poem, but it "cribs" from his cadence. The poem is larger than the author's capacities at any given moment, but the author's life is the sustenance of the poem. Zukofsky seems to be a reader and a writer, but not both at once. He persists in defining himself and his work as two separate, though overlapping, areas. This is not unlike Wordsworth's relation to the "spots of time" that dominate his memory.

Zukofsky's account of his authorship is more significant than any single point he makes. In his analysis he seems to take his methods onto the plane of self-criticism. The experience of making "A" becomes a multiple one. Zukofsky's divided attitude about the activity of making the poem is the important point, not the attempt to divide the recurrences into "conscious" and "unconscious"—terms that are probably not adequate. Though he uses these terms in a letter to Cid Corman, what stands out is his inclination toward multiple modes:

> Anyway what interests me most on top of it as I am—too
> damn close for a guy who can't avoid "ideas" tho these interest him least—is not the ideas but the way the recurrences & reflections . . . come up welling tho I don't *con-*

sciously try anything like plotting 'em, of all the other movements of *"A"*.[14]

On one side is the author, recorder of "recurrences & reflections," and on the other side stand those phenomena. Yet these recurrences are surely a product of his ways of seeing, thinking, and writing. One reason Zukofsky assiduously avoids the middle ground of authorship may be that dependence on unplanned recurrences is extremely useful for the "objective" poet as he withdraws from his work, or, rather, withdraws his ego and writes with his whole self. In the following passage from *"A"*-13, where Zukofsky comments on the recurrences of his art, he again points to a division.

> The blood's music repeats: "cellar door" (1926),
> (1956) *"Neither/nor, nor and/or"*
> Attesting an exchange between an intellective portion
> Of head and that part it calls music
> Meaning something sometime to come back to a
> > second time,
> > > (pp. 296–97)

("Cellar door" concludes line 172 of "The".) Here we have two times, two rhyming phrases, and two parts of the head. So the multiple perspectives that dominate *"A"* extend to the author's own account of them.

The four categories of recurrence mentioned on page 214 are intended as convenient groupings, not as absolute demarcations. The first of these—structural links—has already been covered. Into this category we can put the objective/subjective distinction of *"A"* 1–12 and the sequence (two similar movements followed by a dissimilar one) evident in movements 13–24. I call them structural patterns

14. *Origin*, 2d ser., no. 1 (April 1961), p. 63. The letter is dated August 25, 1960.

because their chief function seems to be to provide distinct areas for working out poetic problems. A few of the links, however, are surprisingly conventional. "A"-13 begins the second half of the poem, and its paternal, prognosticating tone differs radically from the tone of "A"-1. But enough of the themes and objects present in the first movement return in "A"-13 to demonstrate a connection between the movements, even though they were composed thirty-two years apart. Seventy-nine lines into "A"-13 appears a thank-you note:

> The grace of a madhouse—courtesy, *Thanks*
> *for passover delicacies*
> *specially the black bambino*
>
> *(bambini plural) Aint tasted*
> *that kind of ADmired chocolate*
> *for 40 years—* (pp. 264–65)

The voice of Pound returns (heard, we recall, in "A"-1), bearing with it the theme of bondage present in "A"-1. The "nigger babies" update the slavery motif to modern times. Further on in the movement, we find another version of the "great Magnus" lecturing on consumption:

> You have to eat three times a day says our Cyrus—
> two billion in holdings—
> I can very well hear him doing it. (p. 283)

The end of "A" shows a like symmetry. As we noted earlier, the last movement of the second half begins with a quote from the last movement of the first half.

But these structures are outweighed, in number and variety, by the repetition of images and thematic material. One image (and theme) is remarkably prominent, simple, and versatile—circularity. The second word of the poem, which we tend to neglect while scrutinizing the first, is "round." Zukofsky characteristically skews a common word—"around"—and by splitting it renders the familiar strange, thus rescuing it from the inattention it suffers in daily use. (A profitable way to read "*A*" is to be as alert as possible to the deviations from "normal" usage.) Note how the elevation of the letter "A" to a line of its own tends to divert our attention from the odd use of "round" as a collective noun. We accept it without thinking because "round" is a musical term.

Circularity for the most part hides in "*A*"-1, peeking covertly from such juxtapositions as the implication that the "mass movement" of the workers is a recycled version of Israel's exodus from Egypt. "*A*"-2 mutes the motif as well, but it shows clearly in "*A*"-3 and "*A*"-4. The turning meter of "*A*"-3 joins with such lines as "rise and surround" and "Cemetery rounded" (p. 10). The context of the turning horses at the beginning of "*A*"-4 is difficult to distinguish, but they seem to be on a carousel. The suggestion in "*A*"-3 that Ricky is a kind of errant knight seems to produce the merry-go-round. "Carousel" comes from the French *carrousel*, a chivalric tournament. (Just around the corner is the circus of "*A*"-7).

Turning (suggesting, among other things, perversion and conversion) obsesses the Jewish elders in "*A*"-4; "Do not turn away your sun" (p. 13), they pray, punning on "son." The word returns in a line quoted from Yehoash: "creatures turned to sand" (p. 15). "*A*"-4 rings its last change on circularity by associating carousels (which rotate to music) with the grinding millstone that kept time for Veit Bach. "A carousel — Flour runs / Song drifts from the noises" (p. 15).

By the end of the first four movements, we can distinguish two distinct motions in this circulation; one kind of turning produces or assists in the production of music, the other is mere rotation and suggests the passing of time and consequent loss. Bearing this in mind, we can look back at

"A"-2 and find that the effects of circularity are indeed making themselves felt; "the sea grinds the half-hours" suggests the action of time wearing away, grinding things down, as the sea nibbles at the shore. (Blake long ago linked clock-time with "Satanic mills.") Time takes away, but it brings to birth as well. It all depends on which of two points of view one happens to choose.

What opposes the erasures of time? In *"A"*-2 it is the structured growth of organisms: "It is not the sea, but what floats over it" (p. 7). The opposition of decay, death, and time with flowers and music caps the verse of *"A"*-4:

> A carousel — Flour runs.
> Song drifts from the noises.
>
>> "My petted birds are dead."
>
>> "I will gather a chain
>> Of marguerites, pluck red anemone,
>> Till of every hostile see
>> Never a memory remain."   (pp. 15–16)

We can hear "flower" in "flour" and find "sea" in "see." The chain of flowers mentioned is a distant antecedent of the "wreath" appearing prominently in the middle of *"A"*-12.

Circulation subsides in the fifth and sixth movements, perhaps because the poem's premises are in danger (circularity seems to appear when the poem is self-confident). It resurges strongly in the circus of *"A"*-7. Not only are the horses moving around the ring, in the center lurks a round manhole.

"A"-12 marks the most thorough use of revolutionary movement. Alert readers will find Zukofsky giving more attention to a cyclic conception of history; one of the themes of the movement is the similarity of events widely spaced in time. Odysseus, we find, is alive today under the name of Jackie. Jackie's letters to Zukofsky collide with fragments of the *Odyssey*. For example:

—Where the Cimmerii live:
In cloud and fog no sun ever
Broke, or a star. Beached in pitch-dark   (p. 218)

leads into a letter from Jackie describing his voyage to
Japan:

> Friday, April 13, we derk at the port of Yokohama 5,263
> miles from San Francisco. We derk about 1 o'clock in the
> afternoon and stay on the ship until midnight.
>
> (p. 219)

"Derk," in Jackie's orthography, happily suggests "dark."
On arriving in camp, Jackie reports:

> . . . there was a sign at the gate which said in Japanses.
> (This is hell) You can believe that. You couldn't walk any-
> where with out getting all mad. It isn't to bad now, I guess
> we got here after it had rain for a couple of day.
>
> (p. 221)

The letter yields to another snippet from Homer; "followed / The shore to wet hell" (p. 221). Hell, so far as
"*A*"-12 is concerned, consists of the earth and its creatures
turning to water—the dissolution that discord promotes.
To clinch the connection between modern and ancient
strife, the movement observes armies

> Still fighting in northwest Greece
> The 8th division
> In the Grammos Mts.
> Homer described as the gateway to Hades.
>
> (pp. 141–42)

"Division" seems the key word.

The cycles of history have their domestic side. Families,
too, live by recurrences. In "*A*"-12 the loss of Grandfather
Pinchos (Paul) serves as a prologue to grandson Paul's
birth and development. This transition, with each member

of the family taking a step into a new position (the author changes from son to father), is "A" marking the passing of one generation and the advent of its replica. Other famous sons and fathers mingle in the movement: Henry James, Sr., and Henry James, Jr., Aristotle and Nicomachus; Alessandro and Domenico Scarlatti, to name a few.

As "A" enters its second half, the retrospective bias becomes more obvious. At the end of "A"-12, we faced an inventory of notes for unwritten works and discarded attempts, but "A"-24 digests all of "A" as well as other of Zukofsky's works. A tendency toward more specific definition seems present; in "A" 12–24, we find more numbers, relating to the members of the family, friends, and public events, than in the first eleven movements. The mere existence of Zukofsky's own family might be the catalyst prompting an effort at exact understanding, an effort reflected in an arithmetical surge.

The poem gradually assumes the appearance of an accounting, an inspection of the riches of this world. As usual, Zukofsky finds the past present in the most unlikely ways. Vivaldi's red hair, which earned him the nickname "the red priest," prompts Zukofsky to make comparisons with son Paul, the musical prodigy:

> And the red-hair's
>   Concerto in A minor.
> Pinchos knew nothing about it —
> Except the intention
> A song fathers:
> Bit of red hair
> Lost in black,
> Gloss of black
> In my Paul's gold-red-brown   (p. 158)

Paul's bit of red hair provides an opportunity for another connection in "A"-18:

As if one root
went 1000 years deep flew back from Iceland
to round full cycle beginning Eric the Red.   (p. 397)

Eric the Red was the father of Leif Ericson. Paul, flying
back from Europe via Iceland, becomes another discoverer
of America. "Round" and "cycle" suggest that America
has the privilege of continually being discovered.

Giambattista Vico earns a passing nod in "*A*"-12, implying that Zukofsky has followed in Joyce's footsteps in
adopting a theory of history in which nations and ages
repeat events that occurred long ago. This view permits
Zukofsky to employ his favorite methods of squeezing together diverse texts, a case of artistic proclivity determining choice of theory. "*A*"-15, for example, bringing the
death of President Kennedy and the early stages of the
Vietnam War into view, also presents the longest single
quotation of the poem. Some 120 lines from Gibbon's *The
Decline and Fall of the Roman Empire* argue that civilization
can never again lapse into barbarism.[15] Yet his rosy argu-
ments clash with atrocities presented in the same movement and in neighboring portions of "*A*".

The alert reader will have noticed that it is next to impossible to separate theme and image when discussing
"*A*", even though they seem distinguishable at first. All
criticism attempts to match its own terms with the work in
question. If one of the tests of value is the degree to which
the work resists such attempts, "*A*" passes with flying
colors.

We cannot do justice to the last category—verbal similitudes—in a few pages. But we can sample some instances
of auditory and visual punning. Zukofsky's puns seldom
exist as mere witty expressions; they work by combining

---

15. See Gibbon's *General Observations* appended to chapter 38.

themes and images, operating like rivets in the "machinery" of the poem.

Puns dot *"A"* from the start; in *"A"*-1 we find:

> Yeh, but why don't you give us more than a meal
>   to increase the consumption!
> And the great Magnus, before his confrères in industry,
> Swallow tail, eating a sandwich   (p. 5)

"Consumption" is both the use of goods that occurs in a healthy economy and a disease especially threatening to those who have only one meal each day. The captain's pomposity hovers in the pleonastic "great Magnus"; "swallow tail" applies to his coat, but also hints at a predatory nature.

Of course, *"A"*-7 is where puns run wild, since condensation demands that we rummage for multiple meanings. In ordinary discourse, we expect that each use of a word will be unequivocal. By turning expectations on their head, Zukofsky is not "inventing" puns (to do so would require the coining of new words) but only perceiving relations hitherto latent.

Imagine a machine programmed to describe its surroundings. Suppose further that the terms it will use are drawn from an unabridged dictionary that has been fed into its memory bank. If the machine has poor selection capability it might compensate by producing multiple definitions. No machine wrote *"A"*-7; but Zukofsky followed a similar method. Abstraction ("to draw away") in *"A"*-7 seems an alternate use of language, arguably a drawing closer to connections between things as seen from a dictionary's point of view. This becomes more and more the case as time passes; many people knew in 1929 that one name for a type of streetcar was "jigger," since they flourished around the turn of the century, but we have to go to the dictionary.

It is a critical cliché to speak of some modernist writing

as "language speaking here, not the author," but portions of *"A"* do seem to fit that description. The words of *"A"*-7 revel in multiple meanings; the "real" objects are presumably there, serving as excuses for language to exercise its synthetic power. At that point, the terms "abstract" and "concrete" cease to function usefully.

In the second half of *"A"*, Zukofsky increases his engineering of puns. Tipping us off to this new emphasis, the thirteenth movement begins with an obvious pun: "In a trice me the gist us" (p. 262). This ostensibly announces that the poet is about to impart fatherly advice to son Paul. The adjective "Trismegistos" was one applied to the god Thoth, who supposedly authored a number of hermetic works, and therefore also dispenses wisdom. "Trismegistos" means "thrice great," and *"A"*-13 discusses the three members of the Zukofsky family initially in three-line stanzas. Thoth is also the god of just measure—an appropriate patron for a movement that emphasizes exact rhythm.

"A"-13 uses puns to comment on public as well as private affairs:

> Not Nick in Ike nor Ike in Niké
> Could Rhyme *love dove*—tale the
> Stall in crew's chief, earth and
>
> Daughter. . . .   (p. 265)

It seems perfectly appropriate for the poem tacitly to note that Stalin's reign marked a "stall" (delay, structure confining a horse), and that Khrushchev is the chief of the Russian crew, since one of *"A"*-13's aims is the chronicling of the period 1950–60. It also continues the Russian/American theme first heard in *"A"*-8. Around 1960, developments in rocketry began to draw Zukofsky's attention. It could have been predicted, considering *"A"*'s earlier interest in different kinds of transportation. "Niké" names an

American anti-aircraft defense missile. (One rhymer of *love* and *dove* might be Eliot, whose fire-watching experience during the London blitz helped shape "Little Gidding"'s fourth section, which speaks of the "dove descending . . . with flames of incandescent terror" and posits "Love" as the torment's deviser.) Continuing its investigation of missile lunacy, *"A"*-13 sandwiches the following lines between stanzas that detail the impressive distances traversed by rockets and satellites:

> Wandering jew growing
>
> In two fingers of water in
> Desk inkwell—a good thrust   (p. 266)

The plant may be smaller than an ICBM, and so has less thrust, but its power is of a different sort—organic, which probably earns it the apellation "good." Given its name, and considering its location, the plant exists as a model for both the poet and his poem.

As we noted in chapter 5, the events of the 1960s prompt some of the poem's bitterest puns. At times, however, the commentaries on public figures subside into sadness and reticence. Discretion seems to be the watchword when *"A"*-15 records so weighty an event as the assassination and funeral of President Kennedy:

> Eloquence
> words of
> a senator's eulogy
> *da capo* five times:
> . . . .
> Capella, *alpha* in Auriga, little first goat   (p. 366)

Da capo ("from the beginning") suggests the uses of *capo* as "head" or "leader." That the nation's leader was shot in the head is not stressed, but apparently helps dictate the choice of words arrayed around the event. Capella, the brightest (hence *alpha*) star in the constellation Auriga ("charioteer"), means "little she-goat." She-goat? Charioteer? What net of words can we construct to subsume all these meanings? The solution to the problem does not lie with the words this time, but with a physical fact. Capella is situated forty-six light-years away. The light that reached earth in 1963 left that star in 1917, the year Kennedy was born. The overtones of "alpha and omega" hint at the beginning and ending of light and of a life.

By now it should be apparent that the nooks and crannies of the poem are the places where its essence resides. It flowers there in shapes that cannot be anticipated. We can make educated guesses after some acquaintance with *"A"*, but new twists, such as the importance of Capella's distance, are always cropping up.

Zukofsky seems convinced that punning in some cases uncovers not only verbal relationships, but intimate connections between words and things. He goes into the question of what our words show about ourselves and the "tangibility" of words in *Bottom: On Shakespeare*. The passage cited below was one he chose to repeat in "About *The Gas Age*":

> That is the interest of the arts—and even the convolvuli of mathematics (and why may they not be called so) partake of it—the feeling that even the most intellective of them are *tangible*. This is after all a thoughtful word which has perhaps no closer definition than the casual sense of *substantial* or *objective* intending a *solid object*. So when Dante "thinks" a metric foot in *De Vulgari Eloquentia* a human foot stalks him like Cressid's. So the visible reference persists tangibly as print, and the air of the voice in handwriting as notes.[16]

16. Louis Zukofsky, *Bottom: On Shakespeare* (Austin, Texas: Ark Press, 1963), p. 423. See also Louis Zukofsky, "About *The Gas Age*," in *Prepositions: The Collected Critical Essays of Louis Zukofsky* (Berkeley and Los Angeles: University of California Press, 1981), p. 172.

(Zukofsky's letters and manuscripts were always hand-written. If there was typing to be done, Celia obliged.) Zukofsky does not provide a detailed argument demonstrating that words, both spoken and written, have a formal link with solid objects. Yet, as we saw earlier, he persists in his "concrete" theme, and, in "The Effacement of Philosophy," suggests that the history of one particular word chronicles civilization's increasing abstraction from the solid:

> What one acts and speaks about are inescapable to the materialist, but precisely what the sages looked for. Perhaps the fortunes of the Greek word *ruthmos* may elucidate this matter: first it meant *shape*, then *rhythm*, now *proportion* or *style*.[17]

Those suspicious of Zukofsky's argument may point out that the three stages of the word's usage are all equally abstract—that to use words at all is to divorce oneself from things. But Zukofsky is not interested in divisions such as "abstract" and "concrete" for keeping things separate. For him, they are points along a spectrum. He works by analogy, and this comes out clearly in his version of the *ruthmos* analysis that appears in *"A"*-12. It occurs in a passage serving, we are told, as an antidote against the danger that "all will be abstracted":

> So goes: first, *shape*
> The creation —
> A mist from the earth,
> The whole face of the ground;
> Then *rhythm* —
> And breathed breath of life;
> Then *style* —
> That from the eye its function takes —

17. *Prepositions*, p. 55.

"Taste" we say — a living soul.
First, glyph; then syllabary,
Then letters. Ratio after
Eyes, tale in sound. First, dance. Then
Voice. First, body - - to be seen and to pulse
Happening together.   (p. 126)

The nervous, jumpy rhythm of the verse—isolated bits—
gives way at the end of the passage to an enjambment
whose harmonious length assists the message, or, rather, is
the message. "Happening together" describes so much of
"*A*" and Zukofsky's habitual laminating and melding of
matters commonly separated.

Our review of "*A*"'s tangled unities suggests that the
closest we can come to a general judgment about them is
this: they manage the return of the familiar under different
forms. Odysseus has a new incarnation as an American in-
fantryman, Hebrew turns into English that sounds like
Hebrew, and bits of well-known poetry lightly impinge on
the verse ("Sunday Morning" in "*A*"-12). Since the reno-
vations of the familiar cannot be predicted, only detected
when they appear, both poet and reader are always striving
to adjust to a new constellation.

Mathematical Configurations in "A"

TWO PASSAGES of "A"-8 and all of "A"-9 exhibit a most striking, because most rigorously worked out, example of the marriage of mathematics, music, and poetry. We have already noted how Zukofsky's interest in different kinds of development (thematic, fugal, historical, and so on) dictated the design of "A"-8. This fascination with development as such seems also to have produced the passages in question.

About the time Zukofsky began work on the eighth movement, he received some materials from Basil Bunting concerning "Welsh metrics of Selwyn Jones . . . along with his [Bunting's] notes on that."[1] These documents have since disappeared, but some intriguing notes by Zukofsky furnish a few hints about the "Welsh metrics." (The notes he made are fragmentary, in rough form, and have the look of hurried writing.) They suggest that he was most delighted with the way the change of sounds in the Welsh poetry constituted its "sense and structure." The

1. MS, HRC.

material, he writes, "led me to investigate my own work
. . . to determine an "absolute" judgement of the poem as
sounded English."[2] His emphasis on "sounded English"
does not surprise. What does surprise are the peculiar new
strategies for attaining "absolute judgement." Further remarks in the same set of notes indicate how he pressed toward that goal. The friend referred to below was almost
certainly Jerry Reisman, whose contributions are acknowl-
edged in *First Half of "A"-9*.

> The above broodings have led a friend (or an enemy of
> practical prosody) writing a poem the form . . . based on
> any geometrical figure . . . perfectly definable by an equa-
> tion involving two or more variables.
>
> For instance
>
> the equation for a circle
>
> $$a^2 + b^2 = c^2$$
>
> defines any circle where c is a constant equal to a diameter
> of circle & a & b are drawn from ends of a diameter toward
> a circumference thus inscribing a Δ in a semi-circle. What
> we do is to find rate of variation of one variable to rate of
> variation of the other. Then choosing any two poetic quan-
> tities the poem must be constructed in such a way that the
> ratio of the variation of one of these quantities is to the rate
> of variation of the other as the ratio of the rates variation of
> the corresponding quantities of the equation which com-
> pletely describes the geometrical figure.[3]

Zukofsky is describing a fairly simple operation. As a
point (*d*) moves around the circle, the length of lines *a* and
b vary. In the diagram below, for example, line *b* is longer
than line *a* when *d* is located in the left half of the circle.
When *d* moves to the right half, the reverse holds true.

2. Ibid.   3. Ibid.

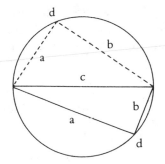

Zukofsky, assuming that the metamorphosis of sounds in the Welsh was essential, searched for equivalents in English. He and Reisman evidently analyzed English rules of distribution with an eye to tight command and exploitation of those rules. Zukofsky remarks that Reisman settled on "two poetic quantities" for his experiment. What they were, or what kind of poem resulted, we do not know. For "*A*" Zukofsky chose two variables—the sounds *n* and *r*.

That he chose them carefully is certain, but why did he select these in particular? Their ubiquity may have helped: *n* and *r* are the most frequent voiced consonants in English. There would be more words to choose from than if Zukofsky—writing poetry in a straitjacket—had opted for a pair such as *g* and *b*. Further, *n* and *r* are polarities; they resonate at opposite ends of the voice; *n* is nasal, *r* pharyngeal. Being opposites, they could readily serve as contrasting variables. (We will come shortly to their importance as opposites in "*A*"-8.)

Reading "*A*"-8 might justly be called a gradual discovery of calculi of movements (historical, personal, imagistic, and so on). The mathematical formulae sorting *n* and *r* also happen to be calculi of motion, tracing the progress of variables through space. In short, the "music" of "*A*"-8 and its mathematics have a similar form.

Speaking of calculus . . . Zukofsky elsewhere points out the connection between mathematical and musical structure discovered during the eighteenth century, and applies it to "A"-8:

> (Newton . . . discovering the calculus . . . Bach consolidating the math. complications possibilities of all possible counterpoint, & Mozart . . . the last who really knew what it wuz about) & it seemed very just to me that the Ballade of "A"-8 . . . be what it is: a desire to get all of a world down into 36 lines.[4]

The ballade referred to is one of the two sections of "A"-8 that distribute n and r contrapuntally. Newton, Bach, and Mozart, apostles of harmony, particularly the harmonies produced by countrapuntal motion, provide Zukofsky with authority for his experiments with variable sound. We have already observed that the poem advances by alternation; here is a new, compact variation on that progress.

Mathematics, like music, has the advantage of relative freedom from doctrinal or didactic import. It therefore serves as a "pure" form for combining sound so that the energy of the spoken word operates in a rigorously plotted field. Perhaps Zukofsky conceived this as an advance on the method governing most of "A"-8. The reader, faced with the movement's simultaneous emphasis on the "music" of the passages and the ideas embodied in them, tends to concentrate on one or the other. But the mathematical music that Zukofsky created last (the formulaic passages of "A"-8 were the last composed) is always present, precisely because we are unaware of it. As we speak the poetry, the effect of the patterning operates, an invisible complement to the meaning of the words; we are better off not knowing the pattern behind the sounds. Lorine Niedecker, refer-

---

4. Undated letter to Lorine Niedecker, HRC.

ring to "*A*"-9, commented on the value of such hidden schema: "Readers will not notice the calculus, only the sound, the energy, and that is the art of it."[5] If Zukofsky had not chosen to reveal the mathematical aspect of "*A*", decades might have passed before someone stumbled across the secret. Yet the poem works. Zukofsky was part of a generation that valued invisible energies; visible light covers only a fraction of the spectrum—a metaphor, and a fact, applicable to much of his method.

Since the mathematical plotting was an extension of matters forming "*A*"-8, Zukofsky carefully arranged for the mathematics to link thematically as well as sonically with the movement. The importance of balance, counterpoint, and opposition shows most clearly in the eighty-one-line section beginning "To this end, Communists assembled in London" and ending "To shunt aims, To each his needs, the Manifesto." "*A*"-8 divides the passage into nine stanzas of equal length, but a chart drawn up by Zukofsky detailing the distribution of *n* and *r* shows that the sonic pattern depends on cutting the passage into twenty-seven three-line sections. Every three lines, that is, the number of *n*'s and *r*'s is adjusted. For example, lines 13–15 contain three *n*'s and four *r*'s, while lines 16–18 have four *n*'s and six *r*'s.[6]

Though the formula governing *n* and *r* placement does not appear on the chart, Zukofsky mentions that the *n*'s and *r*'s deploy according to "ratios of acceleration & deceleration," suggesting the calculus of a curve. The proce-

5. Lorine Niedecker, "The Poetry of Louis Zukofsky," *Quarterly Review of Literature* 22 (1977): 199.

6. According to the chart (now at HRC) that Zukofsky prepared listing the distribution of *n* and *r*, there should be but two *n*'s in lines 10–12. In fact there are three. This discrepancy is the only one evident in the eighty-one-line section. When tallying *n*'s and *r*'s for themselves, readers should remember to count only the sounded ones. Such words as "column," "Monsieur," and "splitting" are therefore passed over.

dure is not greatly complicated. The first nine lines of the section increase the r's (from two to three to four), while the n's remain constant at eight. Thus the ratio of acceleration of r to n is $1/0$, i.e., infinite. The fifth stanza of the section does the same. But the last stanza continues to hold the number of n's constant at 8 while decelerating the r's (from four to three to two). This yields a ratio of $-1/0$, i.e., negative infinity. "So," Zukofsky writes, "IX balances I and V." Arguing the equilibrial merit of the eighty-one lines, he says:

> And the stanzas balancing in ratios of acceleration & deceleration also balancing in "thought," & the whole connected with the 8 themes presented in pp. 1–4 of A-8 & the subject matter of all of A-7.[7]

The balancing of acceleration and deceleration woven into the eighty-one-line section seems to be a smaller version of such contrasts as the decline of the Adamses and the rise of the Zukofskys. Its mathematical precision, reducing the effects of chance, also works thematically. It helps reinforce the poem's animus against speculation, e.g.,

> Who have signed to the probability
> Of a series of 8 red planes,
> Not 7 followed by a black   (p. 47)

The passage amalgamates progress in Soviet airpower, a slap at fascism, the growth of "A", and elimination of roulette, the pastime of the wealthy. Denunciation of the roulette wheel points forward to comparisons of gambling and capitalism: "simple and smooth machinery / Which differs in no essential respect from roulette or rouge-et-noir" (p. 78).

The precision and purity enjoyed by music and mathe-

7. MS, HRC.

matics also provides a means of organizing that eliminates the superfluous. Only indispensable items fit cleanly into a fugue or an equation, and Zukofsky consciously aimed at such severe economy. In *A Test of Poetry* he observed how words and music might be combined.

> Simplicity of utterance and song go together. Song as musical, poetic form is usually defined by a continuous and complete statement of the words. The fitting of words to musical composition seems to have reached its maximum development in English poetry as early as the 14th century. The complications of rhetorical ornament (similes, metaphors, conceits) in later times seem to have created a printed (and worse, a *bookish*) poetry written to be read silently rather than to be spoken or sung.[8]

Of course, mathematically plotted portions of "*A*" can hardly be accused of "simplicity" in the ordinary sense. "A desire to get all of a world down into 36 lines" produces a poetry as simple as it *can* be. The important point is that complications resulting are necessary complications and no more.

The "simplicity" of mathematics and music led Zukofsky to another odd connection. He adduced a close connection between the common people and fine arts as a firm basis for his poetry: "it occurred to me Bach and Mozart start out of themselves but with a short tune of the people which they develop. . . ."[9] How do "the people" constitute a foundation for Bach and Mozart? Zukofsky seems to credit their close relation to the earth as a reason. Making their living from difficult manual labor, they have no use for anything more than the most efficient and economical way of working. The struggle for survival forces reliance

8. Louis Zukofsky, *A Test of Poetry* (New York: C. Z. Publications, 1980), p. 65.
9. Undated letter to Niedecker, HRC.

on basic modes. Zukofsky tends to perceive the poet/musician as an Antaeus:

> Poetry does not arise and exist in a vacuum. It is one of the arts—sometimes individual, sometimes collective in origin—and reflects economic and social status of peoples; their language habits arising out of everyday matter of fact.[10]

(The phrasing has a Veblenesque, not to say Marxist, tinge, especially in the use of "matter of fact.") If music and poetry are rooted in the folk, and the essential virtues of music and poetry proceed from a simplicity and economy inherent in the laboring classes, it becomes logical, even necessary, for Zukofsky to join Bach and folk-songs in the eighty-one-line section. The balancing slant of all of "A"-8 operates in this section in several ways, one of which—the redress of economic injustice—is partly furthered by the frame of the section: the *Communist Manifesto*. Accompanying Marx's call for equalization of imbalanced wealth are snatches of tunes in which freed slaves celebrate the confiscation of their former owner's wealth (stolen from their labor), and Robin Hood gets the drop on the Sheriff of Nottingham:[11]

> I spec it will be all 'fiscated.
> De massa run, ha! ha! De darkey stay, ho! ho!
> So distribution should undo excess — (chaseth),
> Shall brothers be, be a' that, Child, lolai, lullow.
>
> When the sheriffe see gentle Robin wold shoote, held
> Up both his hands.   (p. 50)

10. *A Test of Poetry*, p. 99.
11. The lines ridiculing the "massa" come from Henry Clay Work's "The Year of Jubilee" (1865), which is included in *A Test of Poetry* under the category of "Anonymity" (pp. 43, 102, 164, and 165). The Robin Hood passage can also be found in *A Test of Poetry* (pp. 20 and 158).

Since the victims of unbalanced wealth, the poor, are most interested in readjusting the scales, Zukofsky orchestrates their songs through the acceleration and deceleration of n and r, arranging the thematics of balance through balancing sounds. Even if the assumptions behind this effort are dubious, its elegance is indisputable.

The other part of *"A"*-8 written according to formula is the thirty-six-line section (ballade) ending the movement. The passage consists of three ten-line stanzas and a six-line coda. It uses only four end-rhymes, and the word "earth" ends each of the four stanzas, emphasizing the proletarian theme. But, as before, the ballade patterns n and r in smaller units than the typography indicates. The chart Zukofsky drew up for his own reference shows nine divisions of four lines each. The formula is missing, but apparently it was related to a circular motion through 360 degrees; "revolutionary" sentiment in the ballade seems to be the thematic equivalent.

Only those two isolated portions of *"A"*-8 were formulaic, but all of *"A"*-9 exists as a playground for n and r. A detailed explanation of the formula for, and distribution of, the variables appears in *First Half of "A"-9*, where Zukofsky reveals that

> the first 70 lines are the poetic analog of a conic section— i.e. the ratio of the acceleration of two sounds (r, n) has been made equal to the ratio of the acceleration of the coordinates (x, y) of a particle moving in a circular path with uniform angular velocity.[12]

12. Louis Zukofsky, *First Half of "A"-9* (New York: privately printed, 1940), p. 37. It was easy for Zukofsky to find equations compatible with conic sections. There are any number of them, since "the general equation of the second degree always represents a conic" (W. Gellert, H. Küstner, M. Hellwich, H. Kästner, eds., *The Van Nostrand Concise Encyclopedia of Mathematics* [New York: Van Nostrand, 1977], p. 318).

A circle is derived from a right cone by thrusting a plane across the cone parallel to its base. A cone, of course, suggests the shape of the letter *A*.

Behind *"A"*-8 and *"A"*-9 lies an assumption that the standards for poetry are always the same, that the fashioning of poetry fails if it relies on fashions of the day. It appears that these standards, according to Zukofsky, are based on physical facts, especially the construction of the human body. He seems to have taken to heart Pound's claim that "music begins to atrophy when it departs too far from music. . . . Bach and Mozart are never too far from physical movement."[13] Though Zukofsky does not explicitly state such a theory of poetry, he hints again and again that the eternal standards are based on the unchanging form of the body. Perhaps he would claim that since the proportions and mechanisms of the body are describable in precise mathematical terms, he has reason for pushing his art into the realm of numbers.

The physicality of poetry receives more stress when Zukofsky compares *"A"* to a machine at which the reader stares uncomprehendingly:

> This brings us to the problem of how easy it is for people to read poetry once they learn the poet's machinery. It's like finding out about any other piece of machinery or doing a specific job on the belt system.[14]

Here Zukofsky is tapping a whole generation's fascination with the uses of technology as art, but the letter making these comments was written in 1937, suggesting that the "machinery" he has in mind are the recent innovations in *"A"*.

13. Ezra Pound, *ABC of Reading* (New York: New Directions, 1960), p. 14.

14. Letter to Niedecker of June 7, 1937, HRC.

With the end of *"A"*-9, Zukofsky dropped the use of poetry based on mathematical formulae, so far as we can tell. The special rigor of the experiments therefore seems a limited development from Zukofsky's interests in the early and middle 1930s. But his habit of combining musical modes with words continued in less rigid form. *"A"*-13, subtitled "Partita," and composed ten years after the completion of *"A"*-9, consists of five parts, each with a different rhythm. As Zukofsky reveals in a letter to Cid Corman, they are modeled on the forms *allemande, courante, sarabande, gigue,* and *chaconne.*[15]

15. See *Origin*, 2d ser., no. 1 (April 1961), p. 63.

Index of Movements

The following is a list of the first line (or lines) of passages closely examined in this book, followed by the number of the page where discussion of the passage begins. The column at the left gives the movement and page number of each passage in the California edition of "A". Thus, 1:1 means "A"-1, page 1.

Index of Names

Designer:	Eric Jungerman
Compositor:	G & S Typesetters, Inc.
Printer:	Vail-Ballou Press
Binder:	Vail-Ballou Press
Text:	11 on 13 Bembo
Display:	Phototypositor Times Roman Bold
	Italic, VIP Perpetua Bold, Bold Italic,
	VIP Bembo small caps.